# Words about John Cox

"The thing I like about John is what you see is what you get. There is no pretence or double-talk with him. This makes him someone worth listening to. So, if you're struggling trying to connect with a God who you can't quite 'get,' John is a man you can trust on your googling journey."

—**David Shadbolt,** spiritual coach, England

"John has an innate ability to unravel difficult concepts and reorganize them into language easily understood."

—**Brock Clayards**

"John is not a sofa-comfort Christian leader…His story—when you know it—is not one of ease…I, for one, would have been ploughed under had I been faced with the demands on his life. Yet he has come through. This is a book written by a man whose life has been literally saved and crafted by the real Jesus."

—**Simon Middleton,** senior VP for a major international company in Europe

"Over the 15 years I have known and worked with John Cox I have come to appreciate him as an artist, prophet, and friend…Through various mediums (music, painting, writing, speaking) John has been able to express the love of the Father for us."

—**Dave De Jong,** co-pastor at Jericho Road church

"Here is someone who has seen life on all sides and has discovered for himself core truths…John's optimism and trust in others allows him to have a meaningful dialogue with anyone about the fundamentally important issues of life, whatever their own beliefs and condition."

—**Prof. Dr. Kevan Martin,** professor at Institute of Neuroinformatics, University of Zurich

"John pokes me with wit, intelligence, and creativity. His teaching influences me to not necessarily view God in a logical manner. I approach Him with faith and emotion. I see Him as an inspiration. I see Him as a God who can change my life."

—Helgie and Mary-Anne Naesgaard

"Under John's teaching, I learned of a God who is very personal, who desires to have a loving relationship with me, and in His grace and mercy forgives my weaknesses and failures, picks me up, and continues to mold me, not without many ups and downs, into the person He wants me to be."

—Paul and Brenda Chapman

"As a retired general practitioner, I have known and treated many deeply depressed people. John was among them (although he was not my patient). His anguish over separation from God and the depression was eloquently expressed in his poetry and writings through that time…Restored to God, he has rejuvenated a diverse and bruised group of believers into Jericho Road…church."

—Dr. John and Barbara Jemson

"John is a man of integrity who, more than most, earnestly seeks to walk out the truth of which he speaks. His desire to be real and honest in both his successes and failures is an encouragement to us."

—Wayne and Tish Bernard

"John has lived his life with humility in a culture that expects instant gratification in everything. When money has come into his life, I have seen him pour it out on others' needs rather than himself. He not only talks of God's lifestyle, he lives it."

—Capt. Fred and Glenda Mather
(MV *Uchuk* 111—Gold River, Vancouver Island)

# GOOGLING
# GOD

## JOHN COX

HARVEST HOUSE PUBLISHERS

EUGENE, OREGON

*Cover by Left Coast Design, Portland, Oregon*

*Cover photo © Yamada Taro / Digital Vision / Getty; Back cover author photo © Denis Woodske*

Names and details of people and events mentioned in this book have been changed to respect and protect confidentiality and identity.

**GOOGLING GOD**
Copyright © 2008 by John Cox
Published by Harvest House Publishers
Eugene, Oregon 97402
www.harvesthousepublishers.com

Library of Congress Cataloging-in-Publication Data
Cox, John, 1952-
Googling God / John Cox.
    p. cm.
    ISBN-13: 978-0-7369-2127-5 (pbk.)
    ISBN-10: 0-7369-2127-3 (pbk.)
    1. Christianity. I. Title.
    BR121.3.C69 2007
    230—dc'22

                                                                    2007019259

**Printed in the United States of America**
        08  09  10  11  12  13  14  15  16  /  VP-NI  /  10  9  8  7  6  5  4  3  2  1

• • • • •

To…
…*my daughters, Carmen and Michelle, who have unwittingly led me deeper into the loving heart of God the Father.*

To the memory of…
*Donna, Wendy, and Larry. So tragically hurting in this life, dismissed and not honored. How they dance with joy now in the throne room of the King—dearly loved, whole at last, and so wonderfully free to be…They caught a glimpse of Jesus here—but now they know!*

And also to you…
…*who have longed to know the real God but have been wounded, disillusioned, disappointed, or "bored to tears" by what you have encountered along the way. God is much kinder, nicer, more accepting, more fun, and more intellectually stimulating than you or I may ever have imagined him to be. He is also looking for you and me much more passionately than any of us will ever search for him. You are very precious to him. I pray that these meager thoughts and ramblings will help in some small way to build a bridge and a means of reconciliation between a distant child and an adoring Father–Creator, a God whose heart is warm and filled with such a passionately unconditional love and acceptance for every single one of us.*

• • • • •

·   ·   ·   ·   ·

# Acknowledgments

When I began writing *Googling God* I was never really sure whether it would ever get to a printed page. Thank you to those who kindly endured my first draft and encouraged me to keep going and offered helpful comments: Brock and Margaret Clayards, Michael Welsh, Robin Cox and his daughter Trish, Guy Champagne, Helgie Naesgaard, and Kevan Martin.

Thank you to the staff of Writer's Edge, who provided the first encouraging response when previewing the manuscript. And of course a huge "thank you" to Harvest House Publishers for taking a risk with me and giving me this opportunity to be published. Thank you to all the Harvest House personnel who have been so helpful and kind, encouraging and guiding me through the process; in particular Terry Glaspey and Paul Gossard, whose wisdom and sensitive comments have been deeply appreciated and proven to be invaluable.

And from the bottom of my heart I acknowledge unreservedly the grace and love of the living God, whose son Jesus calls me "friend." Thank you, God, for the gift of life and for the hope and healing you have poured into a heart that was once broken in despair. All that is good in these pages is yours...The rest—well, I guess it's mine...

·   ·   ·   ·   ·

# Contents

The longest journey is the journey inwards.
Of him who has chosen his destiny,
who has started upon his quest
for the source of his being…

—DAG HAMMARSKJOLD

"Would you tell me, please, which way
I ought to go from here?"
"That depends a good deal on where
you want to get to," said the Cat.
"I don't much care where," said Alice.
"Then it doesn't matter which way
you go," said the Cat.
"So long as I get SOMEWHERE,"
Alice added as an explanation.
"Oh, you're sure to do that," said the Cat,
"if you only walk long enough."

—LEWIS CARROLL, FROM *ALICE IN WONDERLAND*

Seek and you shall find…

—JESUS

# Prologue

As a very young boy I had a tough time understanding the world. I don't know how it was for you when you were a brand-new little human being, all freshly formed and wide eyed. I remember sitting on the steps outside our house in Cape Town, South Africa, staring at the mountain, Devil's Peak, rising high into the sky in front of me. With my eyes slowly traced the way through the trees and around the rocky outcrops up its slopes, right to the top. *What would it be like to climb up there?* I wondered. *I guess when you get to the very top you have to wriggle on your tummy until you can't go any farther because you hit the sky.* Then I ran inside to play a game.

On another occasion I watched the trees blowing, and the leaves, liberated from their branches of birth, paragliding down the street, sometimes spinning so high I couldn't see them anymore. After much thought I concluded behind my furrowed brow it was the movement of the trees that caused wind. Therefore the more trees there are the stronger the wind blows in that region—it's obvious! But I couldn't understand why the trees moved sometimes and at other times their branches were quite still. What moved the trees?

The world was a big place all right, and I was pretty small. The garden around our house was about as much as I could handle! So I began to construct my own worlds, where I built little forts with my friends and pretended to be other people who were bigger and braver than we were—like

Superman, Peter Pan, Hercules, or even Davy Crockett, "king of the wild fron-
tier"! On other occasions we constructed road systems in the dirt between
the flower beds for our toy cars to race around, complete with sound effects
screeching from our mouths. When it rained and we were stuck indoors
I read books and drew pictures of boats and discovered that sucking my
thumb was soothing, and that pulling the bedclothes over my head felt
safe and secure.

During the windy gray Cape winters I used to climb the mountains
around Cape Town with my father—meaning going for walks on Sunday
afternoons. We hiked to the summit of a few of the mountains nearby and
I never bumped my head on the sky or had to crawl on my tummy. I also
don't recall ever admitting to my father what I had thought we would be
doing up there. Informed by experience, my understanding changed.

* * * * *

**The key to wisdom is this—constant
and frequent questioning...for by doubting
we are led to questioning and by questioning
we arrive at the truth.**

—Peter Abelard

* * * * *

We all grow and learn by testing what we see and think against our real-
life experiences—taking on board new understandings, jettisoning others,
or having old truths verified. That is probably the simplest and most ancient
method of learning: observing, testing, experiencing, and then adjusting
to what has been learned and storing those memories for next time. We
learn that things "out there" are not always as they appear to be, that our
understanding is somewhat limited, and that the conclusions we draw are
sometimes right and quite frequently not really accurate at all. Slowly we
learn to look, observe, and ask questions before coming to conclusions.
*Why? How? When? What? Where? How long? How many? How do you
know this? Can you prove that to me?*

Where we stand (our point of view) frequently determines our perspective and how we see things. The west coast of southern Africa is famous for the spring flowers that almost miraculously blossom after the rain falls and carpet the hills with color for miles and miles. I drove up there to witness the miracle for myself. When we arrived in the region all I could see was lots of green on the hillsides. "So where are the flowers?" I asked.

We drove a little further and more of the same stretched out ahead. "Look behind you now," said my friend. I turned my head, and those hillsides I had first seen as green were ablaze, with yellow, white, lilac, and orange splashed everywhere. We had been driving into the sun and all the flowers were tilted away from us toward its light and warmth. When we looked behind us with the sun at our backs it seemed as if we had just discovered the place where rainbows are born and assembled to fly. What we saw depended on where we stood and which way we were looking. Don't be surprised if you find a different view opening up in these pages, one you have never seen before…splashes of color might be right behind you and all you need to do is turn your head and look again. It's really cool to be surprised like that—at least I think so!

●　●　●　●　●

**People demand freedom of speech
to make up for the freedom of
thought which they avoid.**

—Soren Kierkegaard

●　●　●　●　●

As I write these words I have a number of lines of sight regarding what I observe and how far I am able see from my desk. If I swivel my chair, I look at the wall with pictures of my parents and children above the shelves stacked full of books. Through the window in front of me I observe the sun lighting up the cedars…it comes out every now and then on the Wet (West) Coast. I can also gaze into the computer screen, and technology enables me to "see" much further than the confines of my physical environment.

From the chair at my desk, therefore, I am able to see a number of layers with varying depths of interest and substance, all telling me something about the world in which I live.

That is what this book is about. Exploring together to see if we can find God through all the various layers around us, some that are really close at hand and others that are further away and more complex, perhaps. Asking questions, learning together, and trying to make more sense of what we observe and experience from our unique vantage point where we stand amid life on earth today.

Right now I am conducting some research for an airline in Europe. Through the miracle of the Internet I can punch a name or phrase into the Google Internet site and retrieve articles related to that topic from around the world within seconds. I then have to sift through the information and select those items that are useful and relevant to my specific research focus. The magic is being able to find so many sources of information relating to a particular topic so quickly. Of course they come with varying degrees of authority, interest, and accuracy, but at least they give me something to work with.

● ● ● ● ●

**I do not feel obliged to believe that the same God who has endowed us with sense, reason, and intellect has intended us to forgo their use.**

—GALILEO GALILEI

● ● ● ● ●

So how about "googling God" and exploring what kind of information might help us make sense of what *God* means? Maybe we already believe he exists and have worked out our worldview, but we have never really tested it (like bumping your head on the sky—or not!). We probably recognize already that some of our perceptions could do with a few questions being asked and answered; hopefully, some fresh insights that will be helpful will appear from these pages.

Others of us may be "googling God" for the first time and are pretty clueless about what will come up on the screen. That's okay too. What matters is that we start somewhere—and asking a question is better than beginning with dogmatic assertions, isn't it? I appreciate people questioning honestly, kicking the tires to see firsthand what is reliable and true. Merely believing, or not believing, in something because you have always done so (without understanding why) is foolish, really. It's a bit like my sticking with my childhood theory about what causes the wind to blow. Sincerity probably wouldn't be acceptable as a sufficient reason for that assertion. If I responded that my belief about the wind was private and personal and not to be talked about in public, and that it was a matter of individual freedom and rights—well, you might just google me a doctor while asking, "What did they teach *you* at school?"

●　●　●　●　●

**Oh Lord please don't burn us
don't kill or toast your flock
Don't put us on the barbecue
or simmer us in stock
Don't bake or baste or boil us
or stir-fry us in a wok.**

—MONTY PYTHON

●　●　●　●　●

*Googling God* is for ordinary people who are looking for meaning (or more meaning), maybe even God, in the world and in their lives—and for those of us who have never been close to "religion," or who have possibly attended church on occasion. Maybe we've been turned off by religion at school, or by an overzealous friend, or by some other unfortunate set of circumstances. Whatever the roadblocks have been, the mystery still remains.

The answers are seldom satisfying and the questions continue to nag and intrigue. They surface unexpectedly from time to time in various contexts and conversations, like an inquisitive seal staring at us with wide brown eyes just above the waterline wondering what we will do next as we look back, perched on the rocks by the shore. Remember, the number of dumb answers is far greater than the extremely rare stupid question. (In fact, the latter may even be extinct—it has been so long since one was asked.)

Maybe your life is quite comfortable and you don't "feel the need" for God at all. That's okay too—there's no pressure here other than an invitation to think and reflect. Not too many years ago we did not feel the need for computers or cell phones because they had not been invented. Once we were introduced to them, a "need" emerged that changed our lives. So who knows what might be out there for us to discover?

*Googling God* is also for those of us who believe we have already discovered some truths about God. Better still, we have gained a healthy mind-set that recognizes we have embarked on a long journey of discovery—one that, in fact, will last the rest of our lives. Most of us have blind spots and gaps in our understanding and as we grow, we suddenly find ourselves curious about an issue that we had ignored before, or not recognized as important. My hope is that something new and fresh in these pages will provide "another answer" or a new perspective for you to consider and be thrilled by.

⚬ ⚬ ⚬ ⚬ ⚬

## Truth is not determined by majority vote.

—DOUG GWYN

⚬ ⚬ ⚬ ⚬ ⚬

My oldest daughter laughingly recounted what happened when she arrived back home from college the other day for the weekend. She was downstairs, when her phone rang. Her mother was calling to find out when she would be home. She quietly walked upstairs, stood right behind her mother while she was still on the phone, and said, "I'm here right now—look behind you!"

The truth is, we're often crying out, "Oh my God, where are You?"…and he is walking up the stairs with a smile saying, "I'm here right now—look behind you!" Keep turning around and looking over your shoulder as we journey through these pages together, just to make sure you're not missing splashes of colorful flowers, or God himself busy "googling you"—wouldn't that be a surprise and an adventure?

# Imagine...

*Imagine there's a heaven. It's easy if you try...*

IT IS ONE OF THOSE CLEAR EVENINGS WHEN THE AIR IS COOL AND CLEAN. The stars blink, a multimillion specks of glitter tossed carelessly and lavishly across the night sky. If we lie on our backs we don't have to wait long before a shooting star scuds across the heavens. The fire crackles in a low glow of hot embers and flicking flames. The warmth radiating from the coals is just enough for us to be cocooned from the encroaching damp. We are friends, comfortable together and not afraid of long silences.

It's the kind of evening after an active day outdoors when our soul grows quiet, our mind is reflective in a calm and tranquil place, and our heart is at peace and open. A thought can drop into our mind like a pebble in a pond and cause ripples to radiate outward, gently lapping upon the shores of our consciousness. It seems very natural when we stumble upon such a clearing in the forest of time to gaze up at the stars, and pondering the vastness of space feel very small. In the stillness of the evening the question quietly slips into the night air, "Do you think there really is a God out there?" And we begin to talk…

That is the spirit in which I hope we can converse as we explore a hugely significant question together. With gentleness and respect, trying not to jump to conclusions too quickly. Taking time to listen to each other with openness, safety, sincerity, and passion. Some of us will hold fairly strong opinions, while others will be more unsure and just want to listen and question as the conversation unfolds. "I believe in God—but I don't understand why, if he loves us so much…"

Our conversation will scan a variety of topics concerning God, and include questions and reflections that will probably trigger hostile reactions sometimes. I am no expert with *infallible* stamped over my words. My family and friends will enthusiastically confirm that I am a very mortal human being in my mid-50s. I have many failures and a few encouraging successes scattered through my very ordinary life, and I've been "around the block" a few times.

●　●　●　●　●

**I may disagree with what you
have to say, but I shall defend,
to the death, your right to say it.**

—Voltaire

●　●　●　●　●

In attempting to tackle the vast, complex, and vexing question of "God" with deliberate simplicity, I am more or less confining the discussion to a consideration of the Judeo-Christian understanding of the deity. This is a historically rooted belief system centered on the existence of a monotheistic deity (one God) with the Bible as the foundational spiritual document and reference point.

I share the perception that most of us are intuitively spiritual and yet for a host of reasons may have neglected that aspect of our lives. Consequently we don't really know what to do with it. This is compounded by the fact that many of our "spiritual" encounters along the way have not left us thirsting for more. From the moment of our birth, while we have been fed with food to nourish our bodies and educated with information to expand our minds, our spirits have frequently been left to wither with little or no input whatsoever.

Fortunately the spirit will not die—however, it can be severely stunted.

It demands the same attention as our other faculties if it is to develop as a strong and healthy component of our unique humanity. The purpose, therefore, of these conversations is to stimulate thinking and facilitate discussion...with the awareness that a work of this modest size inevitably hardly begins to scratch the surface. However, the potential for eternal questioning, great complexity, and perpetual analysis does not mean that a topic is inaccessible to ordinary people like you and me.

It is easy to be intimidated by religious and intellectual snobbery and therefore assume we are disqualified to participate. In fact there are many levels of "knowing" when it comes to God. At the simplest level (which often is the most important and profound) everyone can discover and know enough about God's reality for it to make a significant difference in the quality of their lives. Much like the experience of a kiss and an embrace communicates love at a level where the intellect becomes mercifully speechless and even irritating.

While I respect and admire academic thinking, it seems to be a mixed blessing. It is possible to discuss with great learning all kinds of information and yet at the same time ignore how that information impacts or takes root in the human heart. Learning has the potential to open our hearts to love and truth, but it is also quite possible for us to use words to protect and defend ourselves from experiencing anything.

Lifelong learning is a continuous spiral that tracks around the same course, with more or less the same themes appearing again and again. However, each time we visit a familiar place during the next circuit in the spiral we are at a different age, or in different circumstances. Although we recognize the place, it is never exactly the same, and neither are we. Which is why it is sometimes only when we visit that place called "God" on the fifth or sixth or hundredth revolution that we actually take the time to stop and stare and begin to question. As long as we are alive it is never too late to do that, and it's certainly never too early to start. Repetition is almost always necessary.

Maybe during our informal introduction I'll tell you a little about myself to enable you to know something of my context and background. Indeed, that is the first question I would pose if we were actually looking up at the stars and chatting by the fireside. I would not launch into a discussion about God, but rather begin the conversation with a genuine expression of interest in you.

*"Who are you, and what can you tell me about yourself?"*

I might describe my childhood in Cape Town and how much I loved the beach and the mountains, my thrill when I learned to play the guitar, and the pleasure I find in music. We'd talk about family and friends and influential people. I'd mention my mother's untimely death when I was 12 years old and the subsequent "challenging" teenage adjustments. I would probably recount some of my university years—looking for direction. My compulsory service in the army would be significant, and the debates that tugged within me about whether to become a "priest" when I didn't feel like a "holy man." We would almost certainly touch on some of my wonderful experiences when I assisted in a veterinary practice in Cape Town and in Swaziland, where the First and Third Worlds and cultures wove a fascinating tapestry to embrace and to be embraced by.

I'm sure we would traverse the various mountains and valleys that have contoured my humble existence on this earth over the past 50-some years. Through the web and weave of our conversation I'd share with you my thoughts and experiences about how my understanding of God has emerged thus far. A journey about seeking to know, comprehend, and consider God—asking whether he has any relevance or place in life today. Especially, how to make sense of the struggles and disappointments that sometimes make it hard to believe anyone is out there at all.

●　●　●　●　●

**A day without a friend is like a pot without a single drop of honey left inside.**

—WINNIE THE POOH

●　●　●　●　●

I would most definitely boast to you about my two lovely daughters and show you pictures of them. You would hear me lament my failure in my marriage and the difficult years of questioning that followed a breakdown that included a change of career as well. I would also describe how the experience of being a father informs beyond words my appreciation for, and interaction with, God. And then I'd probably nudge you with some witty remark: *"It's your turn now...what were you doing while I was busy with that stuff?"*

Many people who have been exposed to the Christian religion either intimately, or on the fringes of church activity, have been very bruised. Some have been severely damaged by a defining experience of "God" or religion that has quite understandably caused them to recoil and vow to never go *there* again. Maybe it has been an encounter with a "professional" who patronized us or seemed irrelevant to where our lives played out in the real world. (In the worst scenario we may have, regrettably, experienced abuse in some form.)

Others of us have found "going to church" boring and disconnected from the rest of life. We grew tired of feeling guilty for not finding it more captivating or interesting. Quite possibly our experience with a zealous "believer" was enough for us to press the delete button in our psyche and make a note to steer clear of that topic and those people in the future. Not necessarily because we did not want to believe, but because we did not appreciate being preached at and not respected as a unique person. Some of us took a leap of faith and believed in God and the promise of his love and faithfulness. But despite our genuine attempts, it didn't turn out as we had anticipated at all, and we eventually abandoned the journey, full of disappointment and disillusionment.

Not everyone, though, has had a negative experience severe enough to push them away from their journey in knowing God. Some of us have been raised in homes where faith has been meaningful and alive, and we cannot remember ever not having believed in God. We have many positive memories and are very thankful for our experiences—they enriched us and provided stability and a meaningful context during our formative years. Nevertheless we also want to "kick the tires" for ourselves and be assured that what has been passed on to us is indeed authentic and something we can truly call our own.

There are so many possibilities and justifications for withdrawing, yet at the same time there are also many reasons to persevere. Consider the countless mountain expeditions, polar-exploration attempts, or space-travel odysseys—and how many lives have been sacrificed pursuing those missions and goals. Despite all the hardship, costs incurred, and lives lost, we continue to clamber up mountains, sponsor explorations, and converse excitedly about traveling to Mars and beyond. It is the nature of human beings to keep inquiring, asking questions, and finding answers to the mysteries surrounding our lives on earth.

Spiritual exploration is no different. It is to be expected that along the way there will be casualties, hardships, false starts, and maybe some disillusionment with a desire to give up. But in the final analysis there is something within us that nags, and after a while we return to muse over this strange and wonderful question related to the very meaning of life itself. Is there more than meets the eye, and is there really a power and personality behind the universe, whom we refer to as God?

It is an awesome question to ponder. We look up at the stars and talk about what it means for space to go on and on and on. One analogy I came across states that if an auditorium the size of the Royal Albert Hall in London (which can hold an audience of over 5500) was filled with frozen peas—that would give us some idea of the number of galaxies in the solar system. Contemplate the distances between stars and the planets, and how long it takes to fly to Mars even at an incredible speed. We imagine traveling into space and never coming to the end of it, and our minds crumble because they cannot contain the concept. But even though the subject of space is so large and incomprehensible in its entirety, we still explore and seek to understand what is visible. That's all we can do with God as well. Start where we are and begin to explore, even though we will never comprehend...or ever arrive at the end of the vastness ahead.

We could lie on our backs looking at the night sky every night, as people no doubt have done from the dawn of time and the first sunset, when the glory of the heavens was first unveiled. We could count stars, play games imagining shapes, and see who spies the most meteors. Lying next to me that is probably as far as you'd get, considering I know nothing about the expanse of the universe.

But imagine lying next to an expert—someone who has studied astronomy and spent their whole life peering through a telescope into the night sky! Imagine listening to him or her talk about the stars and "what is out there" based on the research they and their fellow astronomers have completed. Wouldn't it be fascinating to listen as they point out features and reveal truths about the heavens that we would never otherwise have known? Unlike most of us whose heads invariably bend toward the ground, they have spent their time looking upward beyond the earth's horizons. They explore so much more than stars in the sky or pinpricks of light in the blackness of night. They see stories and history, light years, black holes and galaxies, explosions, planets, moons and orbits, movement and change.

●　●　●　●　●

**Be who you are and say what you feel because those who mind don't matter and those who matter don't mind.**

—DR. SEUSS

●　●　●　●　●

Don't we all benefit from having an expert or mentor walk alongside us pointing out features and helping us see through the layers of meaning surrounding us? Our first encounter while making observations is with the obvious and superficial that we easily see without guidance or comment. If we persist, gradually our learning spirals down deeper into many layers of discovery, understanding, and revelation...new thoughts and ideas crystallize and become visible within our sphere of vision and comprehension.

*"I never knew that!"*

*"You mean this rough stone is really a diamond? It looks like a pebble to me—how do you know that?"*

"*You can examine the geography and the dirt on the surface and deduce whether there is oil down there?*"

"*You mean to tell me that just from one microscopic cell you can gather so much information about a person?*"

So the process unfolds, layer upon layer, with a never-ending ability to amaze those who take the time to explore, question, and research further outward or inward beyond the space, paradigm, and mind-set they presently occupy.

We learn to see so much more than our first impression with a little instruction, practice, and patience. It's called observing with a trained eye, seeing through a new lens, experiencing a paradigm shift.

If you have tried to find a picture in a stereogram you'll know what I mean. Those patterns look like nothing at first glance. They contain a hidden image and you have to blur your eyes (or go cross-eyed) to be able to see through the obvious image and discover what you cannot initially see at all. If someone did not inform us that there was more to see we wouldn't even take the trouble to look. When we finally do see the image within the picture emerge, it is amazing! Yet look away quickly and return to the page and you'll have to start all over again to see it. (Where we focus determines what we see.) I found that as I prepared this material initially I struggled to see the "hidden" images (printed below). But once I focused and saw them, I was able to discern the new pictures almost right away because my eyes had become trained to "see" in a new way. Discover for yourself…

●　　●　　●　　●　　●

### Look and you will find it—what is unsought will go undetected.

—SOPHOCLES

●　　●　　●　　●　　●

One question, though—sorry to interrupt. Do you need to understand how these pictures are constructed before you look? Or are you prepared to look and experience and then maybe find out more information later?

It's all about faith, isn't it? Once we start talking and thinking like this we can only give wry smiles because we are habitually so inconsistent and selective about what we need to have proven to us before we decide to act. It really all depends upon how we perceive the end product or goal. If it appeals to us and is fun or nonthreatening we will usually be prepared to jump. If it challenges us or is a threat in any way we will naturally start questioning and adopting other stalling tactics.

Now if you're ready to jump, cross your eyes, be patient, and stare at the pictures below and on the next page—daring to believe that all will be revealed!

*The first picture contains the words "God and..."*
*(You'll have to find the rest.)*

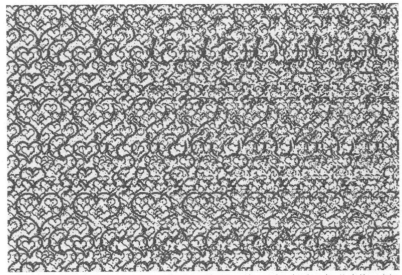

*This picture contains a common form of greeting.*

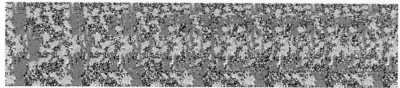

While those who wandered this planet before us no doubt gazed in wonder into outer space, today we tend to lounge in a chair armed with a chocolate latte and stare into cyberspace. We Google-dance with our electronic mouse into the global database that increases in size with every click. We have the capability to download information originating from anywhere on the globe. The opportunity for research, education, and the broadening of our intellectual horizons is unprecedented in history.

So again, why not consider googling God?

Let me pour you a glass of wine or a cup of tea or coffee, throw another log on the fire, and reflect on that question. There is no rush, so feel free to reflect on these matters at whatever pace is comfortable for you. We'll detour and tell stories, recount some sad and hilarious thoughts, and see where we end up.

I'll promise you one thing. I'm not going to try to convert you or slam you up against the wall to get some predetermined response. We're just going to chat and share ideas with a view to learning together. If such an exercise is helpful then we will both have benefited, and if not we can always respectfully close the book and part company. My hope is that you will find the conversation stimulating, thought-provoking, and engaging.

Did you see that shooting star? Whew, what a long tail. Unbelievable!

# Why Bother?

GOD AND JESUS CHRIST CROP UP IN THE MOST UNLIKELY PLACES!

Their names bounce off the lips of people from a fascinating assortment of backgrounds and walks of life. They are mentioned constantly in the conversations of mill workers and fishermen, business executives and bankers, kids in the playground and athletes of every sport. The only problem is, most of the time God and Jesus are referenced as if they do not exist. They are merely included as thoughtless syllables in a chain of other profanities, "God Almighty, what a shot!" "Jesus Christ, did you see what just walked by?" "F——you!" "Christ, why can't you listen more carefully?" "Jeeeeesuz, that was cool!"

The phrase that would likely cause the most surprise or offense in the string of profanities above is "F——you!" Oddly, replacing that phrase with "God Almighty" or "Jesus Christ" is superficially less offensive to many of us. What is even odder is that no other religious figure receives such disdainful treatment. We don't hear people exclaiming "Buddha, that hurt!" or "In Allah's name go to hell!" "For Muhammad's sake shut up!" "Krishna, that was a great strike!"

What has happened to God and Jesus? They dominate the vocabulary of so many and yet are close to the hearts of relatively few. The answer is obvious, isn't it? They are terms that have no meaning to the speaker—therefore they have been swept off the top shelf and relegated to the basement, where they are used to punctuate conversation in a meaningless and arbitrary fashion.

There's no point in complaining and expecting people to listen or change. Why should they? Far better to encourage questioning and provide the kind of example that will cause them to think again. If and when God means something to us on a personal level, then our language will change accordingly. Surely if we have learned one thing it is that long-lasting positive results seldom if ever grow out of negativity, rules, and making threats. In fact, one of the authentic tests for the reality of God (if of course he exists) is that he attracts us through unconditional love and disarming kindness. Which is often counterintuitive to how we tend to approach challenges: by haranguing each other with rules and wagging fingers—a lot easier than manifesting love unconditionally. Such a love can get you crucified...but now we're way ahead of ourselves.

I imagine we probably have all muttered words similar in substance to one or more of the following phrases in our lifetime:

- *"I spent 12 years at a school where we were forced to attend church services, sing hymns, and receive religious instruction. It all seemed so dated and boring—I don't think that kind of stuff really makes a difference, and I'm certainly not interested."*

- *"Religion seems to bring out the worst in people. They become judgmental and holier-than-thou, or are always complaining about 'the world.' Then there is the fanaticism that motivates people to kill and to do all kinds of hateful things to others with whom they disagree—all in the name of God. Frankly, religion scares me."*

- *"If God is real, I just don't understand why there is so much pain and suffering in the world. He does not seem to be very active and I haven't experienced a whole lot of love from people*

*I know who attend church. Most are hypocrites as far as I can tell—you should watch them during the week!"*

- *"I wouldn't mind maybe believing in God, but the leaders don't impress me much. I am so tired of hearing about scandals, abuse, money scams, and other stuff that does not seem to be very consistent with a message of 'love.'"*

There seems to be a huge credibility gap between what God is supposed to be like and the experience many of us have when meeting his followers. A few years ago I attended a business workshop hosted by the Disney Corporation in Vancouver. The guest speaker was talking about customer service and how important it is to minimize "bad experiences." He said, "We have found that every negative customer service experience takes 36 positive experiences to win them back again."

● ● ● ● ●

## If God did not exist, it would be necessary to invent him.

—VOLTAIRE

● ● ● ● ●

I would never have guessed the stakes were so high, but it makes sense to me. It's invariably true, isn't it? We tend to gravitate toward the negative and we allow the positive to be swallowed up by the "one thing" that went wrong. And that is the impression that lingers and invariably gets the airtime in conversations about "religion" or God. The charlatans in general occupy more headlines and sound bites than do Mother Teresa and others of her kind. It is hardly surprising therefore that we grow disillusioned with perceptions about God that become bent and distorted so easily through the prism of other people. It is actually predictable and, I would suggest, even inevitable—because God is portrayed as perfect in every way and those who believe in him are imperfect in every way. There is bound to be inconsistency, distortion, and even hypocrisy visible in the crowd gathered around him, sporting his colors and breathing, sneezing, and speaking in his name.

God, and those who believe in him, are not one and the same. I have heard many people admit, "It's not God I have a problem with, it's the people who say they believe in him who are so judgmental and self-righteous, and so on… That's what turns me off and makes me want to have nothing to do with religion." Yet on the other hand, most people who profess to believe in God will credit a friend, or an act of kindness, or a positive quality they saw in someone as a factor that helped them come to a place of personal faith. (I'll describe a few folk who impacted me a little later.) The truth of the matter is that people who behave badly are an unhelpful advertisement for *anything* they are attached to, whether it is God, soccer, politics, or extreme sports. If we can accept that level playing field, then the first item on our agenda is to learn to separate the disorderly and unattractive crowd from the core activity or person being examined.

It's rather like expecting everyone who watches soccer or enthuses about the game to also be a star player. They are not, and they never will be. Once I accept that reality, then disillusionment will probably be less of an issue, although we'll have to keep reminding ourselves to make the distinction. Our expectations for the players will naturally be significantly higher than for those who merely support, help organize, and watch the game. Nevertheless we still expect the "others" to share some of the values, aspirations, and characteristics of their idols.

If God is real he is going to be really hard to comprehend from where we stand, precisely because he is so entirely different from us! Understanding him with our minds and trying to figure him out may actually be a futile and impossible task. Maybe "believing" begins to grow and be formed from a synthesis of mind and heart, experience, intuition, friendships, and trial and error, all interacting simultaneously until one day something "clicks" for us (like guitar strings, which need to be tuned in relationship to each other in order for the music to be played).

I remember learning to windsurf and spending hours clambering on the board, holding onto the sail, being pulled forward, falling back into the water, and repeating the process over and over again. Eventually I learned that pushing the board with my legs, leaning back counterintuitively into the wind, and trusting the sail to support me was the key to getting it right. Once that fact had clicked, then I began to experience some real progress. Discovering God is not linking up logical dots in isolation. It is rather experiencing an increasing awareness of the possibility that there is more to life than meets the eye—which leads me into a little story describing in another way this challenge of learning and explaining.

> *Somewhere in the north of England a young couple celebrated the arrival of their first child. He chortled and gurgled contentedly, cradled in his mother's arms...*

The voice telling the tale lilted in a melodic Welsh accent from the lips of a gray-haired, balding man who, as I recall, was a "missionary" visiting Cape Town from England. I must have been in my mid-teens when I heard him speak, and for some reason I have never forgotten the story he slowly and movingly recounted to his small audience.

> *Excitedly the proud new mum and dad escorted their baby home and cared for him, doting on every move and gesture as countless other parents have done throughout the ages. However, as the months went by they noticed something was not quite right with their young son. After a visit to the doctor they learned he had been born blind. Tests were conducted, and the subsequent visit to the surgeon informed them of the possibility that an operation could be attempted when the boy was in his teens. The surgeon explained that when the boy's head stopped growing a particular surgical procedure might miraculously rectify the problem and restore his sight, but the chances were questionable. There was nothing more to do other than wait and hope for the miracle that seemed like an eternity away.*
> *One day some years later the boy was outside in the garden*

*of their home. It was a warm summer's evening; he was walking barefoot on the grass holding his father's arm.*

*"Dad, what's this?" he asked.*

*"What's what?" his father replied.*

*"What am I walking on that feels so soft and different?"*

*"That's grass, son."*

*"What's grass, Dad?"*

*"Grass is green."*

*"Dad, what's green?"*

*"Well, green is a color like…" his voice trailed off into silence, at a loss to know how to explain what his son could neither see nor relate to.*

*Many years later the boy traveled up to London with his parents for the long anticipated, even dreaded, surgery. The operation went well and the family returned home to recuperate. The surgeon agreed to come to their home on the day the bandages were to be removed, and very slowly and excitedly the wrappings were taken off. The boy blinked as his parents held their breath and waited. He told them he saw light, then a blur, then shapes, and then…*

*"What's that?" he cried, looking out of the window.*

*"That's green grass, son," answered his father, who could scarcely contain the tears welling up in his own eyes.*

*"Why didn't you tell me it was so beautiful?" responded his incredulous son.*

If it's hard to describe green grass to a blind boy, how challenging it is to talk about a loving God in a cynical and love-starved world?

In the late 1970s I had the privilege of spending three years studying theology in Oxford. It is a beautiful town steeped in history and rich in academic resources; it is a university equal to any other in the world. One of our assignments was to visit and support a church or institution in the area every Sunday. These were allocated every term, and one assignment I received was to visit the local borstel. A *borstel* is a detention center in England for first offenders under the age of 14. My task was to talk to a bunch of rebellious young boys assembled in a small meeting area under guard—about God.

What would you say? How would you start? Particularly when the mention of *father* evoked thoughts of anger and alcoholism, and *love* meant sex. Almost every normal reference point had been grossly distorted by these boys' brutal introduction into a hostile and unfriendly world. I stuttered and stumbled my way through my poor excuse for a talk, and to be honest I was glad to get out of there. I had no idea what to do. I felt blind and dumb and ignorant. An alien visiting a strange and foreign world caged on the outskirts of Oxford—so much study, so little wisdom.

I feel somewhat like that right now as we begin these googlings about God. The only reason I am attempting the task at all is remembering those boys…and the people I have met over the years who have found the local pub or sports club to be far more accessible, accepting, and comforting than the local church.

I have lived on both sides of the fence. There was a time when I thought I had all the answers, that I could eloquently articulate foundational truths about God and persuade anyone of his love, existence, and purpose for their lives. But then there have been other occasions when, despite my passionate conviction, I have fallen silent about a loving God, deeply confused. Silent in the face of the relentless injustice of apartheid in South Africa, the prejudice and hatred displayed among people, helplessness in the grip of terminal illness, anger when confronted with meaningless death and brutal suffering, frustration with the apathy and indifference on the West Coast of North America. Silent when faced with the addiction to political correctness that offends everyone by offending no one.

I have been silent in more recent times, when for a number of years I became imprisoned by my descent into the black hole of depression and despair. A place devoid of hope or reference points, where I felt abandoned by God and cynical toward anything to do with him or his so-called "love."

God was a cruel joke, and the faith I had poured my life into felt like a complete and utter waste of time. So why bother?

I bother because, through all the silence and brooding cynicism, the alternative—"nothing"—made even less sense and ironically demanded more faith. There were lots of people to keep one company in a pub, on a sports field, watching a movie, and for many, smoking a joint or engaging in harder drugs. They were accepting and nonjudgmental and enjoyed laughing and having fun, but despite all the noise the hollow echo and the emptiness was deafening to my ears. It wasn't satisfying enough for me to spend my whole life there. And I genuinely loved the people.

Then there was also another "noise" that would not lie quite so still or be quiet. To add to the puzzle…other experiences and memories refused to submit and quietly dissolve into the gray muddle of time gone by. There were people I had met, like Osbiel, Vic, the blind man in Bethlehem, and "Aunty May." Each one of them demonstrated a quality of life that humbled, mystified, and excited me to the very core of my being. They were ordinary individuals rich with an extraordinary peace and kindness, exhibiting the incredibly attractive essence of what it means to be human. Their demeanor and lifestyles bore witness to a more noble beginning and purpose than a mere random "big bang" that jump-started humanity off on its wild ride through time. But we'll get to that later.

●　●　●　●　●

### Love is friendship set on fire.

—Jeremy Taylor

●　●　●　●　●

I first met Osbiel Matsebula when I must have been about 22 years of age. By then I had graduated from high school, spent a year in the army, wasted two years at the university (because I had no idea where I was going) and, finally, embarked on a career with a veterinary charity in the slums of Cape Town. I loved the work. Within a year I was hitchhiking 3000 miles (via a detour to Harare, Zimbabwe) into Swaziland, to help run the society's recently inaugurated veterinary clinic in the capital city, Mbabane. The head office was located in a small house surrounded by kennels that used to belong to the local SPCA before our society acquired the operation. The property was situated on a dusty road that detached itself from the main highway as it crested the final hill out of Mbabane and descended into the beautiful Ezulweni ("heaven") valley below.

Osbiel was employed as a general helper who performed odd jobs, cleaned the kennels, and ran errands as required. He was a young Swazi man in his mid-20s with a minimal education (he could read and write slowly) and had a simple but deep faith in God. He lived in one room in the main house that also contained the office, and I occupied the other. Rows of whitewashed dog kennels with wire-caged runs in front of each of them surrounded two sides of the property. A cacophony of bays and barking was a constant backdrop to our lives there.

Many evenings were spent in the tiny kitchen around the cast-iron stove. The air was permeated with the smell of wood smoke laced with coffee and boiling pigs' trotters (feet)—to be fed to the dogs. Osbiel and I would swap stories about our lives from our starkly contrasting worlds. We sang all kinds of songs, accompanied by my somewhat erratic guitar strums and his enthusiastic and "interesting" spoon rhythms. On occasion "Madala" (a term of respect for an elderly man) joined us. He also lived on the property in a separate building. Madala always dressed in a blue overall and was invariably smoking a pipe or inhaling something a little more potent. As with many older African men he spoke slowly and conveyed an air of great authority and wisdom. When he smiled his face broke into a hundred lines contouring his mouth and converging on his eyes. We would joke and laugh, sometimes until the tears streamed down our cheeks and our sides screamed in pain for the convulsions to cease.

During the week, Osbiel and I traveled in a mobile clinic through the local towns and into the more remote regions tucked away in the hills and mountains around Mbabane and Manzini. The idea was to maintain a regular schedule and provide simple medical care for a variety of animals, from dogs and cats to goats, horses, cows, and even chickens. Osbiel would act as an interpreter and help explain what the problem was and then describe the treatment we would provide. I was always amazed how one sentence uttered by me could be translated into so many words in Swazi.

I lived and worked with Osbiel for about nine months in 1975. The qualities of his life that so impressed me were his willingness to serve, his contentment and joy, and his simple and quiet faith in God. All his possessions were stored in the room next to mine, neatly placed on his bookshelf or folded behind the curtain draped in front of a few rudimentary shelves nailed across an old doorway.

Osbiel always ran everywhere, and every action was executed with care, pride, precision, and the broadest of smiles. He prepared mugs of coffee as if he were serving a gourmet meal. And in that humble act his gift to me is symbolized—an example of someone who was able to take the simplicity of the ordinary and mundane and transform it into sacramental acts of love and kindness. When Osbiel poured my coffee he bestowed on me the privilege of being the most respected and honored guest in the royal kingdom of Swaziland. And he conducted himself in that dignified manner with everyone.

Three years prior to my adventures in Swaziland I found myself attending a welcome dinner for new students joining a Christian Society at the University of Cape Town. I was alone in a crowd of strangers, when someone tapped me on the shoulder—turning around I was face-to-face with Vic Pearce. Behind a broad smile carved in a face that was wrinkled, weathered, and suntanned like a prune he offered me his hand—"Hello, John—nice to see you, let me buy you dinner tonight, it will be a privilege to have you as my guest." I think I had been introduced to him once before when he was speaking at a local church and I was just about to head out to the army. I was astounded at his graciousness and unabashed willingness to make the first move initiating a friendship.

Vic had been a personnel manager with De Beers Consolidated Diamond

Mines for many years. He was a bachelor and chose early retirement specifically to work on university campuses, befriending young students and sharing the love of God with them. He was quite unashamed and alarmingly forthright. He would rise early and jog around the campus, perched on the slopes of Devil's Peak with magnificent views across the southern suburbs of Cape Town. These routine excursions would invariably include one or two surprise visits along the way. Vic would arrive at a male student's bedroom door at six-thirty in the morning, knock loudly, and wish them happy birthday. He would offer a prayer of thanks with them for that special day as they feigned politeness and groggily mouthed appreciation while yearning for more sleep.

Many young people's lives were enriched and encouraged by Vic's visits, whose sole purpose was to remind them they were not forgotten, they were special, and God genuinely loved and cared for them. They were moved by the vulnerability he displayed by repeatedly making the first move to befriend and encourage students who were a long way from home. He had a knack for disregarding the bravado and macho cockiness of the young and insecure, and he pressed gently through that façade into the places that yearned for love, meaning, and acceptance. And he always made a person feel so appreciated and important!

Some years after my time at the University of Cape Town, Vic appeared out of nowhere. Hearing that I was accepted for training to be a pastor he offered to pay my airfare to study in England. There were numerous occasions when I found a note in the mail with an invitation for lunch with him. His words were always encouraging, expressing a belief in me I had never heard or received from anyone in my life before. Those words and gestures touched me deeply and were a profound gift, freely given to a young man who felt somewhat misunderstood and quite uncertain about his position in life. Vic was undeterred by my joking and teasing of him in a pathetic attempt to keep him at bay. He read and understood me more deeply than I ever realized, and I am very grateful indeed that he did so.

In 1990, shortly after the Gulf War, I attended a five-week study course in Israel at a school based in Jerusalem (now known as the Jerusalem University College). I had long wanted the opportunity to spend time there and taste the history, sights, and smells of that fascinating spiritual melting pot. On my journey via England someone mentioned to me that I should visit the House of Hope in Bethlehem. It was a small home for Palestinian blind, disabled, and abused children, run by three elderly women. One afternoon I finally boarded the bus to make the short journey down to Bethlehem—a visit I shall never forget.

● ● ● ● ●

**Question with boldness even the existence of God; because, if there is one, he must more approve of the homage of reason than that of blindfolded faith.**

—THOMAS JEFFERSON

● ● ● ● ●

I had been given vague directions, and when I disembarked from the bus I was not quite sure which street to follow. I saw a man with a white cane tapping his way down the road holding onto the arm of a friend. I crossed over to ask his friend for directions. "Excuse me, can you tell me how to find the House of Hope, please?" I had expected the "friend" to respond; instead it was the blind man who stopped and turned toward me. Looking right at me he smiled, lifted his cane, and pointed back down the road. "Just walk in that direction for about 100 meters, you can't miss it on the right." "Thank you," I replied and followed the pointed cane. *Only in Bethlehem,* I thought, *would a blind man point a lost man in the right direction.* It struck me as soon as he spoke: The blind see and those who see are blind!

The House of Hope was exactly where the blind man had assured me it would be, and I was ushered in to meet Aunty May. She was drinking afternoon tea with her two assistants and they greeted me with great warmth, joy, and laughter. Our conversation was remarkable in that all three women were in their late 60s or early 70s yet vibrant with life. Aunty May reclined on her bed and apologized because she was still recovering from a broken hip suffered from a recent fall. I only realized much later after my visit that Aunty May was blind. Another of the ladies was also blind and recounted how she had traveled to Paris in her younger days for eye operations that had been unsuccessful. All were excited about the growth of their work and the support they were receiving from people who lived in England and in other regions of the world.

I left their company radiating the life they had breathed into me, deeply humbled by the absence in their speech and disposition of any trace of self-pity or bitterness. I thirsted for the depth and quality of their faith, their obvious contentment in all circumstances, and the selfless love they demonstrated in providing a home and hope for children others of us would pass by. None of them complained about their situation or their health but instead interjected, when challenges were acknowledged, "God is faithful."

Faithfulness, love, encouragement, contentment, servanthood, enthusiasm, humility, vision, courage, and generosity of spirit. Those were some of the qualities Osbiel, Vic, the blind man of Bethlehem, and Aunty May and her friends unwittingly shared with me in our fleeting encounters. Qualities that point beyond the tangible and material toward a richness and a beauty reflected in some human beings. This begs the question, Why in them more than in others? And then again, why do such glimpses of "love" tend to move us so deeply and evoke such respect and admiration, causing an inner murmuring and a hunger for more of these values to be present within ourselves? We haven't even mentioned the more famous examples of the twentieth century, such as Mother Teresa, Nelson Mandela, Mahatma Gandhi, and many artists, poets, and musicians.

The other evening I sat in the pub with a friend whose opinion I respect, and I asked him what he would find interesting in a book about "God." And he said, "What's the point? What difference does it make in my daily life? Why bother?"

These are reasonable and valid questions. The vast majority of people assimilate into their worldviews and experiences a regard for the "Christian Church" as very "traditional and irrelevant" or "hysterical and emotional." Given some of the antics and behaviors manifest in those who attend churches of all denominational stripes it makes sense that some people choose to avoid the whole subject. Although it is understandable, the problem with this response is that it simply caricatures a vast and complex reality in too simplistic a manner. It is invariably inconsistent with other more philosophically tolerant responses in the same individual.

A common example is that we do not refrain from driving because we have been involved in one crash, or because we have experienced traveling in a car driven by an irresponsible driver (be they conservatively slow or emotionally exciting, even frighteningly fast).

●  ●  ●  ●  ●

### Half this game is 90 percent mental.

—YOGI BERRA

●  ●  ●  ●  ●

*What is the point? What difference does God make in my daily life?* That was similar to the question I posed when I first considered buying a microwave oven. After having the use of one for a short while I began to wonder how I had ever lived without it! Or maybe answering the question is more accurately framed by using the analogy of trying to describe and explain a love relationship. Can the answer be given in scientific terms, or in cold logic supported by indisputable facts? To some degree we could substantiate an answer describing companionship and conversation and the experience of "being in love"; but to clearly define the reality is difficult if not impossible. We will throw up our hands in exasperation and say, "Try it for yourself and see—then you will know."

How do you "try it for yourself" with God? Maybe a starting point is being open to possibilities. Similar to initiating a date: quite simply demonstrating a willingness to take the first step with a little risk, introduce yourself—then see what happens. It's all part of the adventure. We can do the same with God as well; in fact I suspect he enjoys a little spice in his relationships. He probably gets tired of formality and people reading to him from books.

"Introduce myself to God?" you ask with a blank look on your face. Sure. You can say something like "Hello, God—I'm not sure you even exist—I'm [insert your name] and if you are real I'd like to know that." You may be surprised what happens over the following weeks. You could find your-self thinking more frequently about God, the topic of God will crop up in conversations more than usual, or you may find an article in front of you, or…whatever. Just relax and have fun and maybe remind "God," if he exists, that you're waiting for some answers. If he exists he may quite enjoy send-ing some creative clues designed just for you. It's your job to let him know you're listening—it is his job to communicate clearly enough for you to be able to hear.

And by the way, if you already have come to faith in God this little exer-cise does not exclude you. "Coming to faith" is like being born into a world where you become increasingly aware of a new dimension. The problem is that many people who "come to faith" tend to stop there and consequently they get stuck in spiritual diapers. The world is absolutely cluttered with spiritual babies crawling around quarreling with each other and behaving as if just "being born" is enough. *End of story! God's great mission is now accomplished!*

No, it is not—thank God! There is much to explore after initially discover-ing I am born into a spiritual realm. Similar to growing infants experiencing their new physical world, through which they tumble and tread largely by trial and error. For those who believe in God it can also be exciting to ask something like, "What do you want to teach me now?" or "Where is a blind spot, attitude, or even belief that is getting in the way of my growth?" Those little questions should keep life interesting for quite a while. The neat thing is that the growing and learning (and unlearning) process will never cease or flash "The End" across our screens.

Imagine if you were on your deathbed and someone told you about a relative who wanted you to inherit a castle in England. Neither of you had ever been in touch with each other. In fact, you did not even know you had such a relative. What difference would that inheritance have made to your life? Maybe God is like that. What difference would it make?

Or imagine meeting God one day after your death, and he starts telling you about all the plans he had for you—but you were always too busy to listen, or too scared to try, or you had limited your relationship with him to be no larger than your own understanding. Or worse still, imagine God has to tap you on the shoulder because you don't recognize him. He is so unlike what you had pictured him to be—much nicer, kinder, and more loving than you had ever imagined; no rule book in sight. He'd rather embrace you than read you the riot act—and you discover it now, after your death. How might things have been different in your life on earth if...

There could be all kinds of interesting possibilities wrapped up in those answers—but that is for you and me to explore and start to unravel.

# 3

# You Can't Prove Anything!

*The flashlight said*
*I have no need of batteries*
*And instead became little Emily's*
*piggy bank*
*Filled with a few measly coins*
*And never once did it ever*
*Shine a single ray of light*
*Through the darkness*
*To illuminate anything at all*

*The car said*
*I don't need wheels*
*I feel quite complete like this*
*And became a shack of sorts*
*Perched on discarded bricks*
*And never once moved an inch*
*To explore*
*The so much more*
*Beyond the horizon of the road*
*Outside its rusting doors*

*The man on the earth said*

*I don't need God*
*And stubbornly wandered*
*On his self-guided tour*
*Stumbling through a world*
*He failed to understand*
*And never once tasted or glimpsed*
*Eternity*
*Or felt embraced by the love*
*His heart so yearned to know*

No one can prove the existence of God any more than you or I can scientifically prove the reality or the authenticity of love. Furthermore, in a pluralistic global village where many expressions of worship and religion jostle for position, there is enormous pressure to be politically correct and to accept every expression of faith as equally valid and true. To maintain that one way to God is the "only way" is to be regarded as extremely arrogant and narrow-minded.

Some people advocate that all religions are equal, and that faith itself is ultimately the quality to respect and value among the various religions. They argue that if the object of faith is determined by culture, one's environment and upbringing, and a host of other variables, how can one person evaluate the "truth" of another person's faith?

Of course there are others who will passionately claim that all expressions of faith in God or a spiritual deity are misguided. Faith merely fills a void in weak people, who are unable to cope with life without a spiritual crutch manufactured from the substance of their desperately wishful thinking.

So what is one to do?

Which way do we go?

What is the right direction? Is there one?

Who knows anyway?

*"Does it really matter what you believe as long as it is meaningful for you and helps?"*

*"Why can't everyone just follow what makes sense to them and leave others alone?"*

*"I wish people wouldn't try to convert me. I've seen examples of people who believe in God, and it certainly isn't what I'd want to be."*

*"Why can't I just do my best and try not to do anyone any harm?"*

*"Look at history, and all the terrible things that have been done in the name of religion."*

The voices are countless, the questions never-ending, the answers few and far between—I mean the answers that satisfy…

Another person says that in every human heart there is a God-shaped void that only he can fill. Another replies that she doesn't think she is missing out on anything and that she has no need for God. A third shrugs his shoulders and walks away.

● ● ● ● ●

## I am not young enough to know everything.

—OSCAR WILDE

● ● ● ● ●

One of the clues to the existence of a "God-shaped void" is the deep desire (consciously or subconsciously) within each one of us to find meaning and fulfillment. This need is met one way or another—in work, sport, relationships, art, adventure, or pretty much anything else we can imagine. Where humans have abandoned the pursuit of meaning the tendency is to self-destruct into addictive patterns of behavior that temporarily fill the void and dull the pain. Maybe a core ingredient of our essential DNA is a propensity to require and find meaning at the center of our lives—an object or focus of worship.

What about those who retort that this so-called need or void is merely rationalizing a crutch for the weak—some people just need "religion." A crutch looks ridiculous in the hands of a healthy individual, but for the wounded it is a strong and helpful support. What is even more tragic is watching someone who could use a crutch stubbornly stagger along the road unaided and unsupported. So who is weak? Who is blind? Who is deaf?

A leper places his hand in the coals of a burning fire and feels no need to remove it when his flesh burns because he experiences no pain. In the case of a leper the absence of the "felt need" to remove his hand from a natural source of pain is an indication of disease. It is not a testimony to his superior wisdom, or the fact that the laws of nature do not apply to him, or will be suspended for him. Insensitivity or indifference to pain in fact is the very condition that will ultimately destroy him...irrespective of how he might subjectively feel about that reality. This fact of objective reality (laws of science and nature) provides us with an interesting segue into considering the universal law of gravity and what it might teach us about God.

Gravity exists on every continent among every people of every tribe and every religion. It does not change and is not altered or suspended for anyone, anywhere, at any time. Gravity does not exist in one form for those who choose to believe it should be so and exist in another form for another group, who believe it should be manifested slightly differently. In other words, the reality of gravity is not relative—it is a law of science that is universally true for all human beings. When a drunken person walks off a roof thinking he can fly, gravity does not change because of his distorted perception. It remains constant, and even though the drunk discovers his mistake in midair he nevertheless plummets to the ground and lands hard (off any rooftop in any country on every continent in the world).

The same truths can be applied to the universal need for all human beings to eat and drink and breathe in order to remain alive on this earth. It matters not what your or my opinion is about "how things work." The fact is, we either accept as a given the basic principles involved in sustaining life, or we risk death seeking some other method of our own design.

My first trip overseas was a very exciting event in my life. I was in my early 20s and flew from Cape Town to Luxembourg, where I had arranged to spend one night before continuing on to London. After booking in at my hotel I decided to walk around the city before darkness descended. Preparing to cross a busy road I looked right, then left, right again and stepped off the curb. A screech of brakes stopped me in my tracks. An oncoming car slid to a halt within inches of my shocked self desperately trying to claw my way back to the sidewalk. I had forgotten that cars drive on the "wrong" side of the road in Continental Europe and consequently was very nearly injured or killed. I was innocent, ignorant, and operating in a country where the laws of driving were not the same as the ones I had grown up with. My "relative knowledge" was absolutely useless in this context; I either had to change my thinking or expect to be knocked flying by objective reality.

There is not much argument over these universal and self-evident truths, and yet…when we talk of spirituality all chaos breaks loose. Discussions invariably insist on relativity to a degree that borders on intellectual insanity. To believe in any form of universal spiritual truth or consistent law for all humanity is usually not regarded as an acceptable point of view. Instead God, unlike gravity, changes with whomever is considering his/her/its existence. Apparently such open-mindedness is rational and intellectually admirable. To suggest otherwise is to be branded narrow-minded, highly judgmental, and certainly not in step with the progressive thinking of our enlightened times!

●　●　●　●　●

### Everything has been figured out, except how to live.

—JEAN-PAUL SARTRE

●　●　●　●　●

What do we conclude from the existence of such a wide array of religious expressions and rituals? Who is right, and does it really matter? What is true, if anything?

Millions of cars incessantly roll and sputter over the face of the earth. What does that reality tell us? Or how about the multitude of planes that traverse the skies and the fleets of ships that sail the oceans? It suggests that transportation is an important issue for people of every nation and tribe. Therefore it is reasonable to conclude that transportation is a common priority throughout the world.

Similarly, the existence of many expressions of religion indicates the universal reality that human beings are spiritually hungry, because we continue to explore and search for a meaning to life that is beyond the tangible. Religion, or spirituality, helps us explain the essence and meaning of life itself, and maybe even equips us to cope more constructively with the reality of death.

With transportation, once we have acknowledged the universal need for it we might consider the various forms that have been invented and are used. These would include shoes for walking, bicycles, Rollerblades, skis, motorbikes and motorcars, airplanes, trains, and ships. The wide array of modes of transport available does not necessarily mean that some are better or others are worse. They all have validity and serve a purpose in helping to meet the variety of needs human beings face in their diverse situations. However, they are solutions that have evolved from the human community as we have collectively applied our resources to solving the challenge of horizontal and vertical mobility.

Is religion similar—a manifestation of the creative response of humanity seeking after something or someone greater than us that we can honor and worship? To some extent it is, but even with that admission we would then be asking, "Why?" However, if that is the end of the matter then we are indeed left with a very one-dimensional situation: humanity seeking to solve the yearning for fulfillment from within the confines of our own self-defined parameters as best we can, utilizing what we know and perceive. That is called relativity—everything is equally true because from my perspective I think, feel, believe, and experience it to be true for me.

Consider the leper again. The fact he cannot feel pain is relatively true but not universally true. His lack of sensitivity actually is a symptom of his disease rather than the basis of a universal truth. Consequently "my" subjective experience and perspective alone is hardly a reliable or trustworthy enough foundation upon which to base and build a "universal truth" or principle. It may indeed provide valuable and valid evidence supporting a belief system, but it will never in and of itself be sufficient to qualify as reliable fact.

How would the discussion change if God does exist in some form?

What might his perspective be? Or should I refer to God as "it" or "she" or a "higher power"? Many of the debates around this topic mention God in a way similar to how one might refer to an inanimate object or thing. The implicit understanding in such discussions is that God can be shrunk down to fit within human parameters, and then we get to decide where to place him, much like we would position an antique on the mantelpiece. Religion unfortunately accomplishes that task rather effectively, and always politely and reverently. It places God in a compartment or box where he is respected, but definitely kept in his place. He is not allowed out to mix with "the secular." (Which means he can't interfere with most of life, where I am god and I rule, or with politics or business or relationships or sports or...)

• • • • •

### There's nothing an agnostic can't do if he doesn't know whether he believes in anything or not.

—MONTY PYTHON

• • • • •

Religion trundles God out into the open arena to benevolently preside over state ceremonies, marriages, funerals, and baptisms. And when the ceremony is over it tenderly places him back on the shelf and the "real party" begins! Or God is an enormous sleeping giant around whom we whisper and tiptoe with some trepidation—a gentle tame "higher power" who awaits our bidding like some genial dumbwaiter. But what if he moved and expressed some initiatives, thoughts, and purposes of his own—quite independently of "us"? What if he stirred like a gigantic Gulliver, snapping the paltry intellectual threads with which we have tried to restrain and confine him? What then?

During a discussion group with professional businessmen we were talking about how our culture worships the intellect and the pursuit of knowledge and money. Yet when it comes to spirituality all reason appears to be jettisoned in favor of personal prejudice or knee-jerk reactions. As if to unwittingly illustrate the point, a man who was a chartered accountant by profession said, "You can't believe the Bible these days."

"Have you ever read it?" I asked.

"No, not really," he replied.

"Well, how can you seriously make the statement?" I responded. "You would not accept such a rationale in your boardroom, so why is it acceptable in this environment?"

I recall a helpful illustration someone gave many years ago when I was attending a discussion on atheism and agnosticism at Cape Town University.

An atheist asserts that there is no such thing or person called God, therefore they do not believe in the existence of a supreme being. How can one prove that God does not exist or that he does exist? How do you prove love, or the experience of being loved, or happiness, or low self-esteem?

The fact that we cannot prove the existence of such realities in an objective manner does not necessarily mean they do not exist at all. The rationale to suggest that an atheist is really an agnostic (meaning someone who is not sure that there is a God) goes something like this...

> *Q: Do you agree that life is made up of a multitude of different experiences?*
>
> *A: Yes.*
>
> *Q: Would you claim to have personally experienced every experience that is available to a human being?*
>
> *A: No, of course not.*
>
> *Q: Might it be possible that "God" could be found in one of those experiences that you personally have not yet entered into?*
>
> *A: I suppose so.*

This little dialogue simply illustrates that it is as intellectually indefensible to assert that God does *not* exist, as it is to claim to "prove" that he does. Maybe there is a more constructive question to explore.

How about examining the evidence concerning the possibility of God in order to determine whether there is a strong or weak likelihood of his existence? The danger many of us succumb to is that we predetermine what we think. When we peel away the layers of reason, the substance of our thoughts is often surprisingly thin and underdeveloped. At its center the kernel of rejection is exposed, shown to be rotten with fear and negativity when we contemplate what acknowledging God's existence will mean to our "freedom."

●     ●     ●     ●     ●

**Atheism is a non-prophet organization.**

—Unknown

●     ●     ●     ●     ●

On a more lighthearted note, if God turned out to be everything we ever wanted and dreamed of in a man or a woman, would that change our response?

What is brought into focus again is the importance of differentiating between the people who express belief in God—whatever the faith, and the deity who is at the center of that faith.

A few weeks ago I was driving across Vancouver Island, where I live, over the mountains to play squash with friends in the town of Port Alberni. As I wound my way through magnificent cedars around Cameron Lake I listened to the radio news report of the space exploration mission involving Titan and the Rover modules exploring Mars for much longer than had been anticipated. It was remarkable to learn that after seven years of flight through space the Titan module was activated and "steered" from Earth to descend and land on this most distant and strange landscape. Likewise the Rovers on Mars communicated with Earth and were used to conduct all kinds of experiments while being driven and controlled from our planet.

I arrived at the squash club early and stood outside in a fairly chilly winter breeze waiting for Lindsay or Wayne to arrive and unlock the door. I tucked myself into the doorway for protection and looked out across the parking lot.

On the road before me was a white paper cup lying quite still. As I watched, every now and then the breeze would nudge it and roll it sideways—just a few inches—first one way and then the other. My mind went back to the Rovers on Mars and the Titan module. *Imagine,* I thought to myself, *if that paper cup was being manipulated from someone sitting on Mars…and they were making it move and could even watch me standing in this doorway!* I'd never believe such a thing was possible—and yet that is precisely what those missions had accomplished. That reality is mind-boggling enough for me—and if human ingenuity can accomplish such magnificent feats, what might be possible with God?

Wayne and Lindsay strolled up at almost the same time. "Look at that paper cup," I said, and recounted my great revelation enthusiastically. "John, what have you been smoking?" was the sympathic response. "Let's play squash."

4

# Is Truth Like a Coke Bottle
# in the Hand of a Bushman?

THE SAND DUNES OF THE KALAHARI DESERT ROLL ACROSS THE UNDULATING LANDSCAPE AS FAR AS THE EYE CAN SEE, SOME WITH SHARP RIDGE BACKS AND OTHERS SMOOTH AND ROUND, RISING FROM BROAD AND GENTLE SHOULDERS. At the edge of this wilderness a man stands holding an object he has never seen before. He is short and wiry, not an inch of fat on his body, clad only in a small loincloth fashioned from animal skins. Across his back is slung a roughly finished bow with lethally poisoned arrows stored carefully in a skin quiver. His ancestors have lived in this region for as long as anyone can remember. He learned the character of this harsh environment and its treasures growing up at his father's side. Now he knows every undulation of the earth and can identify any animal track like the back of his wrinkled hand. What he does not know is where the object in his hand has come from, what it is, and what it means. His father never showed him one of these.

Some years ago the film *The Gods Must Be Crazy* introduced Western viewers to the remarkable people known as the San Bushmen, who live in the southwestern region of Africa. These people have wandered the semidesert expanses of the Namibian and South-West African coast for thousands of years. They lived, and flourished, by developing highly sophisticated skills enabling them to survive in a region that would starve and dehydrate most of us within a few days. They know how to tell the size of

4

an animal and identify all kinds of facts merely by examining its spoor (tracks and droppings) on the ground. They know what plants to eat and which to avoid, and they can extract water from the roots of plants we would pass by and disregard as useless.

The Gods Must Be Crazy begins with one of the "primitive" tribal men stumbling across a very unfamiliar object in their world—a Coke bottle. Apparently it was thrown out of a passing plane and fell on the desert sands of the African coastline—mysteriously appearing and entirely out of context for those who find it. The bottle is a hint to them of a world much bigger than their own. They don't really understand what it is, what it means, or what to do with it. Consequently they do the only thing they can do—they invent their own meanings and interpretations and beliefs around its existence, based upon their perspectives and understanding of life.

To a Westerner observing the tribe's handling of the Coke bottle and their fascination with it, the situation seems comical bordering on ludicrous. How could something so common and disposable in the West provide such fascination for those in this remote corner of the world? The Westerner knows that what the San tribe is examining is a piece of molded glass manufactured for the mass consumption of a carbonated beverage. However, the tribal leaders understand this object as having fallen from the sky and therefore conclude it must have come from the gods—but why is beyond their comprehension.

How do we explain the Bushmen's interpretation of the Coke bottle? As a Western observer my parameters and life experiences are different and broader (not necessarily better) than theirs. The Coke bottle is nothing special or unique in my world, and I understand how it is made, why it exists, and what it is used for. With all that background the reaction of the Bushmen to its presence in their world fascinates and also amuses me. I am amused because I know its real origin and purpose—it is only an old bottle. But to the nomadic tribe it is an object from the sky, and thus from the gods. Which interpretation is true, theirs or mine?

●　●　●　●　●

**Man has such a predilection for systems and abstract deductions that he is ready to distort the truth intentionally, he is ready to deny the evidence of his senses only to justify his logic.**

—DOSTOYEVSKY

●　●　●　●　●

Subjectively speaking, within the Bushmen's worldview their response is quite understandable and their interpretations are true and valid—for them. Objectively though, the Coke bottle remains just that—a discarded piece of molded glass created by an affluent culture, with no spiritual significance to it at all.

Who cares anyway, as long as both parties feel fulfilled and their meaningful explanations work for them? Nobody cares—until they are no longer alone in their surroundings. Until a man in denim jeans crests the rim of the neighboring sand dune clutching a plastic milk bottle and claiming that his spiritual fount is the ultimate source of life, sustenance, and meaning. Then there may be potential for upset, particularly if cherished beliefs determine behavior, impact social interactions, and even influence how one lives on this earth and treats the environment. At such a point we may not arrive at mass conversion or philosophical and spiritual agreement, but it will be important that our common understanding allows for a significant degree of mutual respect, tolerance, and individual freedom.

The first time I saw the city of Oxford it was snowing. Again, this was on my first trip overseas. I had been in England for a few threads of a day after landing at Heathrow, and already I had managed to make a fool of myself! After asking for directions regarding the train to Oxford I dutifully boarded at Paddington Station in London and watched the scenery flash by as the express clattered its way over ancient England. I had understood the journey to be about 90 minutes, maybe two hours in duration. We stopped at a few stations along the way, and after two-and-a-half hours I began to wonder whether I was on the right train. When I saw words with "ff" I knew I was in trouble, and sure enough I was in Wales heading for Cardiff. After explaining my mistake somewhat sheepishly to the stationmaster (I had failed to change trains at Didcot—I'll never forget that name) I was ushered back aboard another Oxford-bound train and I finally arrived after dark.

I would hazard a guess that most of our spiritual journeys are similar to my London–Oxford train ride—littered with missed connections, false directions, and the occasional need to backtrack. Personally, I think as long as we're trying to make progress there are a multitude of tracks, trains, paths, and modes of locomotion for us to utilize during our quest. The challenge we are faced with is, how do we discern the difference between a dead-end and the mountaintop? And is there only one way—which is a puzzle tucked into the folds of these pages throughout our discussion for us to ponder? (I'll take you to where I lived in Oxford a little later.)

●　●　●　●　●

**It was the experience of mystery—even if mixed with fear—that engendered religion.**

—ALBERT EINSTEIN

●　●　●　●　●

At times when we focus on issues that are really important for us we can get so close to the trees and so lost in the undergrowth that we no longer see or remember what the forest looks like anymore. Perhaps therefore it will be helpful to invite one of Oxford's most famous teachers to guide us through a few of the "big-forest principles."

During his many eloquent discussions about God, C.S. Lewis, the great twentieth-century explainer of Christianity to the common person, discussed the philosophical difference between an *open universe* and a *closed universe*. This is important, because it provides the foundation and framework for much of our philosophical discussion and debate.

In a *closed universe* concept, philosophers and others attempt to explain the world and its meaning from the evidence around them. They (humanity) are at the center—and all meaning radiates out from them as they observe, reflect, and interpret whatever they can see, touch, taste, and feel. There is no God, no "Other," no objective independent reality out there beyond the world and ourselves as we know them. Meaning is attributed to life as a by-product of what is experienced by the observer, and as the collective understanding gleaned and analyzed from human observations and learning over centuries of dialogue between the generations. The center of the universe and the source of all meaning is humanity itself, and thus by default we are gods, or supreme beings, with ultimate authority, knowledge, wisdom, and control in our hands.

The *open universe* concept maintains that human beings and philosophers are not the center of the universe after all. They form part of that which is created by the "One" who is greater than all of creation, a Creator. Meaning, purpose, and fulfillment is ultimately discovered in relationship between the Creator and the created—and in the self-awareness of the created to understand who created whom.

●　●　●　●　●

**Believe those who are seeking the truth;**
**doubt those who find it.**

—ANDRÉ GIDE

●　●　●　●　●

For many of us the discovery of spirituality can be somewhat akin to the San Bushmen stumbling upon a Coke bottle in the Namibian desert. It is mystifying and unfamiliar, handled with some trepidation. At the same time many nomadic business entrepreneurs are finding themselves strangely drawn and intrigued by it.

The worldview of the Bushmen is *open.* They have room to allow for and believe in the existence of "the gods" and that they have an impact on their lives and on the universe in which they live.

The predominant Western worldview is closed. All things have only the meaning that emerges from the collective wisdom gathered over many generations. As the Bushman with a Coke bottle is to us, this understanding might be equally quaint and comical to an observer if a larger picture is brought to bear and a greater perspective is found.

Consider how the astronauts perceived the world during their first journeys into space, viewing the Earth from a distance for the first time in human history.

> *The Earth reminded us of a Christmas tree ornament hanging in the blackness of space. As we got farther and farther away it diminished in size. Finally it shrank to the size of a marble, the most beautiful marble you can imagine. That beautiful, warm, living object looked so fragile, so delicate, that if you touched it with a finger it would crumble and fall apart. Seeing this has to change a man, has to make a man appreciate the creation of God and the love of God.*
>
> —JAMES IRWIN, USA

> *From space I saw Earth indescribably beautiful with all the scars of national boundaries gone.*
>
> —MUHAMMAD AHMAD FARIS, SYRIA

How then do we know whether our worldview or belief system is open or closed? How do I know whether all that I believe about life, God, or the world, is really just a Coke bottle? How do I know when or if I am projecting meaning on reality that might be quaint, misguided, or even dangerous—even though it is sincere? And if I could see beyond to the bigger picture, might I also respond, "Oops, that was sure misguided"?

The most pragmatic answer may well be that we will never know for certain either way and that we may well be right and wrong. But if we do not even ask the question en route, then we are far more likely to end up in Wales rather than in Oxford...or maybe even further off course!

A child has a need for toys and play. During the course of following its natural instincts it starts playing with an electric socket in the wall and pushing its fingers into the holes designed for the prongs of a plug. It does not realize that the "game" could end with it unwittingly destroying its own life. Therefore a parent or someone older will intervene and move the child away from its seemingly benign plaything.

Relative truth or innocence does not change the impact of objective reality—electricity will kill unwitting children who come in contact with it as indifferently as it will execute a man in an electric chair. That principle holds true in a wide variety of situations and contexts.

The sausage and cabbage that Kevan and I consumed in his small apartment in Wolfson College was surprisingly tasty—it was all we could afford. I was visiting my friend in Oxford after a stint in the South African Army, an unproductive two years in college in Cape Town, and another few years working. South Africa was a tense and troubled land heaving under the black cloud of apartheid and ruled by a paranoid and insecure white government, which tended to attribute every conceivable challenge to the threat of communism. All white males were conscripted to military service after leaving school, with a real possibility of being sent to fight on the Angolan border.

At the time I left for England there was a fair amount of controversy about whether the South African Army was actually active within Angola itself. The prime minister, Pik Botha, vehemently denied any such suggestion, calling it fictitious propaganda. I was therefore surprised to see BBC reports documenting South African troops operating well within Angola, backed by film footage that was irrefutable. At that time censorship was strictly enforced, which meant that the news fed to those within South Africa was significantly different from what was broadcast around the rest of the world. The result was a "South African version of truth" and an "international version of truth." In actuality it is likely that both versions were slanted, containing biases and inevitable inaccuracies in their reporting.

●  ●  ●  ●  ●

**The opposite of a correct statement is a false statement. The opposite of a profound truth may well be another profound truth.**

—NIELS BOHR

●  ●  ●  ●  ●

Which one was true? Both contained elements of truth. But to gain a more reliable version of the whole truth we would have had to integrate and review both the internal South African version and the external international version.

So how do we know what to believe? Perhaps there is no single simple answer with an absolute solution or formula contained therein. Perhaps to embrace belief and truth we will have to be content to be pilgrims constantly searching beyond the truth as we know it today, which is inevitably and unavoidably shrouded in our own relativity. It cannot be otherwise, for we are finite and limited in thought, vision, and intellectual ability.

Maybe the presence of large amounts of certainty is something I have to accept and acknowledge as being ultimately elusive. I mean the fact that "certainty" will never be absolutely mine to possess, precisely because I cannot see or know every angle or perspective of life, the world, or my convictions juxtaposed against those of others. Nevertheless I can still strive for understanding and clarity—within the restrictions and realities of those finite parameters that inevitably frame my pondering of the infinite and the eternal.

The beginning of an answer is found by inviting the questions, "What am I missing? Is there more? What is the evidence to persuade me to believe that this is not just 'another Coke bottle'?" In other words, adopting an attitude of humility that considers my own finiteness and limitations. (Then again, we can take such an approach to the extreme by stating that nothing is objectively true—relativism—and assert that the only acceptable and valid truth is whatever is true for "me.")

How do I know what is authentic or true? That question opens up a huge debate and possibly a can of worms. Authentic spirituality sets people free—spiritual Coke bottles trap and enslave people by creating bottlenecks of rules and restrictions.

Here are a few pointers, questions to ask, that may be helpful when evaluating a particular expression of spirituality (merely my suggestions):

1. What is the origin of this "brand" of spirituality—historical, factual evidence, length of time it has existed, and so on?

2. What is the origin of its foundation statements or authoritative documents?

3. Who are the key figures? Is one human being too much at the center and in control?

4. How is leadership held accountable?

5. Are finances clearly transparent and audited?

6. What is the basic teaching?

7. Do I have the freedom to say no? To question? To walk away?

8. Am I being asked for money?

9. Does it "ring true"? (Pay attention to your gut feelings.)

10. What can I find out by talking to others and learning from their experiences?

The majority of spiritual Coke bottles are presented with love, meaning, acceptance, purpose, and peace as planks in their platform. Every human being desires such things, and it is natural for us to want to find more of them—nevertheless, explorers beware! In the spiritual "world," deception, manipulation, power trips, control freaks, and money-grabbing abound. Don't submit to pressure to join, belong, or "sign up" too quickly—if such tactics are necessary, then something is wrong.

By the way, Doubt and Certainty are essential companions on the road of spiritual exploration. Both are vital to our growth because they keep us sharp, honest—and humble. Doubt and Certainty invariably sit at the head of the table when faith in God is the topic of conversation. This is where Doubt gets to wear a tuxedo and is welcomed as the honored guest, particularly by spiritual cynics and skeptics who prefer to court Certainty's twin sister and Doubt's dearest friend, Uncertainty. They don't mind parading in public with Certainty on other occasions, but when it comes to God, she gets the cold shoulder and always wonders why. What's the reason for such a reaction?

●　●　●　●　●

**The greatest fallacy of democracy is that
everyone's opinion is worth the same.**

—ROBERT HEINLEIN

●　●　●　●　●

If Doubt were allowed to rule in the matter of believing in God, we would struggle to accomplish anything and would probably be doomed to waver and wander in circles for an eternity. Doubt left unattended will never make a decision. And some people almost worship Doubt as their ultimate form of truth. They will talk about "a healthy skepticism"—or gazing out the window they will muse, "One has to have an open mind, you know." The problem is that if we take such a stance too far when applying for a job, or considering marriage, or booking a flight, we'll probably end up without a job, extremely single, and stuck on the ground for life. Doubt, when it is unhealthy, can be obsessed with avoiding decisions; fear of commitment and the "open mind" can metamorphose into a vast, empty, dry and arid wasteland.

Doubt needs Certainty to prod it along and keep it active and honest in conversations about God. Certainty loves definition, building solid structures based on "truth," and defining the world in which it lives with clear thoughts. It adores boxes and compartments, and once it makes up its mind it can be quite intolerant. Certainty also gets things done, makes decisions and organizes, sets goals and works to accomplish them. However, Doubt can help Certainty come to terms with the reality that growth and change are always taking place and therefore we have to be flexible and adaptable. Doubt forces Certainty to continually redefine itself by asking questions and provokes it to reevaluate its reasoning and repeatedly prove the premises supporting its viewpoint.

When it comes to believing in God, Doubt and Certainty are always present around the campfire of Faith. Certainty will want to pitch a tent, settle down, and dig foundations, while Doubt will walk to the perimeters of the campsite and keep asking, "Are you sure this is the right spot?" In a healthy scenario Certainty will have its way for a while and they will camp out for some time. Eventually Doubt will force a move and the journey will continue until the cycle repeats itself. The motivation for moving might come from within the camp or possibly from circumstances outside of their control.

Doubt never doubts that they have to keep moving, and Certainty is quite certain that faith will grow as long as they keep focused on the ultimate goal.

The good news is that Doubt and Certainty do not have to be avoided, for they are indeed our friends and allies. Despite their personality differences they encourage us to dig deeper, and to make decisions that, although involving risk, will result in Certainty gaining more ground in our inner being. The function of Certainty in the quest for faith in God is to settle and occupy territory in order that we may have some inner security and stability. Doubt's role is that of a scout or a safety inspector who is always out there prodding around making sure that what he sees is authentic, that it works, and that the uncomfortable questions are spoken out loud: "What's this for? Is it garbage?" Trouble is, he's a pack rat, which usually means that Certainty has to make the ultimate decision about what to hoist overboard.

Different types of people require different questions to be asked and answered. They need different kinds of evidence in order to enable them to relinquish Doubt and find some degree of Certainty regarding belief in God. There is not one single absolute or fail-proof method to arrive at certainty about God, or to understand how God works in this paradoxical and complex world. Humility and humor will be required almost every step of the way.

Regard Certainty with a mischievous grain of salt and don't always believe her stubborn assurance that she is right and knows what's best. To be fair, do not be alarmed by Doubt or take him too seriously either. He tends to be a bit of a showman and thrives on attention. Sometimes Doubt just needs to be acknowledged and embraced, and he'll fall into belief despite himself. Here's a little secret: Denial often trips both of them up and muddies their pools—which makes the journey even more interesting.

# 5

# The Great Debate

YOU COULD HEAR THE ROAR OF THE CROWDS FROM OUR HOUSE WHENEVER IMPORTANT RUGBY OR CRICKET GAMES WERE BEING PLAYED IN CAPE TOWN. We lived in the southern suburbs about a five-minute walk from the international rugby and cricket grounds. I used to love working at the cricket ground or sitting under the oak trees watching the game. Some of the international matches between South Africa and England, Australia or New Zealand, lasted three or five days! I was absolutely thrilled shaking hands with Graham Pollock (the Wayne Gretzky of South African cricket in the 1960s) as a timid ten-year-old.

Invariably any North American watching cricket will shake their head in disbelief that anyone could find such a slow-moving sport entertaining (and this goes on for days?). The chances are that if I attended a cricket match with a friend and we described our experiences, after the first day you would hear two very different accounts of what actually happened. While I may describe the excitement or tactical skill of players I suspect there would be a confused and rather bored, less enthusiastic description from my North American friend.

Science and faith (belief in God) can evoke similar responses to that of my friend and I watching the same game of cricket. If I have grown up with a science background and little exposure to faith in God then I will quite likely be bored or somewhat indifferent to that "cricket match," and vice versa if my background excluded much scientific content. These are obviously extremes because many of us have some overlap between the two. Nevertheless the point being made is that our instinctive reactions are often more rooted in misunderstandings or a limited exposure, rather than anything we have really applied our minds, hearts, and time to in order to gain a better appreciation and understanding. It's the way we tend to live and work; until we stumble upon a friend who can enthuse us to "look again" and maybe even learn to love cricket (which could be a more difficult a task then believing in God!).

●　●　●　●　●

**If you want to make an apple pie from scratch, you must first create the universe.**

—CARL SAGAN

●　●　●　●　●

The journey to believing in God will lead us through a wide variety of terrains, scenery, and weather conditions depending upon our background, culture, family, friendships, lifestyles, and many other variables. But whatever route we embark upon we can be assured that somewhere along the way we will come face-to-face with a figure that some of us will be startled by and wish to avoid, and others will welcome as a friend. We're speaking of that moment when belief in God encounters science. This whole scenario also occurs the other way round. Science traveling on a journey of faith in theory, experiments, and proof encounters belief in God and experiences similar reactions. It is a level playing field at that moment of meeting, but the conversation that follows is not always open and honest.

I used to be quite intimidated by the prospect of a face-to-face encounter with science and would admit to some feelings of inferiority. I assumed (falsely) that "science" was intellectual and superior and that only the bright people worked in the laboratory. At least that was what I picked up at school when I elected to do biology rather than physics and chemistry. The arts and literature, psychology and sociology, history, architecture, anthropology, geography, astronomy, and all the other disciplines of study and interest were somehow blurred into the background, denigrated to a lower level of importance and rendered less worthy. Maybe it was the spirit of the time or merely my misguided complexes at work.

Despite my own intuitive sense that the God I was being introduced to in the Christian Bible was "the real thing," I desperately needed the reassurance that it was not all wishful thinking; or rooted in my desire to belong to a group and believe in something (neither of which are negative desires in and of themselves).

My journey toward assurance began in a very nonintellectual way. I wanted to belong to a group (and meet some girls) so I joined a small youth group that met every Friday night. We played games and had lots of fun and on most evenings were also exposed to a short devotional talk by one of the group leaders or by a visiting speaker. While some presentations were better than others I am sure that it was the consistent exposure to a varied diet of Christian teaching and personalities that really began the process of a growing reassurance in the foundations of my fledgling faith. I was learning and experiencing all kinds of things about myself and Christian life and faith. I could see for myself that it was not all "hot air" and a crutch for the weak (which by implication would have been me).

I can think of a bunch of people in that group of "teachers and mentors" during those formative teenage years of my life—the youth group leaders Brian (qualifying to be a teacher) and Keith (a civil engineer), John (a teacher), Vic (a retired human resources manager), another John (school principal), Phillip (school chaplain), Bert (businessman), Alan (book sales and marketing), and other men and women. These men were role models for me, whom I observed and listened to and at times wanted to emulate as I whispered to myself, "I'd like to be like that." Hearing why they believed in God and what difference it made to them and the choices they made incrementally challenged me, inspired me, and molded my life, forcing me to think and to grapple with my own choices, behaviors, and lifestyle decisions.

Along the way I rejected God and faith a number of times. After dropping out of the university I felt disillusioned and walked away from any formal expression of faith for a number of years. I used to think that maybe everyone else was having more fun on the other side of the fence where the grass looked so much greener. So I jumped the fence and camped in that idyllic pasture for a while where I was only answerable to myself and to no one else.

But I soon discovered why the grass was greener. It was plastic! It was actually harder to have faith in "no God" and to live my life in random nothingness than it was to believe in the God I was avoiding. As a result I am a strong advocate of life experience being a crucial component for honest learning in matters concerning personal faith and assurance. Life experience will expose the flaws and force issues to the surface in our lives that cause us to dig deeper, receive support from others, and generally learn how to lean on God.

●    ●    ●    ●    ●

**In theory, there is no difference between theory and practice. But, in practice, there is.**

—J.L.A. VAN DE SNEPSCHEUT

●    ●    ●    ●    ●

When I was studying at the university I received a small allowance from three sources, which meant that there was not much left over. At times when money was very scarce I was naturally asking God to please provide, and I occasionally became quite angry and jealous of others. I was embarrassed to discern a behavioral pattern emerge; when I was nearly broke my "faith" was not quite as self-assured as when I had a small financial buffer in the bank. It was much easier to trust God when my security in the bank balance was assured.

Real life has a way of exposing the degree to which we authentically believe, and it will relentlessly test and challenge our philosophies of life. It separates the more theoretical chaff from the wheat we need for our daily bread—whether that philosophy be Christian or not. The irony is that faith is only really tested and able to grow when it is stretched and challenged at the edges of its comfort zone. If we never allow those fringes to be exposed then our faith will suffer just as our bodies do without exercise; it will remain weak, codependent, and insecure. Which means, to be blunt, that our lives will generally not support our profession of faith with much integrity or an attractiveness that evokes in others a curiosity about what (or who) our source of inspiration and strength is.

As the more relaxed and hippie-like "Jesus freak" movement gathered momentum in the early 1970s, a few personalities trickled down through the long grapevine to South Africa. Musicians were an encouragement to me as I listened to their more contemporary styles and easy lyrics describing friendship with God in denim and sandals. They were a breath of fresh air; at last I felt that one could believe in God and Jesus and still be cool—artists like Larry Norman and Cliff Richard come to mind. Christianity in my young eyes was being translated into my life through so many different windows and doors.

I remember listening to an American Christian singer/songwriter playing his songs in the student union dining hall one Friday evening. There was no sense that he needed Christianity for a crutch or that he suffered from some inferior image problem that screamed that to follow Jesus one had to be a nerd. He was so relaxed about his Christian faith and not at all threatened or dogmatic in his conversational style; plus he had long hair and a leather Bible! I wanted to be like him, and that was the kind of faith I prayed for. A lifestyle that integrated my faith throughout every part of my life and one I did not need to hide or apologize for.

When I had the privilege to study in Oxford I was very intimidated by this intellectual ivory tower and wondered whether I would be totally out of place. It wasn't long before I realized that all the students were human beings with libraries of idiosyncrasies and complexes just like mine. In our theology classes every truth I held dear was challenged and I went through a time of real struggle as I saw my cherished beliefs buckling under the pressure of intellectual scrutiny.

I mulled over this dilemma for quite a few weeks, concluding that if God is real at all then he has certainly been exposed to similar rigorous intellectual challenges in every generation. I therefore did not have to protect him with arguments, but rather take hold of the opportunity at hand to find reasonable responses. I discovered along the way where my confidence lay, and why. I came to understand the reasoning behind these challenges more clearly, and considered how I might respond without committing intellectual suicide. It certainly was not restricted to a cerebral exercise and involved my emotions, passions, preconceptions, and personal background, all wrapped up in one tangled ball of "me."

●　　●　　●　　●　　●

**There is only one nature—the division into science and engineering is a human imposition, not a natural one. Indeed, the division is a human failure; it reflects our limited capacity to comprehend the whole.**

—BILL WULF

●　　●　　●　　●　　●

In fact I was deep into a multifaceted learning curve discovering that *knowing something* is far more worthwhile than *knowing about something.* However, the process involved in knowing was more of a boot camp than I had anticipated. I learned that the intellect is merely one component of a greater whole in the quest for assurance in matters of faith. Other key elements that need to be aligned with intellectual integrity are personal emotions (and that gut feeling about something/someone), morality and lifestyle (practicing what you believe—that is, does it work in real life?), and taking risks of faith and prayer and seeing what happens (does God actually answer or make a difference when I take his promises and guidelines seriously?).

Initially I thought that if studied and earned a bunch of degrees and gained intellectual credibility then people would respond to reasonable discussions about God and embrace Christianity with open arms. Of course people do engage in such discussions (otherwise I wouldn't be writing this book), but I also learned during more than 20 years of putting it into practice that facts and rational reasoning are not the major decision-making factor in most of our lives.

I would dare to suggest that maybe an embarrassing percentage of worldviews, whether science, faith, or both, usually reflect more about the emotional and cultural background of the individual than they do about deep rational thinking. Which makes complete sense to me. I would argue that our core priority or need is actually relational and not intellectual. Which is why doubt and certainty will emerge from an integration of both factors working together toward that very commendable goal called "faith."

I should clarify that whenever I am speaking of faith I am specifically referring to belief in God. I stress that fact because we live by "faith in something" all the time. If we don't believe in God that is an act of faith, if we believe in a solid work ethic and self-improvement that is an act of faith, or being kind and not killing people as the way to live—that too is an act of faith. There are countless expressions of faith impacting the choices we make and the meaning we find in living—therefore it is important to be clear about what we mean by faith in this discussion.

If Faith and Science were to inhabit our bodies, Faith would no doubt occupy the heart and Science would prefer to take up residence in our minds. The premise of this book is, without reservation, that both are welcome, both are important, and both are essential for life on earth and indeed for spiritual growth and maturity. If we caricature these two from an academic and scientific perspective, Science would usually be regarded as the wise and sensible professor with his feet on the ground, and Faith would be a flighty young thing not to be trusted. On the other hand from an academic and spiritual perspective Faith would be the Research Fellow in the faculty of Wisdom, and Science would be a rebellious teenager always out late, asking questions, and making a mess of things.

Science is really all about human beings trying to figure out how things work and what makes this world and universe "tick." We study the universe and everything we can see and get our hands on; we explore it, we analyze it, we make deductions from what we find, we look for patterns, we suggest hypotheses, we draw conclusions, we test theories, we outline principles, we develop universal laws, and we build a logical and analytical basis for explaining the meaning of everything. And it is here at the feet of science (some would maintain) that we come face-to-face with religion's greatest challenge and most intellectually equipped foe—or friend?

The potential showdown between Science and Faith can appear to be very threatening and intimidating, until one rolls back the veils of false alarms and considers the players involved in the drama. They are fellow human beings, displaying very little difference in perspective or worldview from that of the philosophers of past generations.

●　●　●　●　●

**Science can purify religion from error and superstition; religion can purify science from idolatry and false absolutes. Each can draw the other into a wider world, a world in which both can flourish…We need each other to be what we must be, what we are called to be.**

—POPE JOHN PAUL II

●　●　●　●　●

Some scientists observe the universe as *closed* (see chapter 4) and conclude that all meaning is uncovered by scientific research. Science at last provides enlightenment and confirms humanity's growing intellectual understanding of an ultimately meaningless cosmos. Their work of science continues to affirm the brilliance and ongoing evolution of the human species.

Other scientists observe the universe as *open*. For them every discovery is a confirmation of the wonder of a creation infinitely complex with an order and precision that is impossible to intellectually dismiss as randomly created by chance. Their work of science points to the existence of a Creator and is no threat to spiritual belief whatsoever. They regard research as a fascinating journey gaining insights into "How did God do that?"

Consider the words of Dr. John Barrow, winner of the 2006 Templeton Prize for Progress Toward Research or Discoveries about Spiritual Realities (as quoted in a *Globe and Mail* article):

> *You begin to understand why it is no surprise that the universe seems so big and so old. It takes nearly 10 billion years to make the building blocks of living complexity in the stars and, because the universe is expanding, it must be at least 10 billion light-years in size. We could not exist in a universe that was significantly smaller.*
>
> *The vastness of the universe is often cited as evidence for the extreme likelihood of life elsewhere. [But] while there may be life, even conscious life, elsewhere, sheer size is not compelling. The universe needs to be billions of light-years in size just to support one lonely outpost of life.*
>
> *It breathes new life into so many religious questions of ultimate concern and never-ending fascination. Many of the deepest and most engaging questions that we grapple with still about the nature of the universe have their origins in our purely religious quest for meaning.*

The perceived problem between science and faith is frequently created by building theories on very faulty and questionable foundations. Just because science may help explain how the universe evolved, or how the earth turns, or how chemicals in the body influence mood swings, does not automatically eliminate or eradicate an equally important question: "Why?" The "how" of science and the "why" of faith or theology are quite capable of existing alongside each other. They are parallel tracks—far less useful and intellectually honest when kept apart, and a very powerful combination when working together—both contributing to support a more balanced and complete body of knowledge.

In business circles a simple exercise used to help in the problem-solving process is called "The Five Why's." The problem is described and submitted to a five-question cycle asking and probing "why?" Responses are jotted down, with the best one selected to begin the next cycle under the microscope of "why?" The exercise forces participants to question and examine every angle and presumption in order to distil the root causes of the problem or failure.

●　　●　　●　　●　　●

**If you don't ask the right questions,**
**you don't get the right answers.**
**A question asked in the right way**
**often points to its own answer.**
**Asking questions is the ABC of diagnosis.**
**Only the inquiring mind solves problems.**

—EDWARD HODNETT

●　　●　　●　　●　　●

In science the question is "How?" It can be repeatedly asked to help dig deeper and push explanations further back until finally arriving at *"How did the earth begin?"* or *"How was life on earth first formed?"* Faith, on the other side of the table, asks with equal force and intellectual integrity, *"Why did the earth begin?"* or *"Why was life on earth first formed?"*

Albert Einstein and other eminent scientists have adopted worldviews that quite comfortably enjoy and appreciate the co-existence of God and science. Consider some of their words:

- *Einstein:* "Science without religion is lame. Religion without science is blind."

- *Einstein:* "It would be possible to describe everything scientifically, but it would make no sense; it would be without meaning, as if you described a Beethoven symphony as a variation of wave pressure."

- *Robert Jastrow (astrophysicist, self-proclaimed agnostic):* "For the scientist who has lived by his faith in the power of reason, the story ends like a bad dream. He has scaled the mountains of ignorance; he is about to conquer the highest peak; as he pulls himself over the final rock, he is greeted by a band of theologians who have been sitting there for centuries."

- *Stephen Hawking (astrophysicist):* "Then we shall…be able to take part in the discussion of the question of why it is that we and the universe exist. If we find the answer to that, it would be the ultimate triumph of human reason—for then we would know the mind of God."

- *Frank Tipler (professor of mathematical physics):* "When I began my career as a cosmologist some twenty years ago, I was a convinced atheist. I never in my wildest dreams imagined that one day I would be writing a book purporting to show that the central claims of Judeo-Christian theology are in fact true, that these claims are straightforward deductions of the laws of physics, as we now understand them. I have been forced into these conclusions by the inexorable logic of my own special branch of physics."

- *Arthur Schawlow (professor of physics at Stanford University, 1981 Nobel Laureate in physics):* "It seems to me that when confronted with the marvels of life and the universe, one must ask why and not just how. The only possible answers are religious…I find a need for God in the universe and in my own life."

The discipline of science has the potential to either keep humanity extremely humble or to cause humanity to be proud and arrogant as new scientific milestones are reached. However, accompanying these discoveries and their bright new progressive realities are also problems, casting long shadows on the dark side. Those shadows invariably lurk within the human realm as the question is asked about what will happen if this discovery falls into the wrong hands. The hands of those who harbor more sinister and less altruistic motives than might have been initially intended. Examples are the discovery of the atom and the resulting nuclear power threat/struggle, space exploration, and the *Star Wars* scenario now emerging; genetic engineering, and the list goes on.

•　•　•　•　•

**Acceptance without proof is the fundamental characteristic of Western religion; rejection without proof is the fundamental characteristic of Western science.**

—GARY ZUKAV

•　•　•　•　•

One of the latest frontiers is that of nanotechnology, where scientists are exploring the miniscule components of matter. John Robert Marlow gives a summary:

> There are 116 known elements, or types of atoms. The world and everything in it is made up of atoms of one or some combination of those elements. The arrangement and combination of these atoms determines what a thing will be. Consider the element of carbon: arrange a gaggle of carbon atoms one way, and you have a worthless lump of graphite; arrange them a bit differently, and you have a diamond. Combined with oxygen atoms, they become a gas floating through the atmosphere. When arranged in yet another manner, and combined with several additional elements—those same atoms form a human being.
>
> Nanotech is, at its heart, a technology, which will allow us to work directly with the basic building blocks of matter—to

*manipulate individual atoms at will. Because human hands are millions of times too large to do this, we must construct incredibly small machines, or nanodevices, to do the work for us. Such devices are now being developed.*

Most of us cannot fathom these issues and yet we learn more and more as time goes by, until we come to accept as quite normal what was once regarded as impossible. If this is the case with science, is it not possible to accept that the spiritual world might be as credible and fascinating as the nanotechnological vistas now beginning to be unveiled?

A few years ago a red-faced Dickensian-appearing accountant glared at me as he thumped his fist on his desk. "Just give the facts, please!" He was looking for facts and figures that aligned with his world. The problem is, there are many variations of facts and figures depending on the questions being asked. Facts explaining how, why, where, what for, impacting whom, originating from where, revealing what…And we could go on like this.

Lee Strobel was an atheist, a journalist with the *Chicago Tribune,* and a man with an inquiring mind. When his wife became a Christian he started a thorough and intensive research project to find out if there is a God. He documented his journey in a book entitled *The Case for a Creator,* in which he describes how the study of science led him to faith in a Creator.

Science, Faith, and Reason could all be in danger of tilting at windmills as they consider each other from a distance; imitating Don Quixote, they imagine a foe where none really exists. They are all essential strands woven together to form the strong cable of knowledge that emerges from balanced interconnecting and different parts working together. A good example of this approach is the recently published book *The Language of God* by Dr. Francis Collins. He is one of the world's leading scientists and head of the Human Genome Project. In his introduction Collins agrees that much of the reputed acrimony between science and faith is fiction. Recent surveys of mathematicians, biologists, and scientists across North America revealed that about 40 percent profess a belief in God.

*The Language of God* describes Collins's journey in faith and science, specifically focusing on the study of DNA and the humane genome sequence (the "language of God"). Throughout the book Collins articulates and demonstrates how science, reason, and faith intertwine in an exquisitely elegant dance that requires the presence of each party to complement and complete the contributions of the other two. As he delves deeply into the genetic code that unlocks how human beings are made he finds increasing evidence for the existence of a personal God who provides meaning and a moral law for all created beings. It is to that quest for meaning and purpose that we now turn our attention.

# 6

# The Meaning of Life in an African Rock Pool

GEORGE SMOKED A PIPE AND LOVED TO TALK AND WAX PHILOSOPHICAL ABOUT SOUTH AFRICA AND THE APARTHEID REGIME. His perceptive comments, sprinkled with humor and sarcasm I found refreshing and stimulating. He was a man of mixed racial descent in his fifties when I met him during my extremely reluctant army conscription in a military camp in Oudtshoorn in 1971. After three months of basic training, running, marching around on parade, and shooting on maneuvers at all times of the day and night, I jumped at the opportunity to be a chef instead. When I say "chef" I mean learning to cook in an army kitchen, where quantities were measured in bags. Questions such as "How much salt should I add?" were helpfully responded to with "Enough."

I worked in the kitchen, and George fed the boiler with wood and coal throughout the day. The boiler was housed at the back of the complex in a shed that opened out onto an unobstructed view of the semidesert that crumpled into hills and mountains on the horizon. George's job was to keep the boiler hot enough to supply the large steam-heated cooking vats we used to prepare meals three times a day for 600 soldiers or more. He was an eloquent and thoughtful man. He had grown up under the harsh discriminatory laws of the South Africa, which had undoubtedly hobbled him in his opportunities to maximize his evident skills. The pigment in the thin layer of skin covering his body significantly impacted his choices and opportunities within South Africa at the time.

That same thin layer of pigment in my skin, because it was slightly lighter than George's (except in summer when I tanned dark brown), meant that I has access to privileged schooling, accommodation in pleasant suburbs, work opportunities, economic advancement, and consequently a richer range of choices and opportunities.

After chatting with George, who was by far the most interesting person to talk to in the army camp, I would return to work in the kitchen. Three of my fellow chefs were young "White" men from Johannesburg. They were Afrikaans-speaking and had already worked for a few years in the tough industrial steel factory known as ISCOR. Jimmy, the fourth chef, lived about an hour's drive away from the camp in a neighboring town. The guys from Johannesburg were tough and figured they had worked out what life was all about and that they had it by the tail. They constantly competed with each other to demonstrate who was top dog in the world of muscle, women, cigarettes, drink, and sexual conquests. They looked down upon me as soft, fresh out of school, and naïve to the real world.

They disliked George because he was too self-confident and "talkative" for a Black man (they used a more derogatory term). Their security and opportunities in life were also defined by the thin layer of lighter pigment encasing their bodies, providing them with a certain protection against the threatened competition they perceived from the rising Black presence in the country. They could not compete with George's verbal and mental skills so they resorted to the only weapon that remained—the color of their skin, and the legal and political protection provided for them by the state.

I didn't really appreciate the significance of this "Black threat" until a few weeks before we completed our training and went our respective ways. Jimmy, who lived nearby, invited us over to his place one evening after we had driven around sightseeing for the day. We visited the famous Cango caves with cascading limestone stalactites hanging from the roof of an enormous underground cavern, and one of the many ostrich farms for which the region is famous. Later in the afternoon we drove through Jimmy's town and out into the mountains along a narrow road lined with scrub and barbed wire fences. Eventually we crested a rise in the road, and nestled into the side of the next hill was a small house with junk scattered around it and a few children running barefoot in the dirt. I noticed Jimmy growing quieter the closer we came.

His parents welcomed us—very simple folk and obviously extremely poor. We were invited to share a meal that consisted of a tiny scrap of meat with a small helping of mashed potato cooked on a woodburning stove at the back of the house. This was Jimmy's reality, and he was obviously quite embarrassed and awkward. It was true that his life in the army provided far more then he would ever have received at home. What gave his life significance and hope was holding onto the privileges the state provided him because of the color of his skin. I felt very humbled on the one hand because in the perversion that was South Africa I had never seen a "White" family living in such squalor. At the same time I was also angry at the injustices meted out by the insane laws of discrimination that ultimately robbed both George and Jimmy of their dignity in very different ways.

For the vast majority of us life is about surviving (and hopefully thriving) within the context of where we live and the privileges or lack thereof that accompany those situations. Purpose and meaning, although psychologically and sociologically understandable, are not the only realities to be considered. As far as the rest of the world was concerned the apartheid laws in South Africa were abhorrent and indefensible, therefore everything possible should be done to help bring an end to such a travesty. George would have applauded any such initiative while Jimmy and the other men from ISCOR were incredibly threatened by the prospect of equal opportunity for all. At the end of the day the choices and sense of identity we brought to our lives and attitudes (as individuals) had to be submitted to a higher more universal moral law internationally agreed upon as basic human rights.

If we had time we could unfortunately draw on countless other examples of this tension between the freedom of an individual and the safety, security, and inherent rights of all human beings. Examples such as the Jewish Holocaust under Hitler, the Rwandan genocide, the issues relating to Native Indians throughout North America, the Israeli treatment of Palestinians, slavery in North Africa, Aboriginals in Australia, Maoris in New Zealand, intertribal conflicts on every continent, and we could go on. Resisting the current trend to airbrush and revise history to our liking, we confess that human nature is very similar on all continents, among all people, all nations, and all tribes, in every generation. Under scrutiny we are all found wanting. Each of us would no doubt be guilty for some despicable action or human rights failure we would prefer to hide under the rug of forgotten history or rationalization in our defense. All would involve layers of purpose and meaning intertwining, overlapping, and frequently clashing, each justifying its actions.

● ● ● ● ●

## Big Bang Theory: God said it, and bang it happened.

—UNKNOWN

● ● ● ● ●

Without the ability to appeal to a higher universal moral sense that defines individual dignity and opportunity embracing all of humanity one is left with the survival of the fittest as the only game in town. The technological advancement of communications in the past 20 years has made it increasingly difficult to hide, consequently our multilayered collage of choices, opportunities, and privileges is more visible and open to inspection than ever before. The ease of access to information impacts our lives not only in the political and social arenas but also in the consideration of how spiritual truths might intersect and illuminate our common search for meaning and purpose.

I remember sitting alone in a room one day and quietly looking around at everything I saw. The chair upon which I was seated, the carpet, the lamps, the bookshelves lined with books, the walls, the ceiling, the floor, the window, and all the other items, quite ordinary and unspectacular that clutter our living spaces. Everything I observed came from somewhere and had been designed and created by someone for a particular purpose. *If I remove God from the equation and insist that there is no Creator or Divine Mind, then I am the only "object" in this room with a random origin and no greater purpose than that which I can conjure up to satisfy my inner cry for a meaningful existence,* I mused.

Arniston is a small fishing village on the South African west coast, only a few hours drive outside Cape Town. The coast is a mixture of sandy beaches and rocky outcrops against which the ocean restlessly rubs with the eternal rising and falling of its heaving torso. It is a fickle and unpredictable coastline that has nurtured and fed those along its shores while also destroying others who have unwittingly sailed into one of her foul moods. I spent a few holidays there enjoying the beaches, particularly fishing from the shore into the breaking waves rolling in from a deep ocean under a spectacular setting sun. Every cast into the waves was full of anticipation: *Was that a bite of a steenbras or just the action of the wave nipping the fishing line?*

One morning as I was exploring the rock pools exposed at low tide I spotted what appeared to be a round object protruding from the sand at the bottom of a pool. I removed some rocks around it and retrieved an old rusty barnacle-encrusted iron ring about 12 or 14 inches in diameter and quite heavy. I hauled it out and carried it home. It was brown with rust and encrusted with sand that began to disintegrate as it dried out. Over the years the flaking barnacles and sand diminished its substance a little more each time I handled it. Now it is a much thinner ring and I still have it in my home. Why?

For many years I kept it at the foot of a bookcase in my office. When the topic of understanding our meaning and identity surfaced in conversations I would retrieve the old rusty ring and place it the coffee table.

"Do you know what this object is?" I asked, holding the ring in my hands. "Take a guess—what do you think it could be?"

"I don't know, some kind of metal strap maybe? It's difficult to tell..."

"You're right, it is difficult in this condition. I did some research and apparently it was a support band on the wooden mast of an old sailing vessel. Maybe the ship was wrecked off the Arniston coast in southern Africa, which was quite renowned for its dangerous shoreline. For years this ring lay in the ocean slowly disintegrating in the salt water, the tidal motion washing over it, the erosion of sand and movement taking its toll day after day. It was never created to be under the water in such a foreign environment, and the result is this very disfigured object we now have before us, virtually unrecognizable to the untrained eye."

Imagine this ring coming to life right now and looking at itself in a mirror. It would observe a rusty brown object caked in sand and broken shells with a few protrusions here and there. It would see black streaks of oxidized iron with cracks in its surface, and scars where flakes had broken off in the past. I suspect that if I were to ask the ring, "Who are you?" it would reply by describing its reflected image. That is all I could expect, for what it sees in the mirror is its only frame of reference. And the description it gives of its reflected identity would be true, for that is what it has become, and indeed it is—now. But is there more than that?

•  •  •  •  •

**The test of a first-rate intelligence
is the ability to hold two opposed ideas
in the mind at the same time, and still
retain the ability to function.**

—F. SCOTT FITZGERALD

•  •  •  •  •

You and I know that there is indeed more, for we have a perspective informed over a long period of time. We understand that what the rusty ring sees in the mirror is not an accurate picture of what it was initially created to be. We also realize that it would have no way of knowing that perspective by merely gazing into a mirror. Certainly it could embark on self-research and explore the origins of what it observes, and find out what those black streaks mean and why iron oxidizes and how sand is encrusted on its surface. Much helpful information and many clues could be gathered through such a process. But it would always be in the form of speculation searching for confirmation, never able to break out of the confines of its own intellectual parameters and capabilities. The meaning it therefore finds for its own existence is by subjective deduction, the origin of which is a distorted and very disfigured reflection in the mirror.

There are many people who see themselves only as a rust-encrusted ring. They have no sense or expectation there could be any other reality of life for them beyond their immediate subjective reflection. Life and circumstances have eroded and distorted them until hope is a faint echo and a distant memory; they float in a sea of confusion, desperately clinging to any flotsam that might keep them alive for a little while longer. Their sole reference point is the tactile and immediate experience gleaned from a reflection in a mirror, defining purpose and meaning for them. It is the layer of awareness encountered in our pool of consciousness—a layer that is very relative, very true for that specific context, yet at the same time very encrusted and invariably misshapen.

I met Jean (not her real name) after someone in our church in Cape Town had picked her up hitchhiking and offered her a place to stay at their home for a while. Jean was in her mid 30s and had spent much of her life on the street as a prostitute. Her face had a hardened tragic edge that would melt into the tear-stained face of a little girl in a matter of moments and become soft and attractive giving a tantalizing glimpse of what could be. But if the eyes are the windows of the soul then it was indeed a long journey home. Jean did not need proof about God existing—the hurdle for her was feeling that she would never be acceptable or worthwhile. Like many who have been abused she wore shame as a tattered and threadbare mantle. She told me once that all she had ever dreamed of was living in a home where she was safe and where she could grow a vegetable garden.

●   ●   ●   ●   ●

**Once you eliminate the impossible, whatever remains, no matter how improbable, must be the truth.**

—SHERLOCK HOLMES

●   ●   ●   ●   ●

We found her such a place with a generous and caring couple who lived in a spacious home on a large acreage on the outskirts of the city and Jean moved in with genuine awe and gratitude. She planted a vegetable garden, was safe and unconditionally loved and accepted. It wasn't too long before I received a call to tell me that she was gone and then some months later she reappeared again. She was ashamed and in tears as we recounted events and caught up. "John, this is all I ever wanted but I am terrified of it. I know how to survive and fend for myself on the street but I don't know how to handle genuine love." I last saw her in a padded hospital ward fighting a heroin addiction. I joined with many who cried out to God in prayers punctuated with a heart-wrenching "Why?" As far as I know Jean continued her lonely and terrible struggle and eventually died far too young ten years later.

Barbara (fictitious name) was another young woman, from Montreal, without a real home who used to come and talk to me quite frequently. She was the adopted daughter of a Christian minister who disowned her when she rebelled in her teenage years. She was confused and in turmoil about issues relating to her adopted parents and her part Native Indian heritage. She was angry and unable to see any prospect for her future. As is often the case, she had no self-esteem to enable her to believe that she could succeed at anything; rejection was the garment she wore most of the time. Drugs and alcohol became her comforters to dull her inner demons.

Occasionally they would subside enough for a glimpse of the real Barbara to peep out into the sunlight. In those few moments she would smile across the room and tell me that she knew that Jesus loved her. It was almost as if the innocent child re-emerged and started skipping down the road until she suddenly remembered. Then the glare was too harsh and unfamiliar and she soon retreated into a less vulnerable place. One morning the police found her dead in her apartment, where she had lain for four days undiscovered. Barbara was 24 and could not find the strength or hope to grasp onto a meaning and purpose for her life that would lift her out of the destructive pool that had become her security. Her immediate experiences presented themselves as her ultimate truth. She quite understandably believed the lie that no positive land of hope lay beyond the horizon for her.

I'm sure some will read these words and think that Jean and Barbara suffered the consequence of poor choices until their lives spun out of control. I agree. My problem with arriving at such stark conclusions is that we always seem so sure of our assessment of solutions for other people, particularly the poor and the downcast. Choices are not incubated and born in pure and untarnished surroundings. They are made within the context of situations, personalities, and environments that have a direct bearing on what the choice is and why it is made in the first place.

For instance, many abused children make choices to shut down emotionally in order to protect themselves and to survive their trauma. Those choices work effectively and in many cases probably save their lives. However, later in life those same choices usually need to be unlearned if they are to enjoy meaningful and happy relationships. It is a journey into wholeness that requires support, affirmation, and commitment to a long process of healing. It is a journey only worth embarking upon if there is another meaning and purpose other than that which has already defined their lives.

I think of Jean and Barbara with great tenderness and real sadness. Tragically there are many people like them all over the world whose lives are devoid of meaning, purpose, or hope, unless someone else will dare walk alongside them and perhaps be able to reveal to them another way. But there are no guarantees or painless remedies.

●  ●  ●  ●  ●

**All truth passes through three stages. First, it is ridiculed. Second, it is violently opposed. Third, it is accepted as being self-evident.**

—ARTHUR SCHOPENHAUER

●  ●  ●  ●  ●

Earlier we talked about intellectuals not being as rational as they might like to believe. The poor, the lonely, and the addicted are no different, neither are Jimmy and George and the other characters in the army kitchen, including myself. We all ultimately tend to clutch onto any meaning we can find within the close confines of our immediate surroundings—whatever that might be. The challenge is the same for both the rich and the poor. How do I let go of what I know to enable me to explore that which I do not yet know?

A good beginning may be acknowledging that there is a significant possibility that I am living with a distorted perception of myself as I reflect on who I am from my perspective within my familiar but limited rock pool. That is what we define as self-awareness. Where we begin to differentiate between who we are and what impact our environment is having upon us, and the recognition that we can indeed move and change…"with a little help from our friends"!

Meanwhile back in the other rock pool off the coast of Arniston with the rusty barnacle encrusted ring…from such a "self-centered" vantage point there is no possible way the rusty ring can comprehend *my* existence as I observe it and then lift it from where it has lain for so long. It might deduce that it had once been an object of iron that had spent many years in the ocean, but the mystifying question would be, How did I get from there to here? The teasing mystery would be grappling to understand or question whether there might be some force or power beyond itself responsible for such an event. The fact that at its creation it would have looked very different from the figure reflected in the mirror would also be beyond its comprehension or imagination unless…

As I gaze upon the ring I am aware of the limitations and the fact that it does not even know anything about the ship it was once a part of and bolted to. I have an understanding of its true purpose and the reasons it has ended up with such a misguided and distorted vision and perception of itself. But how do I communicate that perspective to the ring in a manner it could receive and understand? Maybe I could become a ring myself and thus communicate on the same level? Or possibly provide a visual model of "the original" before the shipwreck, as a contrast to the misshapen object that emerged after its immersion in salt water for so many years. There would be absolutely no benefit for me in doing these things, but it could make a world of difference to the disfigured ring.

The frustrating and mystifying question with which we still grapple is attempting to explain and comprehend what happened to humanity? How did the "earth ship" get wrecked and its precious cargo fall into such a hostile and destructive environment, where everyone and everything became distorted and corroded? One by one we stir like sleeping corpses awakening. Looking around we wonder, *What was I meant to be? Who am I? What is my purpose and significance anyway?*

If this scenario were true then it would appear to be impossible for a very disfigured human being (rusty ring) to deduce by reasoning alone what he or she was created to be like. For how does one accurately and truthfully understand a concept or reality that one has never seen or heard of before? That would be as impossible as the Bushman who picked up the Coke bottle being able to describe the pop it once contained, the people who consumed the pop, and the culture of North America from whence it came!

The only possibility is for an outside source to enter into the human world and environment and provide the "missing piece." Just as the Westerner interacted over time with our Bushman friend and slowly led him into an understanding of the so-called civilized world. Such crucial input from an outside source is known as *revelation;* and without that input the conclusion reached would be very different.

•  •  •  •  •

### The purpose of life is to live a life of purpose.

—RICHARD LEIDER

•  •  •  •  •

If we reject revelation from an outside source for creation then the only alternative becomes an evolutionary explanation boxed into the confines of our closed universe. From the chaos of some explosion, a random big bang that killed any prospect of God as well, the earth was formed with incredibly intricate patterns and designs. Quite by chance the right conditions resulted in life emerging out of the oceans in a very primitive form. By mere chance again the evolution of animal life caused the creation of the unique, self-reflective, reasoning, highly emotional and sophisticated human being, who then crawled onto the summit of creation and proclaimed supremacy.

It is on this summit, where many questionable assertions are made about purpose and meaning, that we find perched the rickety self-glorifying temples, business empires, egocentric careers, and even churches of "religion." Somewhere within the midst of that pile of psychological and spiritual flotsam and jetsam maybe we will discover the gold vein that is more than just "fool's gold"—and truly is the hand of God, the essence of life, the heartbeat of love with all of its goodness and purity. A hand that always beckons us closer, inviting us to discover who we were created to be before we descended into the rock pool. Before barnacles and sand encrusted and distorted our image, and hid the exquisite beauty created in Eden from our gaze.

# 7

# Religion Is Everywhere!

I WALKED THROUGH THE NIGHT FROM THE OXFORD RAILWAY STATION UP TO CARFAX, THE CITY CENTER, AN INTERSECTION OF ROADS DISSECTING SHOPS AND COLLEGES, CHURCHES, BANKS, GRAVEYARDS, TOWN AND GOWN. The streetlights glowed yellow and illuminated snowflakes quietly falling and melting on the black, cobbled ground—it was magical! It was as if I had walked onto an opera stage or a magnificent theatrical set. How many heads and shoulders cloaked in white from falling snow trudged with me across this ancient place on a cold winter's night I wondered? Was it a peasant, a Roman soldier, a stonemason, a student, an Oxford don? No doubt all of them and many more—history creeps up on us sometimes. It whispers in our ears and provides a fresh perspective, reminding us how brief is the time we personally have on this earth in the grand scheme of things. As Shakespeare scribbled in *As You Like It:* "All the world's a stage, And all the men and women merely players: They have their exits and their entrances..."

From Carfax we stroll north along Cornmarket Street lined with stores normally bulging full of shoppers during the daytime. At one corner where a narrow side street leads to the aroma-filled indoor market, we pass an old timber-frame building that has subsided slightly on one side and totters like a dignified elderly man. This is the oldest surviving three-story house in Oxford; it was built between 1386 and 1396, and has good reason to be weary.

We head past St. Mary Magdalen Church and the Martyr's Memorial along the broad St. Giles Road lined with cars and bicycles toward Wood-stock (home of Blenheim Palace where Winston Churchill was born) and the town of Kidlington. On our left is the Eagle and Child, the cozy pub where Lewis and Tolkien used to meet and chat over a pint. Across the road is the stone façade and entrance to St. John's College. Choosing the right fork in the road we continue up the Banbury Road less than half a mile before making a right turn toward the Park. A short way down Norham Gardens Road on the corner, at another fork in the road is a tall three-story redbrick house that was converted into student "digs" (not very far from where Tolkien wrote Lord of the Rings in his living room).

●　●　●　●　●

**Somebody loves us, too—God himself. We have been created to love and to be loved.**

—MOTHER TERESA

●　●　●　●　●

My room was situated on the third floor and once a week a group of students from a variety of countries gathered to explore the question of God. Is God real or not? Is there a Lord of the Universe or is that also imaginative fiction? After considering whether there is even the possibility of a God or Higher Power our discussion turned to the audacious claims of Jesus Christ. We carefully considered the foundational beliefs of the Christian faith, where God is revealed as personal, involved in human history, and loving toward his creation. A few more weeks passed and then one young girl from a Buddhist background in Japan quietly said, "I was raised a Buddhist and spent an hour every day praying to a God I did not know, and now I discover he is personal and real, and he loves me; it is wonderful!" I was humbled by the commitment and perseverance this girl demonstrated in seeking after a true and authentic experience of God.

It might be relatively simple walking from Carfax to my room at Norham Gardens, but finding the path to spiritual truth is a veritable maze of twists and turns with many false and questionable endings.

Religion describes someone's beliefs about the world and how that belief system impacts daily choices and lifestyle. It is a worldview that helps us make sense of the meaning and purpose of life, or the lack thereof. Everyone has a worldview and believes something. Some taglines available in the Philosophy/Lifestyle section of the Meaningful Life Superstore include...

- Survival of the Fittest
- Believe in God
- Create Your Own Future
- Work Hard
- Don't Worry, Be Happy
- God Helps Those Who Help Themselves
- Money Makes the World Go Around
- Live for Today—for Now
- Smile, God Loves You
- Follow Your Inner Voice

All major religions are interested in understanding and teaching how we can draw closer to God. This is true for Buddhism, Hinduism, Christianity, Judaism, and Islam. However the nature of God and how one accomplishes this task is very different indeed when these belief systems are placed side by side (comparative religious studies). In the next few pages we will take a brief overview of each of these faiths in order to illustrate the point. Comments will be cryptic and inadequate, but if you are interested there is plenty more information to google on the Internet when you punch in "world religions."*

---

* While I have drawn from a multitude of sources I gratefully acknowledge the Web site dedicated to religious tolerance for some of the information regarding the various world religions: www.Religioustolerance.org.

●  ●  ●  ●  ●

**A religion that gives nothing,
costs nothing, and suffers nothing,
is worth nothing.**

—MARTIN LUTHER

●  ●  ●  ●  ●

**Buddhism.** Buddhism is the fourth-largest religion in the world, originating around 595 BC as an offshoot of Hinduism. It is often described more as a philosophy of life or a "way of wisdom" than a set of religious beliefs. It is the predominant religion in China, Japan, Korea, and much of Southeast Asia.

The word *Buddhism* comes from *budhi,* which means "to awaken." The founder and first Buddha was Siddhartha Gautama, who claimed to have been "awakened" (enlightened) at the age of 35. Buddha did not claim to be God but taught about the path to enlightenment based upon his own experience.

The path to "awakening" (The Four Noble Truths) includes: leading a moral life (discipline), being mindful and aware of thoughts and actions (meditation), and developing wisdom and understanding (wisdom). It encourages the renunciation of the material and physical as a means to happiness and points to the source of peace and love as being found "within"—hence an emphasis upon meditation. One of Buddhism's key insights is that there is nothing permanent in our existence. Suffering *(dukkha)* arises out of our misguided searching for an attachment to what is actually only temporary. The focus is on achieving liberation from suffering which is accomplished through learning to be detached from the self and its desires, which are all impermanent including the self.

Buddhism does not really define or acknowledge a Supreme Being or God. Consequently there is no need for personal reconciliation with God, as humanity is the ultimate authority. The identity of Jesus as the revelation of God on earth is rejected by default. The central beliefs have their roots in Hinduism and the belief in reincarnation which are cycles of birth, living, death, and rebirth until one attains to a state of ultimate freedom from attachment/desire/suffering and enters into *Nirvana* (which is never really described by Buddha). Nirvana is reached by following the Noble Eightfold Path consisting of the right View, the right Resolve, the right Speech, the right Action, the right Livelihood, the right Effort, the right Mindfulness, and the right Concentration.

There is no soul that is reborn, but rather one process leading to the next. How one is reborn is determined by the cause and effect of our actions (*karma*—an impersonal ethical law).

Karma is frequently misrepresented. It literally means "action" and refers to the intentional acts—verbal, physical, mental—of sentient beings. Intentions result in acts that have effects that will give rise to further intentions and actions. This chain of interlocking causes and effects operates at the level of individuals and societies and of course across lifetimes. The important point is that in Buddhism this karmic causality is not preordained or due to a divine mechanism—it is a fundamental natural process.

Buddhism is extremely tolerant of other religions and does not seek to convert anyone but rather responds to requests for teaching. Meditation is the key to escaping suffering by means of enlightenment. Buddhist scriptures are called the *Tripitaka,* or the "Three Baskets," consisting of the *Sutra Pitaka,* the Buddha's sermons, the *Vinaya Pitaka,* the monastic rules, and the *Abhidharma Pitaka,* early philosophical treatises.

Some of the core philosophical principles of Buddhism are as follows:

- *Momentariness.* Nothing exists for any length of time. There is no *substance* or duration to things. Each moment is new and unique in its existence and is followed by another equally new and unique existence.

- *Relative existence.* Nothing has an essence, nature,

or character by itself. Everything only exists in relation to other things that exist.

- *No atman.* There is no self (*atman*) in Buddhism, either as an essence or as a substance.

- *No God.* There is no Brahman or any other (no objective Creator).

- *Dependent origination.* Everything has a cause. A momentary existence occurs as it does because of a previous momentary existence, but the cause itself is also momentary.

**Hinduism.** There are about 750 million Hindus today, with the vast majority living in India. The name *Hindu* comes from the Indus River that flows from the mountains of Tibet through Kashmir and Pakistan and drains into the Indian Ocean.

Hinduism (third-largest religion in the world) has many gods (which are all aspects of the cosmic unifying force/God) and preaches the reincarnation of the soul as a perpetual cycle of the journey to wholeness and perfection. Hinduism does not have a single founder, a specific theological system, a single system of morality, or a central religious organization. It consists of a multitude of various religious groups that have evolved in India since 1500 BC and is a fusion of many religious beliefs and philosophical schools.

Hinduism is a very difficult religion to describe, with so many varying expressions and aspects included beneath one large umbrella. Because one of those beliefs is that there are many paths to God there is no problem with such diversity even within Hinduism itself. However, unlike many Western religions, Hinduism is integrated into every part of life and is inextricably bound up with everyday life all the time. In practice Hindu devotees wor-ship gods and goddesses of their choice, whoever they believe will help them with their daily lives and problems. Three of the main Hindu deities are *Shiva* (the Creator destroyer), *Vishnu* (the Preserver), whose most well-known incarnations are Krishna and Rama, and *Devi* (the Protecting Mother) sometimes known as the Goddess. They regard the multitude of gods or deities as merely being consistent with the greatness of a Supreme Being who has many facets that can be accessed depending upon the needs and preferences of the individual.

The Hindu devotee believes that objects or icons are their entry point facilitating communication with a particular god—a practice called Punja. The artistic merits of the object are of sec-ondary importance to their spiritual value as a focus for the cosmic energy of the particular deity and as a means of honoring them. Worship is offered either in a temple, a shrine at home, or at an outdoor facility. Hindus usually worship their deity on a daily basis and believe that a deity will leave a temple if that place is not properly maintained. Priests therefore attend to the needs of the deity at the temple (normally dedicated to one deity) and con-duct Punja four times daily (sunrise, noon, sunset, and midnight). The essential part of Punja, however, is not visiting the temple or participating in congregational style worship (as in Christianity, Judaism, or Islam) but rather the individual's offering to the deity. It is quite acceptable for different members of a family to worship different deities within the same household. As children become adults they have the freedom to select deities to worship that they find are inspiring and meaningful.

In the Hindu faith, God is not separate from creation; rather they are one and the same. Many shrines to deities are found outside throughout India in probably as a many and as varied a number of locations as we could imagine. There is no such thing as evil because if God indwells all his creation evil has no place to exist. Life is an endless cycle of reincarnations until one escapes into nothingness, which is known as *Nirvana*. The means to accomplish Nirvana is through practicing meditation and yoga, thereby reaching a higher state of consciousness.

The aim of Hinduism is to encourage each individual to become one with the eternal universal spirit, Brahman, the ultimate reality. This goal can only be attained through a completely transformed consciousness as opposed to attaining perfection through growth of character. It is not possible to accomplish perfection in one lifetime and therefore the cycle of reincarnation or the wheel of karma is the means to that end. Karma is the outworking of divine justice. The consequences of actions performed in previous lives determine where someone has earned the right to be placed in their present life or incarnation. A person can move higher or lower on the incarnation cycle including being reincarnated as an animal. This cycle can only be stopped by liberation from the finite consciousness of individuality (the opening of the third eye).

The sacred writings of Hinduism are known as the Vedas, which consist of four basic vedic books: the *Rig-Veda,* the *Yajur Veda,* the *Sama Veda,* and the *Atharva Veda.* Each book is divided into four parts: hymns to the gods *(Mantras),* ritual materials *(Brahmanas),* guidance for hermits *(Aranyakas),* and philosophical treatises *(Upanishads).*

**Islam.** Islam, the youngest of the major religions, is speculated to become the largest of the world religions by the mid-twenty-first century if the current growth rate continues. It began in Arabia about 1400 years ago and now has approximately 1200 million adherents worldwide. Regions with the largest Islamic populations are in Asia with Pakistan, India, Indonesia, and Bangladesh, each having more than 100 million adherents to Islam in each country. However, the holiest sites for Islam are located in the Middle East at Medina, Mecca, and Jerusalem.

The name *Islam* is derived from the word *salam,* meaning "peace" or "submission." A Muslim is a follower of Islam. *Muslim* is an Arabic word that refers to people who submit themselves to the will of God. Submission means living and thinking in the way that Allah has instructed.

God is called *Allah* (the One who is God). There is only one God who has 99 names, he is all-powerful, and he has always existed. His last great prophet, Muhammad, is revered as God's messenger but is not worshipped. Followers of Islam are all members of one community, the *ummah.* They regard the *Qur'an (Koran)* as their holy book through which Allah's will is recorded and revealed. They have one life to live after which they face judgment.

Muslims worship at their local mosque (from an Arabic word meaning "place of prostration"). Every Muslim is expected to practice what is known as the Five Pillars.

1. *Shahada:* The Muslim profession of faith said first thing in the morning and just before going to sleep: "I witness that there is no god but Allah, and that Muhammad is the prophet of Allah."

2. *Salat:* A precise prayer ritual performed five times a day by all Muslims over the age of ten (preferably in the company of others to affirm the unity of all Muslims). This practice of prayer keeps the faith central in every part of life.

3. *Sawm:* Abstaining (between sunrise and sunset) from all bodily pleasure including food each day during Ramadan, the ninth Muslim month.

4. *Zakat:* Giving alms to the poor. Muslims are expected to give 2.5 percent of their savings over and above donations made to other charities. This is to remind them that all things belong to God and to be less attached to money.

5. *Hajj:* At least once in their lifetime all physically able Muslims should make a pilgrimage to Mecca.

The main articles of faith (Shahada) are as follows:

- Allah is the one true God and his will is supreme.

- The angels are instruments of God's will.

- The divine scriptures, which include the Torah, the Psalms, the rest of the Bible (as they were originally revealed), and the Qur'an (which is composed of God's words, dictated by the archangel Gabriel to Muhammad).

- The Messengers of God, including Adam, Noah, Abraham, Moses, David, Jesus, and Muhammad. Muhammad's message is considered the final, universal message for all of humanity.

- The Day of Judgment, when people will be judged on the basis of their deeds while on earth, and will either attain reward of heaven or punishment in hell. Muslims do not believe that Jesus or any other individual can atone for another person's sin. Hell is where unbelievers and sinners spend eternity.

**Judaism.** Judaism is one of three Abrahamic religions (with Christianity and Islam)—faiths that recognize Abraham as a patriarch (the three patriarchs/fathers of Judaism are Abraham, Isaac, and Jacob). It is the oldest of the monotheistic (one-God) religions and also the smallest, with about 12 million adherents based mainly in Israel or the United States. (The Holocaust drastically impacted Jewish numbers—without that dreadful event there would be approximately 30 million Jews living today with a sub-stantially larger presence in Europe.)

God is known as *Yahweh* or *Jehovah*.

Being Jewish means belonging to a community and living one's life in accordance with God's Law, the *Torah* (Five Books of Moses: Genesis, Exodus, Leviticus, Numbers, Deuteronomy) and the *Talmud*. The Jewish Scriptures also include the writings of the Prophets *(Nevi'im)* as included in the "Old Testament" of the Christian Bible. Jews take great pride in their identity as Jews and that sense of identity is often more important than matters of faith. For instance, there are many secular Jews in Israel as well as the more orthodox religious Jews.

The Jewish holy day is Saturday—the *Shabbat* (from Friday at sunset to Saturday at sunset). Jews worship together in a syna-gogue, and their leader is a rabbi, who does not have the same status as priests do in some of the other religions.

Judaism believes in one God who is the Creator of all things. God created all people in his image and therefore all are created equal. The Jewish people interpret the meeting between God and Moses (receiving the Ten Commandments) on Mount Sinai 3500 years ago as an indication of their special status before God as His chosen people. They do not have a central creed but live in a covenant with God that is expressed through obedience to the Torah. They look forward to the coming of the Messiah (from Hebrew *Mashiah*—the anointed one) who will inaugurate the kingdom of God on earth—a time of great peace in the world (the Messianic Age).

The famous Jewish scholar Hillel (70 BC–AD 10) encapsulated Jewish belief in his response to a question asking what the central teaching of Judaism is: "What is hateful to you, do not do to your neighbor: this is the whole of Jewish Law; the rest is mere com-mentary, now go and study."

All Jewish boys are circumcised when they are eight days old as a sign of the covenant God made with Abraham. At 13 years of age the boy becomes a full member of the Jewish community in a ceremony known as the *bar mitzvah,* which is also a rite of passage into manhood. Other ceremonies within the Jewish community include the *Passover* (celebrating the exodus out of Egypt), and *Shavuot* (celebrating God's gift of the Torah on Mount Sinai). A number of other festivals throughout the year commemorate historic events of victory and deliverance that have taken place in Jewish history.

**Christianity.** Christianity has its roots in Judaism and was founded on the life, death, and resurrection of Jesus Christ, who is believed to be the long-awaited Messiah of the Jews and who lived in Palestine (4 BC–AD 29). There are estimated to be about 2000 million Christians worldwide, with a wide variety of denominations providing various expressions and interpretations of the core faith.

God is separate from his creation but is intimately concerned with all that he has created. He is personal and revealed himself through the person of Jesus Christ as a compassionate, loving, caring, "suffering servant." Jesus was himself a Jew who claimed that he was the Son of God and the fulfillment of all the Law and the Prophets as contained in the Jewish Scriptures. God reveals himself in three persons who are mysteriously both separate and one (the Trinity)—referred to as the Father, the Son, and the Holy Spirit.

Christians believe that all humanity is responsible for their actions. God will judge each person and the precise nature of how that "judgment" is carried out is something of a mystery. God also offers to forgive and help those who acknowledge their "rebellion" and who seek to follow his commands in a personal relationship with Him. No one can be reconciled with God through their own efforts or by keeping laws; instead they are invited to accept what God has done for them in love through the unique life, death, and resurrection of Jesus Christ. Jesus is God's gift of himself incarnated (becoming human), dying on the cross (as an atonement for sin), and rising from the dead. We will explore these topics in more detail later in this book.

Christians believe that the Bible is the Word of God and consists of the Old Testament (same as Jewish Scriptures) and the New Testament (about Jesus' life, death, and resurrection, and the beginning of the church). The Bible contains a variety of written material gathered from many sources over a period of about 1500 years, all of which describe aspects of God's character, his interaction with human beings through the ages, and his purpose for all creation to participate in a loving and dynamic interactive relationship with him.

Christians study the Bible, pray, and worship God together on a regular basis, meeting in a church or home. The gathering together as community is important because their faith is understood to be community-based with interdependence forming a vital part of authentic spiritual growth. Sunday is regarded as a special day set aside to worship God together and as a "day of rest" from work. There are many expressions (denominations) of community and worship under the broad Christian umbrella arising from different convictions regarding the interpretation of biblical teaching, worship style, and Christian lifestyle.

**Me Inc.** This is a very widespread religious movement (possibly the largest in the world) with a multitude of devotees in the Western world. It is surprisingly complex and sophisticated. There are many deities who are worshipped—money, sex, power, and leisure—all aspects of the "I believe in nothing" philosophy that is somewhat akin to self-worship in camouflage. The primary focus is on self-fulfillment and self-gratification. Devotees follow no uniform creed preferring to rally around a mantra that advocates "live for today and look after yourself first." Freedom and "fun" are revered and worshipped as deities to be honored. Enormous amounts of time, integrity, money, and personal relationships are sacrificed to appease these seductive icons.

"Whatever makes me feel good" is another core teaching of Me Inc. Disciples display a high tolerance and respect for the multitude of ways in which adherents find gratification in realizing and sustaining this state of consciousness. There is a strong commitment to moral neutrality and to challenge another devotee's means of gratification is regarded as blasphemy, insensitive, and highly judgmental.

Me Inc. is probably the most subversive religious movement because it is able to superficially align itself with any of the other religions while still being the main focus and driving force. It actually never draws attention to itself and will seldom if ever even publicly admit to being a faith movement at all. In fact it usually masquerades as something that is more publicly acceptable, which could be "good works," religion, business, or any other activity. This chameleon-like ability to blend into its surroundings means that the faith movement is difficult to identify and any attempt to do so will generally be interpreted as insulting, self-righteous, and insensitive.

Adherents of Me Inc. have no formal organization, and meetings are ad hoc and can be held anywhere. The high priests of this faith phenomenon rotate in and out of the role depending upon their popularity at the time; the media machine constantly promotes them through television, music, and magazines. Because the nature of worship revolves around instant gratification the tenure of these priests is usually of a relatively short duration as their popularity wanes.

While we examine the topic of spirituality with care and humility we nevertheless want to beware of being fooled into attributing to spiritual Coke bottles a significance that is misguided. Because it is highly unlikely that we will ever reach absolute agreement in this area, it is important that we validate the legitimacy of every human being's search to know God, and to find meaning, truth, and purpose. However, we also want to be careful not to be duped into believing that every idea or concept using the word *spiritual* is authentically spiritual (placing a stone in a cookie jar doesn't make it a cookie). We are all tempted (unwittingly) to project what "I want to believe" onto something (and thus define God/spirituality in "my" own image). Some checks and balances are essential as a means of alerting us to our own blind spots, and helping minimize the distortion that we bring from our culture, our social upbringing, and our "traditions."

●　●　●　●　●

## To listen to some devout people, one would imagine that God never laughs.

—UNKNOWN

●　●　●　●　●

The popularity and sheer number of religious movements around the world is evidence of the natural inclination and propensity human beings exhibit to worship something or someone greater than the individual. However, that acknowledgment does not automatically lend credence to every religious movement under the sun. Before we make statements about the integrity and substance of a particular religion we will be wise to examine the claims it makes, explore its belief systems, and check out the lifestyles of the founders and current leaders.

Appearances can be very deceptive. In the West we are generally extremely naïve when it comes to understanding the power or impact of the spirit world. This week a story was broadcast about a polar bear that was killed by a mosquito! The mosquito was a carrier of the West Nile virus and is believed to have bitten the polar bear on the nose. That was all it took to pass on the infection and for irreparable brain damage leading to death. Who would ever think of a tiny mosquito being able to fell a mighty polar bear! It is indeed a strange world in which we live with plenty of surprises.

●   ●   ●   ●   ●

I was walking across a bridge one day, and I saw
a man standing on the edge, about to jump off.
So I ran over and said "Stop! don't do it!"
"Why shouldn't I?" he said. I said, "Well, there's so
much to live for!" He said, "Like what?"
I said, "Well…are you religious or atheist?"
He said, "Religious." I said, "Me too!
Are you Christian or Buddhist?"
He said, "Christian." I said, "Me too! Are you
Catholic or Protestant?" He said, "Protestant."
I said, "Me too! Are you Episcopalian or Baptist?"
He said, "Baptist!" I said, "Wow! Me too!
Are you Baptist Church of God or Baptist Church
of the Lord?" He said, "Baptist Church of God!"
I said, "Me too! Are you Original Baptist Church
of God, or are you Reformed Baptist Church of
God?" He said, "Reformed Baptist Church of God!"
I said, "Me too! Are you Reformed Baptist Church
of God, Reformation of 1879, or Reformed Baptist
Church of God, Reformation of 1915?"
He said, "Reformed Baptist Church of God,
Reformation of 1915!" I said,
"Die, heretic scum," and pushed him off.

—EMO PHILIPS

●   ●   ●   ●   ●

8

# Religion—No Thanks!

*ONE OF MY EARLIEST RECOLLECTIONS OF "CHURCH" WAS ACCOMPANYING MY FATHER TO ST. PAUL'S ANGLICAN CHURCH IN RONDEBOSCH, CAPE TOWN. Situated on the slopes of the mountain that towers over the southern suburbs (ironically called Devil's Peak) the church stands on a small hill surrounded by trees. It is built of warm rusty brown and yellow sandstone and is quite large and imposing, particularly when viewed through the eyes of a seven- or eight-year-old boy. When little boys walked through the arched doors of St. Paul's they were unsure whether they were entering a dungeon, a palace, or a castle.*

*Inside the church soaring buttresses and beams lift a peaked roof up to the heavens. The windows rise majestically, filtering God's light through magnificent stained-glass scenes depicting biblical themes of shepherds, and prophets, and truths of another world. Closer to earth reality is more harsh; the seats are solid and hard, wooden, and rigidly placed row after row like trenches to be occupied by soldiers engaging and preparing for battle. Prayers are prayed on knees cushioned by kneelers, and one can spend a lot of time crouched on them desperately trying to look "as if you mean every word."*

*Strange words are spoken from musty books in the kind of English that little boys don't begin to understand. The organ plays and its mighty sound rolls around like a giant's pinball bouncing off the sides of the chiseled sandstone and pounding into young unappreciative ears. The procession begins with choir and robes and candles and singing. The priest enters last in line with his Pinocchio nose tilted upward singing sonorously as he slowly follows the other "lesser beings," the fringes of his ornate vestments silently sweep the marble floor around him. Finally, on arrival at the altar, which seems very far away, he stops and bows, turns and speaks to no one in particular—the service has begun while little boys are already wondering when it will end.*

—FROM *INTO DEPRESSION AND BEYOND* BY JOHN COX

If you were asked whether you believe in God, you may reply with a variety of responses:

"Well, I'm not really religious, I don't go to church regularly."

"I try and keep the Ten Commandments."

"I don't read the Bible every day, I'm not one of those—you know, holier-than-thou types."

"I am kind to other people and I haven't done anything radically wrong."

"I worship God when I'm walking in the mountains, and sailing."

I suspect that "compartmentalized religion" has emerged most starkly in the Western world where there has been a tendency to attempt to separate church and state and dispose of religious belief by defining it as private and personal. Examination of the Hebrew and Jewish experience in the Old Testament will reveal no such lobotomy exists between the sacred and the secular, nor in some of the other world religions such as Buddhism, Hinduism, or Islam. It was regarded as quite impossible to separate the two and to hold them as distinct entities without impacting the other. It would be as futile as attempting to separate the mind from the body and have them exist without the presence of the other. It cannot be done.

The word *religion* spells tension when we attempt to describe or define it. On the one hand we dislike hypocrisy and insincerity while on the other hand we are suspicious of enthusiasm, and hastily brand those who take any specific form of spirituality seriously as "fanatics." When *religion* is used to discuss Christianity at the individual church level it does not usually convey a warm and dynamic image or meaning. Instead it confines religious practice to forms of worship and dogma devoid of life, crammed full of tradition and things we do every week within church buildings.

Religion depends upon institutions, professional clergy, and rituals, and a God who is distant, predictable, and mysterious. This translation of religion begins with our interpretation of what God requires, and then is sustained by the belief that our interpretation has mysteriously become congruent with God's will. Religion is what people do to try and please their god or gods. It involves activities, time, money, rules, rituals, membership, teaching, tradition, and other such things. Some people's god is their work, for others it is sports; it can be anything that consumes our time, passion, money, and devotion.

● ● ● ● ●

**Men rarely (if ever) manage to dream up a god superior to themselves. Most gods have the manners and morals of a spoiled child.**

—ROBERT HEINLEIN

● ● ● ● ●

The unifying factor among most religions is the common commitment to peace, nonviolence, and the harmonious coexistence of all people in the world. Social and personal ethics providing evidence for, and expression of, a genuine spiritual faith form the basic tenets commonly shared among all major world religions. Unfortunately there are also militants in every major religion who distort and exaggerate some of these basic tenets until they are skewed enough to justify a political extremism that is not so peaceful.

The human ability to tarnish "good" and to seek to share the power and influence of the gods we worship while on this earth is legendary. Little wonder that many walk away from organized religion in disgust. Only to find that disorganized atheism, muddled and eclectic agnosticism, or expediently neutral materialism are just as guilty of corruption, distortion, and power politicking.

So what do we do? Give up with a smug and self-righteous cynicism that pretends to believe that we are different, that we would never have been guilty of such atrocities, or that we would never behave like *that* if we had been *them?* We can try, but as long as we're alive on this earth we're in the thick of the dilemma along with everyone else. Which leaves us with an involuntary choice of merely "going with the flow along the path of least resistance," or persisting in our search with honesty and self-awareness that gladly (or maybe reluctantly) acknowledges that we are rather fragile and bear a striking resemblance to cracked clay jars. We are also aware that our imperfections make us quite susceptible to being gullible and too easily seduced and fooled by appearances.

Having briefly reviewed some of the dominant world religions are they all merely different ways to accomplish the same end? If we understand spirituality as something we do to find fulfillment, needing to express ourselves in whatever way is culturally, emotionally, and intellectually meaningful (including Me Inc.), then the answer will be "yes." Which is a stance embraced by some proponents of religious pluralism, although that is a term open to misinterpretation as well.

Religious pluralism in its extreme form is the philosophical worldview that regards all the great religions of the world as essentially the same, each ultimately leading to God. To its credit, pluralism attempts to grapple with the real problem of how can only one religion be "right"? How can everyone else in the world be condemned or damned to hell because they have been born in the wrong culture, country, or religious tradition?

A well-known analogy often used in this discussion describes four blind men each touching a portion of an elephant. One blind man states that an elephant is like a great flat wall. Another that it is like a hard pointed object, cold and sharp after touching the tusk. The third blind man would advocate that an elephant resembles a solid tree trunk as he touched the leg. And the other blind man would strongly suggest that this large animal is like a long thick rubber tube after he had felt the trunk. All the men would be correct in one aspect of the truth and all would be incomplete in terms of their perception of the whole.

This is similar to what takes place when each religion describes God. All have elements of the truth but none have the full picture in absolute clarity—so the argument goes. Therefore all religions complement each other and inform the total knowledge we have of God. No religion is regarded as more superior than another. The true pluralist would go further and suggest that if the blind men talked and listened to each other they would indeed have a more accurate picture of the whole elephant.

● ● ● ● ●

### Wherever you go, go with all your heart.
—CONFUCIUS

● ● ● ● ●

At first blush such an approach appears to be quite reasonable and indeed feasible. However, they do not logically connect when we examine the foundational claims of each religion and place them alongside each other. Furthermore, when the Christian claim maintains that God entered into the human context in the person of Jesus, then blind men interpreting truth is not the determining factor. Because when God spoke through Jesus he revealed the whole elephant (and more) to all the blind men and women—which includes you and me. In other words he enters into the blindness and reveals himself, taking the initiative from his side to provide the solution to the picture puzzle. However, he does not force revelation upon us and crush our freedom under its weight, he invites us to explore the revelation and discover its integrity and authenticity for ourselves.

The Christian faith at its core does not allow for any competitors or multiple viewpoints regarding the nature of God—in the final analysis (and these last four words are vitally important). The assumption so often made is that if God is revealed in Jesus as the greatest revelation of himself then it is bad news for everyone else. Such a conclusion is only true if the revelation implies that everyone else is automatically "damned" or excluded.

Religious pluralism is a reasonable viewpoint with strong foundations in mutual respect for our great religious diversity—which I wholeheartedly support. But here is where the discussion hinges upon the worldview we are embracing as the basis for our reasoning. Religious pluralism is probably completely accurate and reasonable within a closed worldview perspective. However, as soon as the windows and doors are open and the possibility is allowed for God to exist outside of human "influence, logic, or understanding" then the position of religious pluralism is not as secure.

At the same time religious exclusivism (not only prevalent in the Christian faith) is also on shaky ground. In this instance the attempt is made to defend and explain how a loving God can condemn so many to hell if they do not come to God through Christ (or according to the guidelines of any particular religion). Fair question, and one that is not easy to answer. The dogmatic assertion that everyone not in my particular spiritual pasture will be "damned" is far too small-minded. It reeks of our own logic, twisting and turning like a mad cat to find an explanation.

Maybe there are other possibilities. If God's character is truly revealed in the person of Jesus as being deeply compassionate and loving then surely I can entrust into his hands what happens to "everyone" when they die? That is not an abdication of the question so much as an admission of my intellectual limitations and my very finite spiritual comprehension. If I am concerned about fairness and justice, then I can be confident that he is perfectly fair and just toward all of his creation? God's purpose in Jesus was to draw all people to himself while they are still alive on earth. The reason being is that his intention from the beginning of creation was for us to live on earth in a personal relationship with him. Faith is not merely concerned with life "after death" but also with how we live and find fulfillment in a personal and loving God today—before the funeral!

I own a 1976 Triumph TR6 that I drove for a number of years and then left it standing for quite a while due to other priorities. This summer it was running beautifully until one day I tried to start it and the engine turned but would not fire. In attempting to diagnose and fix the problem I have had to dismantle the fuel pump, check the spark plugs, dare to fiddle with the carburetors, clean up the distributor, and test the coil. Any one of these items could cause the engine not to fire and idle if they are not working efficiently.

When discussing religion, faith, and spirituality some of us can turn the key and just "turn over" without ever firing on all cylinders. We get disheartened, kick the car, and walk away concluding this "spiritual stuff" is not for me. In the case of a motor vehicle there are those who are intrigued by how they work and others of us are not at all interested. If we are disinterested we usually seek help where mechanical matters are concerned and we certainly require a manual when we do attempt any initiative ourselves. The same principle is true when trying to understand human behavior, particularly our own.

● ● ● ● ●

## Life is a promise; fulfill it.

—MOTHER TERESA

● ● ● ● ●

An alternative to "kicking the car" is to accept and embrace the paradox of "us" that is both simple and complex. We all have a multitude of systems and circuits that contribute to the total picture of "who I am and how I view and interpret the world in which I live," and how we fire on all cylinders to get the maximum out of life. Some of the contributing factors are consideration of our childhood, culture, personality type, health, exposure to "faith," self-esteem, and no doubt plenty of other variables. Some people dismiss this kind of discussion as "psycho-babble." But caricaturing something unfortunately is not a very persuasive argument to challenge it. If we are intrigued enough to study space, engineering, science, and medicine, it would seem equally valid to believe that the careful study of human behavior might also contribute to our appreciation of the whole package "that is us."

In the Bible (which is really the equivalent of my TR6 manual for humans) God is far from indifferent about matters of faith and belief; funnily enough, He also seems to hate religion! Hardly surprising really, as within that definition he doesn't get to do much. Imagine a marriage where the couple only communicates through formal ritual—fulfilling the laws, rules, and requirements of marriage but without expressing any spontaneity and spark. Or how about reading responses of love and devotion to each other from old manuscripts because they could never come up with anything quite as meaningful! What is missing are spontaneity, vulnerability, joy, and the ability to make mistakes or feel foolish—relationship, in other words.

One of the greatest punishments or tortures for any human being to endure is to be placed in solitary confinement. We are essentially and fundamentally social creatures who need human interaction to live and thrive. Would it come as any surprise to discover that we reflect something of the nature of our Creator who also desires relationship rather than formality and ritual? Christianity, stripped of all its unfortunate manifestations through various church practices, the Crusades, and other distortions, is the only "world religion" where the core truth hinges on the *identity of a person.* The claim of Jesus Christ to be the Son of God is something no founder of any other major world religion has had the audacity to proclaim.

It is as if the dimmer switch is thrown into its highest setting and God announces, "If you want to know who I am, then take a serious look at Jesus Christ. He is the most complete revelation of my existence offered to the world. I have sent him into the world to help you to comprehend my love, my priorities, my personality, and what I am really like." Jesus himself reinforced that truth when he matter-of-factly stated, "If you have seen me, you have seen the Father."

In the person of Jesus God swims upstream, moving in the exact opposite direction to the other world religions. There focus is upon what we must do to get to God or to find "oneness with the deity." In Jesus, God comes to us and enters into our messy environment. He picks up the rusty ring that is this world and invites us to participate in the first global recycling initiative ever witnessed.

Why is relationship so important when considering the possible reality or even the existence of God? We can only have relationships with others who live and communicate as we do. One of the great tragedies of religion without relationship is that God is reduced to the "object of faith," an impersonal higher power/powers, or a myth. If the object of faith cannot communicate and is reduced to mantras and rules then invariably that object of faith becomes whatever we want him or her to be for us. When that happens the image of God is distorted and confusing. It's rather like trying to find the North Pole and never having heard of magnetic north.

I remember as a young schoolboy being introduced to the wonderful mysteries of science and magnetic fields by scattering iron filings on a piece of paper above a magnet. We watched the filings arrange themselves in arced lines as they were drawn into the magnetic field and then Mr. Clarke explained why this happened. Similarly when using a compass; even if I do not comprehend the science of magnetic poles, at least knowing they are a factor to be considered will help ensure a more accurate reading of the compass in my hand.

● ● ● ● ●

**The artist is nothing without the gift,
but the gift is nothing without work.**

—EMILE ZOLA

● ● ● ● ●

When it comes to our understanding of God, the greater our self-awareness the more likely we are to discern what influences our perceptions. One significant "field of influence" that can tug us off center is our personality type. Some people fear these kinds of studies and discussions put labels on people and place them in boxes. That does not have to be the case at all; it depends on how we utilize the insights and knowledge we gain from our multidisciplinary advances to gain a better understanding of human behavior. Our various personalities shape our communication and tend to influence the way we most naturally relate with others. They are lenses through which we perceive the world and can provide us with insights regarding our approach to religion and to God.

I grew up in South Africa and still after 25 years living abroad most people will pick out my accent and know I am not a native of North America. Similarly our primary experience and exposure to spirituality and faith will leave us with a "core accent" (even if that be atheism or nonparticipation), which will inform and color our thinking and our responses.

To complicate and muddy the water a little more it will be wise to consider what exposure if any we have had to God, the church, or religion in our formative years. The "emotional" response and memory we carry with us will significantly influence how we "think" about God as adults. I attended an Anglican-based private school in Cape Town for 12 years where we had "divinity classes" and compulsory chapel attendance. Instead of attracting young boys to the wonder and creative excitement of a living God, most invariably turned away from "church and religion" as adults. It has fortunately changed since then. At the time the message was unmistakable; to be enthusiastic about sport meant you were a hero or a "jock" and to be enthusiastic about God left you branded as a fanatic. The formal presentation of the Christian religion and our "church experience" appeared to be so irrelevant or foreign to where we boys lived, the language we spoke, offering few meaningful answers to the questions we had. Was it the message or was it the messenger?

There are also personal childhood experiences that cause deep scars. Julia (not her real name) sat in my office in Cape Town not quite sure what she was doing there, but she was having some problems in her life and needed to talk. We talked about her childhood and family life and as is usually the case in a first response, "Everything was fine." We chatted a little longer and then I asked her again about her relationship with her dad. After a period of silence tears welled up and she said very quietly, "For five years he abused me and then he would make me kneel and ask Jesus to forgive me for tempting him."

There are many stories unfortunately similar to that of Julia's. Her picture of God was of someone who did not care or who was angry with her because she was in fact guilty (in her mind). That is probably one of the deepest fears and anxieties of people who have been abused. The fear that if they do open up and allow God into that secret area, their nightmare will be proven to be true—that he is indeed angry with them and does hold them responsible for what they endured. The exact opposite is of course true, but that is not intuitively obvious because their vision and perception have quite understandably been skewed by the trauma of their experience.

The paradox is that we are all so alike and yet we are also unique. Our commonly shared patterns are usually good news for people who feel shame about who they are; it is a great relief and encouragement to discover that "I am not the only one." All of our personalities have also been submerged for a great deal of time in the rock pool with the rusty ring. They have become discolored and infested with barnacles as they have been separated from God and subjected to a harsh foreign environment. We refer to that reality as being in touch "with our dark side."

As we therefore reflect on our thoughts, beliefs, and attitudes toward God and his existence, being aware of our own "magnetic north" will make a difference in determining how we process information. It will certainly set the tone for any conversations we might participate in. If we are to honestly explore the question of God's existence then we at least have to listen and allow him the chance to speak and enter into the conversation as well. Maybe he is not like we think he is at all.

There are a variety of places where we can learn about God's desire for us to have a relationship with him. The first is by reading the Bible where all sorts of information is gathered and where our formal invitation to meet with him anytime we choose is printed. The second opportunity to learn about God is by meeting his Son, Jesus, and experiencing him at work in our lives. And finally there are the shared experiences of all kinds of people on the earth today. Those who have discovered that Jesus has indeed changed their lives and helped them know that God's love is very personal, powerful, and present.

I think it's time that we met Jesus, don't you?

9

# Jesus—What a Troublemaker! Or Not?

I LAUGHED, AND SNAPPED A PHOTOGRAPH OF THE SIGN. "NO FOOD, NO SHORTS."

I stood outside a church on the slopes of the gentle hills that roll across the north shore of the Sea of Galilee. The church commemorated where Jesus had walked and taught the crowds who followed him 2000 years ago. After teaching for a while Jesus was aware that the large group of men, women, and children had been with him for a long time without food, so he instructed his disciples to feed them. They were flabbergasted. How were they going to find enough food to feed a crowd of 5000? A little boy with a few loaves and some fish that his mother had packed for him offered his lunch to Jesus. The boy was brought to Jesus by one of the disciples who was probably being somewhat facetious in his response to the impossibility of the directive.

But Jesus was not bothered and was no doubt used to being misunderstood. In this instance the boy's meager lunch was enough for him to perform the miracle of multiplying the fish and loaves to feed a multitude. All these years later here I was standing in the same place next to a sign commemorating Jesus' generous abundance, power, and resounding yes! Except the sign warned in somber religious respectability, "No!" Whatever God does that is astounding and fun and magnificent we seem adept at discounting or shrinking down and taming until everything is back under control, tidy, rational, believable, and dead boring.

Earlier that morning I had left Tiberius by boat and sailed across the Sea of Galilee to Capernaum, where Peter lived and Jesus spent some time. Not far from Peter's house is the synagogue where Jesus taught, or at least you can see the black rock foundation of the original building that stood in his day. I sat amid the ruins of white weathered marble in the sun, ran my fingers across its smooth surface,and looked at a carving of people carrying the Ark of the Covenant upon their shoulders. The history pressed into my soul as I savored every breath.

This was where Jesus had lived and walked on earth at a specific time in history and the archeological evidence was overwhelming. Mosaics of fish (the secret sign of the early Christians), symbols of the cross, places for baptisms—the fingerprints of the early Christians were everywhere. This man was no myth, as some philosophers have easily dismissed him with unconvincing sleight of hand and pen. It was in this very village, certainly within earshot of where I was seated, that Jesus had spoken the word and the dying servant of a Roman centurion had been healed.

Maybe it was here where Jesus instructed his fledgling disciples about how the greatest among them was to be a servant. They had been walking along the road arguing about who was the most important person and Jesus had caught them at it much to their embarrassment and shame. But he did not beat them up, he merely used the opportunity to springboard into sharing his insights and priorities. He did that all the time; teaching from real life while they were on the way to do something else. Not far from the synagogue, actually just across the road he had healed Peter's mother. People marveled at this man who was so unlike all the other religious leaders they had ever met.

This was also the region and town that Jesus cursed, because despite all the healings they still would not believe. No towns stand along these shores today except the black ruins of Bethsaida, Korazin, and Capernaum. Around the curved coastline Tiberius remains a thriving tourist haven, much as it did in the time of Christ. Strange.

I left Capernaum and walked into the hills through golden grasses bending with the wind and from time to time paused to gaze out across the water. On my left the Golan Heights rose steeply, and before me the hills sloped down crumbling to the waters edge in flat expanses of rocky beaches. On my right the road to Nazareth traversed the cliffs rising to higher ground, and in the distance Tiberias perched on the shoreline. Jesus loved these hills and would often come here to escape the crowds and to pray. He never utilized the TV or Internet; he had no cell phone; no international paparazzi ever covered his teachings or followed his movements. He never caught an airplane, traveled in a train, or hitched a ride in a motor vehicle. He walked everywhere between these hills and Jerusalem and Nazareth and never wrote anything down. Yet his words, his teaching, his life, his death and his life beyond death have impacted human beings on this planet more than any other person in history. So what in God's name was he up to?

We have discussed the possibility of God's existence. But what would it be like if he actually *did something* to demonstrate that he is alive and well? If he were merely a figment of our imaginations or a crutch for the weak, then such independent action would be impossible. He would remain a religious projection of our psyche taking whatever form the historical human community conjured up.

•  •  •  •  •

**If we don't stand for something,
we may fall for anything.**

—UNKNOWN

•  •  •  •  •

I have had the privilege of spending countless hours over the course of 30 years listening and talking with people in England, South Africa, and North America about "religion" and this person called Jesus. The vast majority of people are fed up with "religious ritual" and the directive to "go to church," where leaders drone on, harangue them, or beg for money. In almost the same breath many of those same people are also hungry for something authentic and meaningful, if they can only get past the strident dogma and the fear of having to be "religious." Many turn to Eastern religions because they sense a greater depth and integration of their whole life and soul, a quality frequently missing from Western Christianity.

When the conversation focuses on Jesus Christ and his outrageous life and claims, the interest level rises. The battle for a meaningful conversation for most of us is being able to reach beyond our preconceptions, into a space where we are not afraid to look and listen with fresh eyes and open ears. That means getting past the idea that God is a killjoy figure who delights in making life miserable.

Jesus Christ is so unlike the God whom I met at school and in the church—where he appeared to my impressionable mind to be very stern, very boring, very English, and very unexciting. Jesus was and is much more attractive than that! He lived and walked among fisherman, farmers, house-wives, children, soldiers, prostitutes, and bankers. He visited with them and met them on their home turf in the marketplace and during the course of their daily lives. They were attracted to him—much more than they were attracted to the religious leaders of their day. Jesus did more than talk; he modeled before their eyes the meaning of life and the love of God in their language. He communicated in the familiar lingo of the Galilean market-place rather than the theological vocabulary of a lecturing professor from Jerusalem University.

Jesus' most disarming quality was his unconditional acceptance of people whom he had never met before. He was absolutely genuine and authentic, nothing fake or conjured up for another photo opportunity to boost his campaign or percentages in the polls and TV ratings. He accepted people and actually liked those whom he met. Whether they agreed with him or not he still vulnerably loved them first, as only one who is deeply secure within themselves can. They knew this intuitively as they witnessed firsthand his attitude, his touch, the look in his eye, and the tone of his voice. As he listened and conversed with them—they felt special. When their interaction was finished, people were free to leave or to follow him further—without any heavy pressure or emotional blackmail. The unconditional love and acceptance God feels for each person was powerfully and personally communicated whenever anyone was in the presence of Jesus. He never ever persuaded people by accusation, guilt, condemnation, humiliation, or pressure tactics.

●  ●  ●  ●  ●

**Nothing is more difficult and
nothing requires more character than
to find oneself in open opposition to
one's time and to say loudly: NO!**

—KURT TUCHOLSKY

●  ●  ●  ●  ●

A psychological study some years ago attempted to measure the relationship between individuals and their fathers and correlate the result with their subsequent perception of God. The findings revealed that in instances where the father was a kindly figure, God was perceived as benevolent; where the father was cruel or abusive, God was perceived to be brutal and authoritarian. When we consider our own relationship with our fathers we may gain some insight into where our gut-level emotional response to God originates (not every time, but it is a factor to consider).

Unless God (if he exists) provides me with some new information originating from his perspective (which I am suggesting he has done in the person of Jesus), I will not be able to fathom who he is or how he can possibly exist. All I have to work with is my limited brain and the evidence of a very fractured and distorted world around me. From where I stand, the leap of faith is virtually impossible to make based on logic and the tangible alone. Maybe I can conclude that there must be something bigger behind it all but beyond that open-ended possibility I am left dangling in conjecture and confusion.

In order to identify "God" with love and any personal characteristics that are not mere projections of my own wishful thinking, I will need a revelation. If I cannot get to God with my own resources, then if he is real he will have to take the initiative and make himself known to me; somehow coming over to where I am dangling at the end of my intellectual and emotional rope and introducing himself.

That's exactly what God did—believe it or not! He had the nerve to step out of the shadows and provide us with tangible evidence of his existence. He ventured across to our side of the map, and we neither recognized him nor quite knew how to react, other than to give a knee-jerk response of hostile alarm. He provided a point and person for us to focus upon and respond to that is quite specifically rooted in history. Jesus' life and death is historically verifiable and is not challenged by any reputable historian.

We had looked around and laughed and justified our stance by challenging God, shouting, "This world is such a mess—how could God be real? If you exist, prove it to me!" He called our bluff and responded. Now we find ourselves faced with the reality that we may have bitten off more than we realized. Now we're hassling with the stark truth that if God is real then we may be the one's who ultimately have some questions to answer, not him. Deep down we are afraid of his existence because it feels like bad news; but that's only because of our deep-seated misconceptions.

Fortunately the God revealed in Jesus is very patient and kind and not at all disillusioned with us—because he has always known who we really are and what we are like. He actually likes you and me a great deal—more than we comprehend. I suspect he has quite a sense of humor and maybe even delights in watching us awkwardly scratch our heads wondering, *Shoot, now what do I do?*

One of the cardinal rules when counseling couples is never to believe everything one party says without first checking in with the other person involved. It is so easy to become sympathetic to one side and to judge the absent person, only to discover after meeting with the "other" that there really are two sides to every story. In discussions about God the information is invariably one-sided and usually focuses on "what I think" with my horror stories interspersed to justify my position. Then God appears on the scene in the form of Jesus and wants to enter into the conversation and set the record straight. All of a sudden all hell breaks loose because it was much more convenient to present untested observations and conclusions—or was it?

If you or I were God and we wanted to communicate with our creation, what would we do, and how would we do it? Send them a message? How, and what would we say? Why didn't God just announce his existence one day with a message in the sky, or have a special broadcast saying: "Good morning, my human subjects, this is God speaking. Sorry for the inconvenience, I just wanted to get your attention and demonstrate to you that I am in fact here, and a reality. Please resume your activities but remember, I am watching."

What might God say that would make a difference...other then tease, irritate, or terrify? We would probably be left wondering what to do now after the broadcast ceased and silence followed. No doubt lectures and books would be written about "The Day God Made a Special Broadcast to the World." Some would start speculating that it was not really God but an elaborate stunt by some bored and wealthy entrepreneur, or even a new Microsoft gimmick from Bill Gates. Then the "Broadcast Believing Church" would rise up and issue news updates and weekly messages from God (who still speaks) to the world.

What was so unique about Jesus and his message? When Jesus was born into this world God moved dramatically and powerfully. He broke through our small mind-sets and limited vision and did something we could not fully comprehend. How can a virgin give birth? Not possible, we protest. Until we reflect that if God can create a virgin in the first place he surely is able to create life within her without help from anyone else. It all depends where our starting point is.

It is unnatural for us to begin with God from a place of belief and acceptance, isn't it? The negative always seems to overcrowd the positive. I spent 20 years following and serving God and then everything I loved and believed in crashed to pieces all around me and I went through a major depression, a broken marriage, and a very hard time financially. I cried out to God and in frustration turned my back on him and gave up on church altogether for more than six years—and I had been a pastor! The one factor that I held onto was a deep belief that God is incredibly loving and compassionate and was able to handle me in my stress and despair. The fact that I am writing at all in this manner is a testimony to that reality.

What I really want to emphasize is that I slowly began to change my own perspective to see that God is truly wanting to partner with me to get the best "we" possibly can out of my life. He is not against me at all but desires more for me than I can imagine. I am a father of two beautiful daughters and I know what it feels like to want the best for them. When bad things happen it is not at all congruent with what I hoped and planned for them. That is just a small window of understanding into how God feels about me—and you! Jesus hinted at this when he told people around him, "If you then, though you are evil, know how to give good gifts to your children, how much more…" (Luke 11:13).

Begin with the premise that God exists and can theoretically do whatever he chooses and anything becomes possible. Begin with the premise that everything has to be comprehended by the human intellect first, and severe restrictions are immediately clamped upon what God is capable of accomplishing.

It is very easy to shrink God down to a human size. Before we know what has happened we have rejected his existence because we cannot explain everything about him. Surely God, by his very existence as the Creator, would by definition be way beyond our understanding. The question then becomes one of discussing what evidence and reasons there are that may lead us to conclude that He is indeed real? If God is the Creator, and Jesus Christ is who he claims to be, then what we see in Jesus is God trying to simplify himself to a degree whereby we can comprehend enough about him to believe with integrity.

When it comes to talking about life from God's perspective we are all probably rather similar to the Bushman holding a Coke bottle—we don't really have the worldview or intellectual capacity to comprehend him. Therefore he has to resort to communicating very simply, kneeling down by our side and looking into our eyes like an adult would with a young child whispering, "Don't be afraid, now listen to me." Which is precisely what he was and is doing through the person of Jesus Christ.

The point is that if God is real then surely he is capable of speaking through people, doing all kinds of remarkable things, and initiating actions quite independently of our exceedingly limited understanding. Instead of arguing to prove that God is real and living, maybe for a change we could begin from a position that accepts his existence, and place the onus on the skeptic to prove that he does not.

Continuing therefore with our (new) supposition that God is indeed real, how would he communicate in order to demonstrate who he is and what he is all about? The classic description often follows this line. We would expect him to…

- enter into this life on earth in a unique and unusual manner— virgin birth

- manifest complete unity with God—be without sin/rebellion

- have the power to manifest supernatural works—miracles

- possess a unique perspective and self-awareness—different from any other living person

- speak words unlike any other person—authority

- impact world history significantly—disciples

- fill the spiritual emptiness or void in people with a new reality of God—inspire faith

- provide a way for human beings to be reconciled with God—forgiveness at cross

- demonstrate power over death, if indeed this life is not "all there is"—resurrection

What are God's options? More than I can comprehend, no doubt. If we want to communicate with teenagers about drug use, what is the most effective way to get our message across? Find a teenager who has experienced the horror and reality of drugs and who no longer uses them. That person is able to talk about addiction with great sincerity and knowledge in the vocabulary that other teenagers will relate to.

When I was leading a youth group in Cape Town, one of the most effective speakers was a guy who had been a hippie surfer and probably into a variety of other activities as well. Brian was deeply converted and his "market" in central Cape Town became a meeting place for those who wanted to know more about this Jesus who had made such an impact upon him. One of the attractive qualities about him was that he had not been "groomed" by church and consequently he was fresh and without inhibition in the manner in which he communicated to a contemporary culture.

It's not difficult to understand the challenges facing Jesus walking on this earth claiming to be God's Son, is it? Yet despite all the obstacles and cynicism his presence in the Galilee region of the Middle East 2000 years ago changed the world. No one ever lived the quality of life Jesus lived, or taught as he taught (the truth of which all hinged upon his identity as truly being the Son of God). No one (certainly no other founder of a world religion) ever seriously made the claims that Jesus made and neither did they ever do the things that he did with such consistency and with so many witnesses—including rising from the dead!

If one explores the possible existence of God openly and honestly then Jesus Christ cannot be ignored or dismissed in a phrase or two. He is the only spiritual leader of the world's main religions to link his message directly with his identity and to his claim to be the Son of God. Furthermore his resurrection after a bloody and excruciating crucifixion is also unique. People in Roman times could not kill God (which makes sense if he is real) and neither will we be able to. The blunt reality is that if God does exist, what we ultimately think of that fact, or whether we like it or not, does not change anything. We then resort to playing games like children, pretending that if I close my eyes you do not exist, "because now I can't see you."

Don't you find it remarkable that when we discuss God we so quickly disregard the parts about Jesus that are difficult to believe? We are generally willing to agree that he existed as a historical figure and that maybe he was a great teacher and a good man (we alluded to that in history at the university), but to go beyond that point is not automatic or easy.

We talk about God, if he exists, being great and powerful, but when presented with possible evidence we seem to respond in a very negative and defensive fashion. Maybe something like school kids coming to the realization that the school principal has seen all their activities after all, so now what? Does that tell us more about our own distorted preconceptions about God and his character as one who will spoil our "fun" if we ever take him seriously?

When we turn matters around and start from the premise that God is real, it is not at all a stretch of the imagination to believe that he might choose to reveal himself in human form, perform miracles, walk on water and be raised from the dead. No more remarkable then asking a salmon in a British Columbian river to believe that life extends beyond the ocean or that "something" is out to get him. Let's think about that metaphor for a moment.

How would you respond to being told that evil is a reality and that satan actually exists and is working against the purposes of God?

In British Columbia there are beautiful rivers with salmon spawning and swimming in many of them. Imagine you're a salmon and you're heading in from the ocean toward the mouth of the river you left as a young fish a few years earlier. As you make your way "home" you strike up a conversation with another salmon and he starts telling you some very strange things. First he says,

> Do you know that the whole world is not all wet and liquid and that there are other living creatures beyond this watery world that we call home? Also, my friend, you need to be very careful what you eat, because there is a power that exists in that other world that wants to kill you. You will not recognize him because he is very clever and does not look anything like us. He offers you your favorite food by just tossing it in front of you to float quite innocently in the river. As soon as you take hold of that food you will discover to your shock that there is a hook inside that pierces your flesh and you cannot escape. If that ever happens you'd better shake your head and fight like mad. If you're lucky you will shake it off, otherwise you're dead.
>
> Don't laugh, it happened to me. I thought I was dead for sure when I found myself unable to let go of a scrap of food. I struggled for my life as an invisible force pulled me through the water and out into a place where there was no water, and I could hardly breathe. A very frightening large creature took hold of me, freed the hook from my gasping mouth, and then threw me back into the sea. I was stunned for a moment and then swam away as fast as I could. Heard someone up there say something about catch and release, but I don't know what they were talking about. Now I'm extremely careful about what I eat!

Do you think the salmon swimming alongside would believe him, or would he retort, "Huh? Are you crazy? What ocean have you been swimming in, 'cause it sure has done something to your mind."

As Jesus flexed his muscles and began teaching and healing people he caused quite a stir around Galilee and Jerusalem. First, he looked pretty ordinary and spoke in the common language of the day. He was humble and everyone who met him seemed to feel respected and loved in a manner that was much deeper than a superficial Hollywood teardrop rolling down the cheek. Jesus was a paradox. He communicated with profound gentleness and tenderness to the degree that little children loved to be around him because he was fun and kind and included them. On the other hand he could stare into the eyes of a religious leader and snap words of rebuke that cut through the religious hypocrisy and exposed the real motives and agendas in a flash. Political correctness was not something Jesus participated in, and this was one of the reasons why he ended up on a cross so quickly.

Where we humans become inexorably stuck is as we struggle to consistently "live" the tolerance we profess to uphold. This is glaringly evident in the ongoing scourge of racism for example. Although we talk about the evils of prejudice we still practice discrimination in a multitude of discreet and less than subtle ways. In our attempt to protect the rights of pretty much every "interest" group one can imagine we frequently witness the group's spokesperson uttering intolerant phrases in order to legitimize their own particular brand of victimization.

● ● ● ● ●

**It was the best of times, it was the worst of times, it was the age of wisdom, it was the age of foolishness, it was the epoch of belief, it was the epoch of incredulity, it was the season of Light, it was the season of Darkness, it was the spring of hope, it was the winter of despair, we had everything before us, we had nothing before us, we were all going direct to Heaven, we were all going direct the other way.**

—CHARLES DICKENS

● ● ● ● ●

Jesus would be crucified today just as viciously as he was "silenced" 2000 years ago. And many of us would be washing our hands of his blood around the basin with Pilate, protesting our innocence while practicing compliance.

My friend in the pub pointed out that the rock music industry is one place where freedom of expression is most likely to be tolerated. Maybe the only point of this discussion is to demonstrate how hard it is for any of us to be consistent. And that idealism and pragmatism, expediency and deeply held beliefs, all clash and compete for a place in our everyday lives. This is both a dynamic part of life as well as an infuriating liability and responsibility, even more so when it exposes our own blind spots in dealing with these important issues maturely and fairly.

The religious leaders of Jesus' day were much like many leaders in the church today. They liked control, had God all figured out within their miniscule theological music boxes, and had developed a power base and job security with benefits. Controversial topics were avoided or suppressed and they knew how to use spirituality and religious jargon to camouflage, manipulate, or derail pretty much anything they encountered that challenged their view of the status quo. They tended to be defensive and had a "them and us" mentality and attitude. The result was an image of God being presented that was an aloof and a somewhat frightening figure, very distant from ordinary people (with whom he was usually disappointed and angry).

Sound harsh? Maybe. But scratch many theologies and churches and you'll find that our tendencies are not that different from the Pharisees. Jesus called them whited sepulchers "full of dead men's bones" (Matthew 23:27). The irony is that Jesus could see that fact as clearly as those who don't go to church can discern it today—which is why they do not attend.

Jesus was not at all what the religious leaders expected. They portrayed God as a judge and a power who was preoccupied with ensuring that human beings kept the law passed down through Moses. The Pharisees used to devise all kinds of laws that they erected like hedges around "God's law." People were bombarded with rules and regulations, sacrifices and taxes—all in the name of God. They stated that if you concerned yourself about not breaking their "hedge" laws you would be protected from transgressing the really serious ones. They took the Ten Commandments and beat people up with every rule and word in what was ultimately reduced to a priestly power struggle.

Jesus came into the world and said, "I have come to fulfill the law (see Matthew 5:17) and by the way, if you have seen me you have seen God—the Father." *Father?* God is about rules, not parenting, isn't he? God actually *likes* people?

Amazing. Think about this. If it were not for Jesus there would be no revelation or indication that God is personal, that he loves you or anyone else, or that he is kind and compassionate and caring. When I spent time exploring these truths with others they were almost immune to the word "love," but stopped short when they considered the fact that God actually likes them! When you come into the room God turns around and smiles, gets up, and embraces you saying, "How wonderful to see you, Jackie—I'm so glad you're here. Let me get you something to drink and then we can catch up."

That is exactly what Jesus was doing all around Jerusalem and Galilee, and it absolutely blew people away because it was everything they had ever thirsted for in their wildest dreams. For God to like me, and to love me, to accept me with all my "issues," and to tell me that I am not too bad or rejected! Such certainty or even possibility would be the most healing and profound revelation of my life. That would be good news indeed!

I can see Bill sitting across from me right now with tears in his eyes. Leaning forward he shakes his head and tells me about how Jesus' love and acceptance changed his life. He had killed a man and served many years in prison to pay for his crime. But nothing on this earth was strong enough to alleviate his guilt or to give him the assurance and the hope that despite his awful deed he was not lost forever. There's a raw honesty in people who have nothing to hide and have had to face the reality of their own failures publicly. They either become very hard and bitter or they develop a disarming transparency that tells it as it is. I love and respect that quality when I find it. It is so refreshing in a world of vanity and image, hair dye and liposuction.

Bill wept because despite all that he had done wrong, it wasn't enough for him to be rejected. He knew in his heart the presence of a love and a hope and an acceptance that he had never experienced before. God's love for Bill that was made real in the person of Jesus and in a community of people "with skin on" that welcomed and enjoyed his company as well. The truth is, Bill gave to others so much more than he realized, and when he died a few years ago I mourned the loss of a man who had certainly shown me unconditional love and acceptance.

God's love heals the heart; knowledge merely describes the event or debates and discusses the angles. Most of us have too much information and precious little love that heals. Bill knew what he had done, and he also knew what God had done anyway—and the focus was on Jesus.

One of my favorite TV shows is *Extreme Home Makeover,* where a team goes into the home and lives of a deserving family and creates a dream home for them within seven days. The family is sent off on a vacation and when they return they have a brand new home that has been tailor-made for their personalities and needs. I always have tears in my eyes when I watch their responses because they are so overwhelmed with gratitude, awe, and the magnitude of what has been done for them. That's what it will be like when each one of us gets together with Jesus and his Father. No dry eyes, and an indescribable sense of love and generosity which he wants us to begin to taste while we are alive on this earth (and I'm not talking about making every one of us materially rich).

I have lost count of the number of people with whom I have sat and conversed about how we see God and how he views us. When we unlearn some of the nonsense we carry around about God as the big monster with a stick or as the genial and weak old man in the sky, and rather consider the possibility of him loving us and genuinely adoring who we are. A God who desires to interact with us as with a favorite child, something inside breaks open. Tears well up and the cry of the human heart surfaces with a whisper of disbelief intermingled with relief:

"Could it really be so?"

"Yes!"

"How can I know it's not just wishful thinking?"

"Look long and hard at this person called Jesus, brush aside the rubble of hearsay and find out for yourself whether who he is and what he claims is really true. Of course you can start by using your mind but somewhere along the way lighten up with the intensity of your own need to understand. Wave your hand in the air and ask Jesus to lead you into a real experience of his reality and see what happens."

God loves interaction with his creation and is more than willing to meet us half way. The God of religious people is straitjacketed in traditions, rituals, ceremony, and "the right words." It is almost impossible to get through to him because of all the personnel trying to protect him. When Jesus was alive the disciples tried to do the same thing and told people not to bother him and they warned children to stay away and keep their distance. Jesus became highly frustrated with their attitude and instead brushed his disciples aside and said, "Let the little children come to me" (Luke 18:16). The God revealed in Jesus is extremely sociable, loves to visit in all kinds of venues, and doesn't mind being interrupted by you or me at all. We have always tended to misunderstand the place of rules and respectful attitudes and behavior where God is involved. Take the most famous of them all for one example, the Ten Commandments (Exodus 20:1-17).

* * * * *

### Being Politically Correct means always having to say you're sorry.

—CHARLES OSGOOD

* * * * *

The Ten Commandments were never meant to be rules that people could actually live up to. They were intended to describe God's character and his ultimate purpose for human beings. They were a benchmark that people could look to, as if into a mirror, and see how far they had strayed or how disheveled they had become. They could see quite clearly in that reflection why they needed help, a Savior, rescue.

The purpose of a mirror is to reflect back to us the way we actually are in order that we may do something about it! The purpose of the Ten Commandments is to reveal to us that we are unable to be what God created us to be without his help and participation in our lives.

When we look into the mirror and conclude that maybe we need to clean up, have a shower, and wash our clothes that is usually not depressing or extraordinary. We recognize that this cycle is part of the consequence of living on earth. We get dirty on a daily, if not hourly basis. We accept the reality, adjust accordingly, and we go off and do something about it. The same principle and cycle is true in the spiritual dimension. We reflect on the Ten Commandments and then do something about it on a daily basis—not just at Christmas and Easter. If that's our practice then no wonder we are spiritually disheveled and reek to high heaven!

Jesus Christ demonstrated what it looks like for a human being to live according to those commandments when they started from a center of a love relationship with his Father. The Pharisees (emphasizing external rules and obedience) were the ones who kept exhorting people to obey those commandments. When someone who actually did obey them confronted them—they accused him of insolence and then used the same law to justify killing him.

● ● ● ● ●

**As long as I don't write about the government, religion, politics, and other institutions, I am free to print anything.**

—PIERRE-AUGUSTIN BEAUMARCHAIS

● ● ● ● ●

Why did they do that? They were serious and sincere people not much different from you and me. Their problem was that they thought that God expected them to harangue people into obedience and compliance. They did not know what else to do, so they reduced God to rules and religious rituals. Long ago they had lost sight of any hope of relationship such as David had written about in the Psalms, or Moses had experienced, or Abraham before him. Similar attitudes are prevalent in many churches today where God's message is conveyed with hostility and anger that makes love difficult to discern. Usually the love is tough and like a parent chastising a child. Alternatively at the other extreme one hears a message of compassion that also masquerades as love where there is never any discipline and love has become sentimental and weak.

Many leaders delivering the "tough love" message have forgotten how to love people. They have fallen into the trap of elevating the commandments into baseball bats of rules and rituals that batter and bruise those with whom they come in contact. Leaders delivering messages of compassion without discipline reduce God to a sentimental grandfather. He constantly binds up wounds but never helps mend the fence to prevent the same accident occurring again tomorrow.

The solution is childlike in its simplicity. Jesus was once dining at the house of a wealthy man when a young woman entered the room carrying a jar of very expensive perfume. She had been a lady of ill repute in the community, and when she met Jesus he had responded to her with a love that no other man had ever given to her, a love that dignified her and did not demand anything of her at all. She had obviously been overwhelmed and came into the room weeping. Kneeling at Jesus' feet she anointed them with the perfume and expressed her gratitude and thanks in the only way she knew how. The people around muttered, "Do you know who this is?" and Jesus quietly but firmly held their gaze and said, "She who has been forgiven much, loves much" (Luke 7:36-50).

It is only when we know how much we have been forgiven will we truly love others unconditionally and with authentic humility. Jesus really is so much kinder then we tend to be—certainly that is true in my case.

*Woman—I see you*
*Woman—I hear you*

*Woman—I love you*
*Be not afraid...*
*I don't condemn you*

*It's been so long*
*In your lonely place*
*Hiding inside*
*Behind your painted face*
*Pushing down pain*
*But all in vain*
*Today it's back again*
*Looking for hope*
*Longing for peace*
*Yearning for love*
*But finding none*
*You settle for less*
*Feeding on crumbs*
*And your hunger never leaves*

*Surrounded by thieves*
*Stealing at night*
*Under cover of dark*
*Into the light*
*Their fingers accuse*
*Beating you down*
*'Til you don't know who you are*

*Stand up, my child*
*Look around*
*There's no one, no sound*
*Not a stone's been found*
*No, you're not alone, come and walk by my side*
*Together we'll learn to love again*
*No, you're not alone, come and walk by my side*

*Together we'll learn to laugh again*
*No, you're not alone, come and walk by my side*
*Together we'll learn to dance again*

—BASED ON JOHN 8:1-11

The Pharisees struggled with the radical message and revelation of Jesus just as much as we do today. But unlike the Pharisees, or any other spiritual leader before or since, Jesus was also accomplishing a greater purpose that was frankly beyond their and our comprehension. Even now we argue and debate over these matters precisely because they are so foreign to our natural way of thinking. They are the discussions relating to the death and resurrection of Jesus Christ—what on earth was he doing, and what's the big deal anyway? He is so counter-intuitive it will drive you crazy—or turn your perspective delightfully upside down!

# 10

# Tombs with Rolling Stones

"PSST!"

A solitary bearded figure in black beckoned to me through the veiled dim light with wisps of incense and ribbons of sunlight draped across the high stone walls. Curious, I wandered over. Smiling, he pointed to the ground. "You can touch it," he said pointing to the ground on his right. He was gesturing toward the corner of a large marble block that had been cut away. In the lamplight surrounded by cheap crucifixes I was invited to bend down and touch the corner of the tomb where Jesus' body had been laid. And while I was on my knees he said, "How many children do you have, wife, brothers, sisters?" For each reply he reached into his pocket and placed another crucifix into my hand...And then said, "Donation in there." I felt sorry for him but could not bring myself to succumb to this exploitation of Jesus' life, death, and resurrection. "No, thanks," I responded as politely as possible and handed back the trinkets.

I was visiting the ancient Church of the Holy Sepulcher in Jerusalem. Built in the fourth century AD, its walls surround the Rock of the Skull (Golgotha), where Jesus was crucified and the tomb where he was reputed to have been buried is. The rock and the tomb are only about 200 feet apart, maybe a little more. The paradoxes, ironies, and humor of this place are mind-numbing. Like a tragic comedy they perfectly capture the fumbling manner in which we have struggled to comprehend the astoundingly radical revelation God gave the world in the person of Jesus Christ.

One of the first sights as you walk into the Church of the Holy Sepulcher is a flat slab of marble where it is reputed that Jesus' body lay as it was prepared for burial. Above the slab hang seven lanterns. Out of reverence and awe for God's incredible sacrifice? No, because the various churches represented here cannot agree on who should have access to what, and when. As a compromise solution, various sections of the church have been apportioned to different Coptic denominations. The church itself has been traditionally locked and unlocked each day by a Muslim family because the Christians cannot agree on who should have responsibility for the task.

All over the world it is the same sad predicament, before we dare point fingers. The multitude of denominations and splintered churches that exist is astounding, each of us clutching to our chests our fragment of truth while explaining why it is very important and using the Bible to justify our position. Fortunately Jesus cannot roll over in his grave, because he's not there; but he must be disappointed at times at how little of his message we have understood.

The classic Christian analogy describing what God the Father accomplished through Jesus, his Son, is played out in a courtroom scene. A judge is presiding over a court case and the person before him is unquestionably guilty of the crime that has been committed. The sentence will be substantial and for justice to be carried out there is no alternative or extenuating circumstance for the accused to plea bargain.

The judge pronounces sentence and the accused is condemned and resigned to imprisonment and possible death. What is more complicated in this scenario is that the accused is also the son of the judge. Understandably it has been an extremely painful process for both of them to endure. However, the greatest surprise comes after the verdict has been passed down and the accused is about to be shuffled off in leg irons and handcuffs under escort to serve his sentence. The judge rises from his chair, removes the robes that signify his office, and makes his way down to where his son stands condemned. "In order for justice to be satisfied I had to acknowledge your guilt and pronounce the sentence as judge; however, I am also your father. Because I love you I will serve your sentence, and pay your fine even though you do not deserve it. You may go free."

Through the death of Jesus on the cross God has made it possible for any human being to find reconciliation with him by aligning with that sacrificial event. A Christian is essentially someone who willingly acknowledges that they have not been obedient to God for all kinds of reasons that are sometimes deliberate and many times ignorant (in theological jargon, a "sinner"). The spelling of "sin" gives us a clue to its meaning. Sin has "I" in the center which means "I" has taken the place of God as the supreme authority in my life—classified as mutiny or rebellion. With that acknowledgement the Christian also recognizes what God has done through Jesus by allowing his Son to die on the cross in his or her place, thus paying the price or serving the sentence on their behalf.

A Christian is not a "good" person. This has nothing to do with earning the right to be accepted by God. It is all about receiving the gift that God has given through his Son. A friend of mine was chatting the other day and I asked him what was the most significant thing he had learned when attending a basic Christian course about 12 years ago. "When we talked about the fact that we are all sinners. I always thought I was a good person and I never understood myself as a sinner before God; I had to go home and think about that," he said with a big grin, shaking his head at what is so obvious to him now.

If God said that no one could come to him unless they had taken a shower, and water was not available, then it would be a cruel joke—as no one would be able to come before him. We could accuse him of being unfair or placing us in an impossible situation that is ultimately no fault of ours. However, if he not only points out what is required but also provides the facility and means to meet the requirement, then anyone can have a shower who admits they need one.

It is obvious that those who come to him "clean" have taken advantage of the opportunity provided for them by him. The credit goes to the one providing the shower, not to the one who needed it; all they did was respond to an invitation to appropriate something they had not earned. That's why it makes no sense to claim, "I'm not good enough..." If we're not good enough we are first in line to qualify. It's the same as saying, "Whoa, I'm filthy!" and then, having been offered a shower, replying, "No, thanks—I can do this on my own." Remaining dirty is not a merit badge proclaiming our humility; it is more of a flashing light advertising our stubbornness, pride, or blindness. If I am unaware of my state of "dirtiness" it is probably because I cannot see dirt in the dark. The more light that is available, the more obvious the dirt becomes. Jesus is not called "the light of the world" for no reason.

•  •  •  •  •

**When you look at electrical things you can see that they are made of small and big wires, cheap and expensive all lined up. Until the current runs through them there will be no light. Those wires are you and me and the current is God. We have the power to let the current pass through us, use us and produce the light of the world or we can refuse to be used and allow darkness to spread.**

—MOTHER TERESA

•  •  •  •  •

The handle for God's shower is designed in the shape of a cross that is only activated when we individually take hold of it. The gift or purpose of God does not end with Jesus dead in a tomb, having accomplished the status of ultimate sacrifice and a reputation as the world's greatest martyr. If that was the only intention, wonderful as it was, then God may as well have left the situation at the level of animal sacrifices. Remember, the goal is reconciliation in order to participate in a relationship with God as Adam and Eve enjoyed in Eden. It's no more about keeping rules than a healthy marriage is about following written commands. If we remove the love from a relationship then we are left with a framework of "duties" that end up being similar to rules. However when the love is vibrantly at the center the duties or rules become "just what we do to help each other." The same is true in a relationship with God.

Here is the disarmingly simple essence of the Christian faith—a living relationship with a living God focused in the person of Jesus Christ. Remove the life and heartbeat of the relationship and all that remains is an empty shell. The spiritual beach along which we sometimes stroll looking for something beyond the materialism of our day is littered with shells. Many of us pick up some beautiful objects and we eagerly hold them to our ears to hear the surf echo and sense the hint of something that once was. Some of us (like those in Jesus' day) have no idea there is "more to God" than empty shells. Consequently we settle for what we do have and we jealously guard that "experience" or "tradition" and faithfully continue to collect shells—because they are beautiful. For countless reasons we have never been able to find our way beyond that shoreline to the place where those shells actually contain life!

Jesus was very clearly reframing life and death for us. In God's eyes "death" means rebellion and separation from him. The first Christian disciples would understand. Everything about this Jesus whom they followed for the best part of three years was a challenge to their paradigms and intellectual boundaries. His approach to them was challenging, his healings and miracles were challenging, his acceptance of all people was challenging, his teaching was challenging, his love was challenging, his anger in the temple was challenging, his serving them was challenging, his washing their feet was challenging, his submission was challenging, his humility and suffering was challenging, his crucifixion and death on a cross was challenging...

After the crucifixion of Jesus they wandered in their grief along the edge of their existence where all their hopes and beliefs lay scattered and broken across the entire breadth of their own spiritual shorelines. They found the tomb where Jesus had been laid, empty—like a shell on the beach...And they concluded that his body had been stolen; any other interpretation was scientific madness and way beyond their ability to even consider, let alone comprehend.

But if God is...then nothing is impossible! What a wonderfully mysterious, unexpected, exciting, terrifying, humbling moment when Jesus appeared to them while they were holding shells to their ears "remembering." He said something along these lines, "Here I am, I am not locked in those shells, I am alive and will be with you forever...That which is created cannot kill their Creator."

God detests rules as the basis for relationship as much as you or I do. Therefore his ultimate purpose through Jesus was to enable a change of heart and mind (repentance) that would re-ignite love and passion where hardness, indifference, and cynicism had been lodged like cancer for generations. God's purpose in allowing Jesus to be nailed to the Cross and bleed for the "rebellion" of humanity certainly meets the requirements of perfect justice. However, that is not all! It is also to raise him from the dead, demonstrating his ultimate power and authority over evil, satan, and death. It clearly communicates that no matter what we may do or say, we cannot "kill" God; whether we resort to crucifixion, legislation, force, denial, or even "religion." All that these actions accomplish is to delude us into believing we have "taken care of God," which is as about as effective as burying one's head in the sand like that funny looking bird, the ostrich.

Three days after Jesus' friends had removed his lifeless body from the cross, wrapped it in grave clothes, and placed it in a tomb with a huge stone rolled across the entrance, the discovery was made that he was no longer there! The grave clothes were exactly where the Jesus had been placed except the body was gone. Many theories have been suggested to explain the empty tomb. The body was stolen, Jesus never really died, even that he faked the whole charade and went off to live in India.

It is when confronted with events like the resurrection that many of us fail to consider the evidence, dismissing the extraordinary event out of hand as too unbelievable. An honest examination of the evidence and consequences surrounding this incredible claim has astounded, humbled, and persuaded many. The conclusions are actually surprisingly compelling and provide an intellectually credible basis for faith. One of the classic accounts examining the evidence for the resurrection is *Who Moved the Stone?* by Frank Morison, an English journalist. He began his research as an agnostic and when faced with the evidence became a committed Christian and wrote the book he never intended to write.

The unbelievable aspect is always amusing. It would seem to be self-evident that when the infinite God is involved with finite humanity it does not take long before we are shaking our heads saying, "How did he do that?" If crowds can be mesmerized by the conjuring tricks of David Copperfield the illusionist, why is the fact that we cannot explain everything about God sufficient reason to disbelieve? I have no idea how this computer on my desk works; I marvel at the technology that is now part of everyday life. Do I have to understand how it works as a precondition of my utilizing it? Of course not—in this arena I am quite comfortable accepting my limitations and ignorance and I certainly do not feel awkward acknowledging that fact of life. I am grateful for the skills and expertise of others and I gladly appropriate what they have designed and made available to me.

After Jesus' disappearance from the tomb he appeared to his disciples and various other people over the course of a few weeks. The conviction grew that God had indeed raised him from the dead! The disciples were amazed, as they had never expected such a turn of events. Although in hindsight they began to recall some of his teaching and scratching their heads, musing, "So that's what he meant when he said those things."

One of the aspects of Christianity that has always impressed me has been the honesty contained in the biblical accounts. Very ordinary people wrestle quite openly with the question of God and how encountering him overwhelms, confuses, and amazes them. Matthew, Mark, Luke, and John all share their perspectives concerning the resurrection of Jesus and the events of his life on earth. None of them doubt that he rose from the dead, but they each speak with their own personality and "accent."

• • • • •

It was while I was in the Holy Land for the purpose of making three B.B.C. television programs on the New Testament that a curious, almost magical, certainty seized me about Jesus' birth, ministry and crucifixion...I became aware that there really had been a man, Jesus, who was also God—I was conscious of his presence. He really had spoken those sublime words—I heard them. He really had died on a cross and risen from the dead. Otherwise, how was it possible for me to meet him, as I did?...

The words Jesus spoke are living words, as relevant today as when they were first spoken; the light he shone continues to shine as brightly as ever. Thus he is alive, as for instance Socrates—who also chose to lay down his life for truth's sake—isn't...The Cross is where history and life, legend and reality, time and eternity, intersect. There, Jesus is nailed for ever to show us how God could become a man and a man become God.

—MALCOLM MUGGERIDGE

• • • • •

The Gospel accounts describe a motley collection of people from all walks of life whose lives and hearts were changed forever. Because of Jesus' life, death, and resurrection they discovered a God who was extremely personal, rather than a distant and terrifying CEO. There is no question that they struggled intellectually to comprehend what happened and did not arrive at their convictions easily or superficially. Despite the inevitable gaps in their understanding they still found enough that was powerful, real, and relevant to cause them to continue along their strange and exciting path.

In fact their commitment to follow "the Way" eventually led many of them to accept death rather than renounce their affiliation with Jesus of Nazareth. They insisted on confessing him as Lord and the only true God, and would not bow down to Caesar who desired the same adulation. Early documents describe the courage and bravery of Christian leaders and ordinary men and women. They endured death by torture and hideous barbarity in the Coliseum where they faced wild animals to "entertain" the crowds. Despite all the persecution the "Christian sect" grew in the first 350 years after Christ in a quite astounding manner. One of the reasons was undoubtedly that its message touched a nerve among people everywhere who yearned for love and a deeper sense of the living God. That yearning has never really changed down the ages.

C.S. Lewis used to insist that we couldn't be neutral about Jesus precisely because he was so absolutely specific and clear about who he was and what he claimed to be. Lewis is often quoted as saying that Jesus was either mad like someone who believed he was a poached egg, bad in terms of a liar and a fraud, or authentically true and indeed quite uniquely and unbelievably God in human form.

Jesus revealed the heart of God to humanity as the heart of a father for his children. When the children are lost the father is grieved. A situation movingly described when Jesus recounted the tale of the prodigal son.

This is a story about a son who insults his father by requesting his inheritance (before his father's death) and then leaves home to squander it. He travels to a distant land and spends his money on wine, women, and high living. Eventually all his resources are gone and he is reduced to herding pigs to survive. Reflecting on his situation the son decides to head for home and offer to do any menial task just to be allowed to have a roof over his head. He is embarrassed, remorseful, and without any excuse for his dilemma as he heads for "home."

However, the point of the story is really about the love of the father more than it is about the foolishness of the son. It is about a God who aches for his creation, and stands every day in the doorway looking down the road waiting for his boy or girl to come home. When that moment finally happens, Jesus describes the prodigal son nervously trying to rehearse his speech as he approaches the house. He is not anticipating this homecoming as being a moment of great joy and he is bracing himself for the tirade that he knows he deserves.

Instead, before he can say anything his father is running to meet him no doubt with tears pouring down his cheeks as he embraces his beloved son. He wraps him in his cloak, puts a ring on his finger, and orders the servants to prepare a feast. The son keeps interrupting, "But dad—" And the excited father hushes him and kisses him…"Welcome home…my son who was dead, is alive again!" While the son focuses on the squandered inheritance, the father's priority is on a squandered life being turned around with an opportunity to start again (Luke 15:11-32).

*You are wonderful*
*So very kind*
*And you never—never*
*Never—break the bruised reed*

*How can I thank you, Lord*
*How can I give you praise enough*
*For you have loved me from afar*
*And you have drawn me near*

*You are merciful to me*
*Giving hope to the poor*
*You bind up and heal*

*The wounds of those who bleed*
*Yes, you did, you do, you will*

*You are gentle to me*
*Slow to anger or condemn*
*You give new life*
*To those dying in despair*
*Yes, you did, you do, you will*

*You are faithful to me*
*Giving strength to the weak*
*You give new vision*
*To those who struggle so much to see*
*Yes, you did, you do, you will*
*How can I thank you, Lord…*

God raised Jesus from the dead in order that every one of us may also be raised from the death of separation and rebellion and be welcomed home in an undeserved and astoundingly gracious and merciful manner. If you're like I am then you'll find it hard to come to grips with this possibility actually being true and real. We're so conditioned to a stereotypical picture of God that is a strict killjoy, and lacking in any humor. The only way I can comprehend the deeper meaning of the prodigal son was to imagine myself as the father, and the prodigal son as my daughter (or son). When I do that it is easy to comprehend in some measure how the father longs for such a homecoming and behaves with such uninhibited extravagance and joy!

One of the most significant moments of healing within every human spirit is to experience a homecoming as the one who is the prodigal. To stand before God the Father deserving absolutely nothing, and instead of receiving condemnation allowing ourselves to be kissed by him. To witness firsthand the tears of joy in his eyes as he rejoices quite publicly, "Welcome home—my child who was dead is alive again!"

When we celebrate graduations the successful students walk across the stage one at a time and shake the hand of the visiting dignitary and receive their certificate. The graduation ceremony for reconciliation with God is turning around and walking back into the embrace of his loving arms. There is no other way and there is no substitute either.

Far too many men and women are still frantically striving in business or a multitude of other arenas to earn acceptance and the accolades and approval of their fathers (whether he is dead or alive). Standing on the dusty threshold of God the Father's house is truly the only place such healing, peace, and affirmation will be released. And even after that initial embrace it still takes the rest of our earthly lives to learn how to fully accept it and appropriate its meaning to any degree of fullness.

This is not empty sentimental rhetoric. It is exactly the kind of greeting God the Father extends to every child of his creation, including you—with absolutely no exceptions. Nothing you or I have ever done is bad enough to exclude us. A few years after Jesus' resurrection Saul of Tarsus, a man who persecuted Christians and had them killed in the name of God, found himself with his face in the dust outside the gates of Damascus in a very undignified fashion. God spoke to him, "Saul, Saul, why do you persecute me?" (Acts 9:5). Saul was struck blind for three days and when his eyes were opened at every level of his being he too received the same welcome and response the prodigal son had.

Saul, later known as Paul, became one of the greatest Christian leaders and intellects in history. Every word he wrote contains within it a deep humility born out of his Damascus Road experience. God could have killed him because of his arrogance and his brutality and Paul knew that only too well. Instead his "Father" touched him firmly and mercifully, and Paul rose from the dust with a new heart and a humbled mind that could now be used for its real purpose. In actuality, that transformation probably had to be worked out in Paul's life over many years—God rarely does deep work instantaneously because it is the process that builds the character to sustain lasting change. There are very few people who discover an authentic relationship with God who escape being facedown in the dirt at one time or another. It is the logical place for our self-opinionated attitudes and actions to land when we at last come face-to-face with the living God who will not submit to our somewhat infantile utterances and actions.

● ● ● ● ●

**The person who tries to live alone will not succeed as a human being. His heart withers if it does not answer another heart. His mind shrinks away if he hears only the echoes of his own thoughts and finds no other inspiration.**

—PEARL BUCK

● ● ● ● ●

We have all heard the phrase, "Never say never." I was a Christian pastor for 17 years and was strong-willed and relatively effective and successful at what I was doing. I never saw the possibility of my marriage falling apart or my betraying trust; I never saw the possibility of deep depression and years of wandering in the wilderness with feelings of the deepest abandonment I have ever experienced. I never saw the possibility of not being home every day and night for my children or being unable to support them financially. I never thought I would experience such loneliness and an absence of friends. Then, I never thought I would ever be alive to God again—as I am now! The fact is that life has a way of tripping us up and exposing just how weak and naked and lost we really are much of the time. The good news is that when we feel most dead God tends to become most alive—not because we need a crutch, but because our true condition becomes most visible when the buffers and trappings are removed.

January 1971 is a month I will never forget. I was 18 years old and had to comply with conscription in South Africa and report for my army call-up. The rallying point was in the historic old castle that has stood beneath the shadow of Table Mountain in Cape Town for nearly 400 years. The sun was shining and for most people this would be another day at one of the beaches draped around that magnificent coastline. Instead a motley group of long-haired youth began to congregate with suitcases in their hands and girlfriends on their arms, parents and brothers and sisters all chatting and saying their final farewells.

Eventually the orders were barked out and we arranged ourselves in straggled lines, answered the roll call, and then sort of marched across the road to board the train bound for the military training camp in Oudtshoorn. Leaning out of the windows we waved goodbye as the train pulled out of the station and our links with civilian life were severed together with our freedom to do whatever we wanted to. I remember one mop-topped boy sitting next to me with a pimpled face and a sharp nose who probably felt as apprehensive and awkward as I did. Next to him was another fellow with longer hair, sporting cowboy boots. He was nonchalantly smoking a cigarette and almost mocking us with his smile as he mouthed smoke rings into the air then shattered them in a stream of blue smoke. He looked as if he had carefully honed his image from one of Clint Eastwood's characters out of the Wild West.

We arrived at the camp early the next morning and were herded through the routine welcoming procedures, finding our sparse accommodation and collecting uniforms. When the preliminary work was completed we were ordered to change into the army-issued khaki coveralls and report to the military barber. The "haircut" did not take long; none of the gentle hair washes and discussions about "What style today, and how much would you like to be cut off?" This was radical surgery—after a few snips of the scissors and a couple of passes over the scalp with an electric razor the job was done. In less than an hour our individuality lay with our clothes in the barracks and on the floor beneath the barber's chair. The guy without cowboy boots and no cigarette in his hand was newly shaved and looked thin and uncomfortable, big ears sticking out the side of his head—just like me!

God is not at all like an army sergeant and his "home" is not an army camp. But when we do finally meet him there will be no one but us standing there—hopefully still with hair (if that's what we had before). His greatest priority is for us to become who we were created to be in terms of character. Possessions, money, houses, and business status, reputation, press clippings, and important roles will all be lying somewhere else at that moment of final recognition. What we did or did not do will not even be discussed so much as, Who did we become while we were alive on earth?

"What did you do with the dual gift I made available, John?" God will ask. "The gift of your life and the gift of living that life in relationship with me through Jesus? Did you live life with your own resources or did you utilize the power and love I offered to enable you to become what is naturally quite impossible for you? Was the life I gave you spent well, spent on others? Or was it a waste of time, spent entirely on your own indulgences and self-gratification?"

Jesus' life, death, and resurrection resemble a Russian doll that repeatedly opens to reveal yet another one tucked inside. There is so much more to Jesus than a crucifix or an Easter egg, a Bible story or Christmas carols. He is more like God's Swiss Army knife, with possibilities and applications that you and I never imagined when we first took hold of it. As we keep finding new parts rising out from the body of the knife and discovering what they are for we exclaim, "This gift keeps getting better and better—who would have expected so much from this little gadget? They have thought of everything!" That is what hanging around and getting to know Jesus is like. Once we overcome the fear of cutting ourselves we will discover many new and relevant ways that his resources and our lives can intertwine in order to make a real difference—deep within ourselves and in our relationships with others. Let's see what else there is...

Jesus did not rise from the dead to be the resident ghost in Galilee for all eternity. His appearances there lasted about six weeks and then he told the disciples he was leaving them to return to his Father. However, he was not going to abandon them and expect them to "imitate me if you can." He promised to empower them with his Holy Spirit, which would touch their hearts, their minds, and their relationships. Now we're getting to the real reason for Jesus…Not a negative statement about dealing with everything that you and I have done wrong, but rather a positive outcome enabling God to empower us to become more aligned with his character—one day at a time. That's where the Holy Spirit comes in.

The Holy Spirit is not as crazy as it may first sound, even though it receives a lot of bad publicity by Christians making all kinds of outrageous and self-serving claims. Actually "it" is "he" because he is another aspect/ part of who God is. He is the power of God given to enable ordinary people to do extraordinary things when God's power is alive in them.

Visit any hardware store and consider the wide variety of electric light bulbs, halogen lamps, and fluorescent lights. None of them is particularly impressive and the parts are not of great value. However, their function is not realized on the shelf; they come to life when plugged into a power source and radiate light that is extremely useful. The same principle is true for human beings who are actually created to "light up" when plugged into God!

Jesus on earth was the first human being the world had ever seen who was "plugged into God"—an example of the Holy Spirit empowering a human being perfectly. That is why Jesus told his disciples that they would do greater things than he was doing. He was really saying that when the power of God is active in us there is no reason why we cannot love others "as I have loved you."

The commands Jesus gave were all based on the understanding that human beings cannot fulfill those commands in their own strength alone. Furthermore, the command to love others was understood to be an action, not an emotion. The crucifixion was supremely an act of love that Jesus would never have "felt like doing." In effect he said, "Start by acting in a loving way and the feelings will usually follow on behind. If you wait for feelings…well, I'm not sure we have that much time to wait."

After documenting the life of Jesus in Matthew, Mark, Luke, and John the remainder of the New Testament is all about how the Holy Spirit empowered a group of very frightened, disillusioned disciples. Luke's account in Acts particularly describes how this motley, largely uneducated bunch was transformed almost overnight (actually the groundwork had been done day in and day out with Jesus during the previous three years—there just is not a quick, painless, and easy way to grow)! They became a strong band of men and women who not only spoke about Jesus being God, they knew him personally as their friend and worshipped him as the risen Lord. Furthermore, they did not hide behind locked doors and build a memorial to what once had been, they continued the work that Jesus inaugurated—building a community of people who had rediscovered the love and reality of the living God. Their lives and actions backed up their words (just like Jesus had) as they demonstrated amazing miracles of healing, teaching, and courage in the face of hostility and persecution—which was their new partnership with the Holy Spirit beginning to bear fruit.

● ● ● ● ●

**Christianity, if false, is of no importance, and if true, of infinite importance. The only thing it cannot be is moderately important.**

—C.S. LEWIS

● ● ● ● ●

If you walk through some portions of the old city of Jerusalem today you can visit excavation sites that descend 20 to 30 feet beneath the present ground level. The city that existed 2000 years ago was buried under successive mounds of rubble as Jerusalem was sacked and destroyed by invading armies. After excavation we can now walk along a few streets that existed then and sense something of what life was like in those days. When God's Holy Spirit is allowed to work in our lives we are given a taste of what it must have been like in Eden where he had open and unfettered communication and relationship with his creation. Unfortunately it is similar to the excavation site and all we can access is a dusty Eden under generations and millennia of rubble, nevertheless some of the original paths and plants are still visible deep within each one of us. Take another example from archaeological digs. In 2005 a botanist successfully germinated a date palm seed that was 2000 years old, found on Mount Masada near the Dead Sea.

If the germination of life is possible in ancient seeds what might be achievable in the human spirit with a God who is the ultimate gardener and creator of all life? Of course these matters under discussion are incredible and hard to believe. But that is the essence of what we are exploring. Being reunited with someone, God, who is utterly fantastic and is able to bring life out of nothing, raise the dead, or turn a heart of stone into a warm pulsating heart of flesh. The Holy Spirit is the power and presence of God on earth that in mysterious ways accomplishes his purposes. He's probably even stirring in you right now as you read these words. Part of you will be saying, *No, this is too bizarre and beyond my comprehension,* and another little voice will be saying, *No, it is exactly what I am like, and I can bring you to life as well if you will give me the chance.*

God is not unreasonable and quite understands our skepticism. He realizes that we are not used to the kinds of claims Jesus makes and the power to change lives that is possible through his Holy Spirit. He has therefore gathered together a wide variety of stories and teaching aids that will help us come to terms with the reality of his presence in the world and potentially in our own lives as well. The Bible is one of the most incredible resources you and I could ever hope to lay our hands on. Blow the dust and cobwebs off the old and negative impressions that have settled in our minds concerning that book and lets see if we can germinate some excitement around God's powerful and moving collection of love letters to us.

# 11

# Put It in Writing

IN THE WAKE OF THE MASSIVE POPULARITY OF THE BOOK *THE DA VINCI CODE,* A LOCAL VANCOUVER NEWSPAPER REPORTED THE RESULTS OF A RECENTLY CONDUCTED SURVEY. Seventeen percent of Canadians surveyed believed that Jesus had married Mary Magdalene, fathered a child, and that the church had conspired to suppress the truth. I wonder what the people surveyed base their opinion upon?

The incredible popularity of Dan Brown's novel illustrates why is it important to provide reasons for establishing the reliability of the Bible. I have read *The Da Vinci Code* and enjoyed the story and the ingenuity of the plot. However, it astounds me to read how threatened some Christians appear to be by the publishing of this book; as if it is going to discredit and undermine Christianity (Jesus has been the center of controversy from the moment of his birth). At the same time it is interesting to observe how little it seems to take for many people to believe whatever they read in print.

If an opinion poll told me that 50 percent of Canadians did not believe the Bible I would not conclude that the Bible is unreliable and unbelievable. I would conclude that 50 percent of Canadians probably know nothing about that book and therefore it would appear to them that it is not very significant—which is fair enough.

Fortunately the authority of the Bible is based upon more substantial foundations than a few telephone calls and some poorly worded questions next to a check box. Determining its authority and reliability means exploring how the books of the Bible were selected (the Canon of Scripture), what documentary evidence substantiates claims of authenticity, and authorship, and what can we learn from archaeology? Very importantly—does what I read in the Bible ring true for me as I appropriate the teachings into my own life (in other words does the teaching work)?

The first barrier is our preconception that this is an old and awkward book, difficult to read, hard to understand, and littered with awkward-to-pronounce names and irrelevant history. The original biblical writings were recorded in Hebrew, Aramaic, and Greek. This is not the place to delve into all the translations that finally emerged in a wide variety of English versions as well as numerous translations in different languages around the world. There are plenty of "user-friendly" translations available that do not demand the reader to wade through old English terminology with thees and thous and "thus saith the Lord" everywhere. Please do yourself a favor and use a contemporary English translation.

●　●　●　●　●

**If Christians would really live according to the teachings of Christ, as found in the Bible, all of India would be Christian today.**

—MAHATMA GANDHI

●　●　●　●　●

In the first few centuries of the early church there was a group called the Gnostics who professed to have secret knowledge about God that added to what Jesus has revealed, and this knowledge was only accessible to a small select group. Throughout history there are always those who try and complicate what God does and how he works. The basic Christian faith does not require special knowledge, a great education, or any knowledge of ancient Greek or ancient texts.

This was underscored when I attended a talk in Oxford that Billy Graham delivered to about 700 theological students and clergy one evening. I was struck by how many people were gathered and how little impact the group had on the culture and faith of those around them. We were all engrossed in theology, philosophy, languages, and world religions, and for the most part had lost touch with the simple message of God's love Jesus revealed to Galilean fishermen. I admired Graham's courage and conviction as he spoke about the simple truths of the Christian faith and did not attempt to impress academics. He knew that the vast majority of the world's populations are not university graduates and that complexity seldom helps a broken or wounded heart find healing. A lost and wandering child needs to be picked up, reassured, and hugged. It does not need a lecture or a library. God loves to pick us up and embrace us first and foremost, later he'll teach us through his collection of stories that describe how he has worked with other tribes and people throughout history. The bottom line is, don't be afraid of simplicity or be tempted into getting too complicated either.

The Bible is not meant to be an end in itself no more than a menu is meant to be the substitute for the meal at a restaurant. A menu points to what we can eat and experience at the restaurant, to what is available. If the food is never served then it does not matter how well written, accurate, reliable, and "authentic" the menu is—we'll be somewhat distressed—and hungry I would imagine! The same principle is true for the Bible. It is a handbook that tells stories and recounts how God encounters human beings through the ages. It describes who God is, what he is like, why he cares about the world, why he loves us so much, what he offers, and how he desires to work in us and through us. The ultimate point of the biblical menu is to enable the reader to enter into a fresh and fulfilling relationship with God that will fully satisfy a deep and somewhat mysterious spiritual hunger within ("Taste and see that the LORD is good"—Psalm 34:8).

John was probably still in his teens when he followed Jesus for three years. He was one of Jesus' closest friends, so much so that when Jesus was about to die he asked John to take care of his mother, Mary. Many years later John wrote his account of Jesus' life and he began by describing Jesus as God's word became flesh who lived for a while among us (John 1:14). Later John would record how Jesus referred to himself as the "Bread of Life" (John 6:48).

If I could give you a picture of what the Bible is meant to be like I would describe an exquisite weathered ancient building hewn out of rock with lots of scratches and marks left by thousands of years of use. This old building would look like it had been standing forever, and it would have large doors made of solid wood that swung open on hand-forged hinges that moved them as if they were as light as feathers. Before you even turned the corner in the road to see the Biblical House in the distance you would know you were getting close. The air would be filled with the fragrance of fresh bread that wafted from the big stoves continually fired just inside the entrance. Nobody ever entered those doors without a hunger rising in them. And they were never disappointed and never departed hungry. Guests would be warmly welcomed and could help themselves to as much bread as they wanted from the great oak tables laden with a wide variety of baked goods always fresh from the ovens.

People would be laughing and chatting as they bustled around— nothing like the miserable shackled convicts working in chain gangs that you and I imagine, burdened and stooped under the heavy "Word of God." The large living room would be alive and vibrant and the people natural and unassuming, no airs or status to be seen anywhere. Whether you visited the Biblical House by day or night another breathtaking feature would leave you standing open-mouthed in awe for hours. Huge stained-glass windows lined the walls depicting all kinds of historical events in vibrant colors and the most brilliant images you had ever seen in your entire life. These were not sensitive delicate renderings of Jesus with a lamb on his lap, but great chunks of colored glass portraying strength and boldness, confidence and life! At night the color would pour into the darkness outside as the light blazed through, and during the day those inside were treated to cascading rivers of rainbows draping them in multicolored capes of light—it would be absolutely stunning.

You'd never want to leave the Biblical House, because it would be so rich in meaning, warmth, ambience, love, and life. But the visiting rule would be strictly enforced so you would have to comply. Each person could only visit for an hour a day and once a week the visit could extend to four hours maximum. The reason was that the Biblical House was not actually a museum, an art gallery, or a bakery. While it contained those elements, its primary function was to nourish the heart and the soul of each visitor, to inspire and equip them to go out from there and to put into practice the love of God in the real world…as Jesus had modeled in the Galilee region and around Jerusalem. Each person would be encouraged to allow their personalities and skills to become a small stained-glass window in the world, through which God's love could shine and touch others. They too could radiate the fragrance of fresh bread that always seemed to linger around those who had spent time there, evoking a hunger for the living God in the people around them.

●　●　●　●　●

**It ain't those parts of the Bible
that I can't understand that bother me,
it's the parts that I do understand.**

—MARK TWAIN

●　●　●　●　●

That is my picture of the Bible and what I have tasted and learned as I have explored for the past 40 years. It is what I am talking about and imagining as we take hold of this book that drips with meaning, and is a treasure trove of life for those who are willing to take a little time to be guided through its pages.

Yesterday the piano tuner visited to fix some keys and tune the piano

I recently moved into my renovated house with the help of some friends. He told me that he had tuned the piano to the international pitch (that is, A=440 cycles per second). "It's the only thing the world has ever agreed upon," he muttered. That's what the Bible is for as well. Revealing to us the universal "pitch" that God has designed to enable all of humanity to live in harmony in the midst of all the differences. Just as a piano cannot tune itself, neither can we "be tuned" without the help of the one great maestro and piano tuner. When he works we not only discover inner peace and harmony but there is also a greater harmony in relation to other people as well.

The Bible overflows with history, with stories and accounts of how God changed people and how they wrestled with faith. It contains archaeology and mystery, simplicity and complexity all interwoven as it tackles the vexing questions of God, meaning, life on earth, death, and eternity. The New Testament describes God's radical revelation of himself when he entered into history in the person of Jesus Christ. It outlines how the first Christian believers stumbled through their surprising and unexpected journey of faith as pioneers trying to comprehend the enormity of what had been unveiled. It is also a historically accurate book; a collection of documents quite remarkable in its origins, unique in its content, and most relevant for every generation. To ignore what it offers is equivalent to a starving man refusing a meal (a feast!) because he thinks he will not like the taste of what is being offered (before he has even tried it).

A few years ago I was planning a trip to visit my brother and his family in New Zealand. I chatted with my two teenage daughters and we thought it would be a great idea to break the long journey by stopping over at the Cook Islands for about five days. We also knew that the Cook Islands are surrounded by coral reefs, clear water, and beautiful conditions for scuba diving. Although it was a stretch financially I suggested that maybe we should all learn to dive together and then go diving when we arrived at the Cook Islands. I joked later that diving is a good thing to do with two teenage daughters. Put something in their mouths and send them underwater and there was a blissful silence as we shared this unique activity together!

For the next four weeks we gathered with an instructor at the local swimming pool and were taught how to operate the equipment, use the inflatable vest for buoyancy, and monitor our depth and oxygen supply. We learned together in the pool the rudimentary points about diving and applied what we learned immediately by putting on the gear and getting wet.

Coming to grips with the Bible is similar to learning to scuba dive. First, an instructor is crucial. Then learning to apply what we read by "getting wet with God" is the only way to "smell the bread" and "taste and see." There is nothing more boring in life, and frustrating, than for a hungry person to watch someone else eat in front of them. I was a poor student when I spent a week in Paris roaming the streets marveling and absorbing this city of artists, the sculpture of Rodin and others, and the whole French culture. I remember looking through the windows of restaurants at red meat steaming and slowly turning on a rotisserie, people wining and dining, and I salivated at what was on the other side of the glass—which I could not afford.

The wonderful thing about God is that he never teases us through the window of the Bible with "stuff" that he is not prepared to give us. He also reads our hearts, not our lips, so there need be no great concern that he will misunderstand us because we are using the wrong words. Anything we dig up and find in the Bible we can have, but it will take a lifetime to learn how to utilize much of the substance within its pages. It is often easy to grab hold of these truths, but it takes years to chew on them and to fully digest their meaning—which is precisely what makes it so nourishing!

Is the Bible an authoritative document? The case is compelling and is very well supported by archaeology, historical manuscripts, and a multitude of books and articles by writers with great integrity and wisdom. There is certainly validity in questioning sources and not automatically assuming that everyone is in agreement. However, if one is going to dismiss the Bible then we also have to throw out the works of Aristotle, Plato, and many other ancient historians and writers who have a substantially more fragile basis to support the authenticity of their works.

What does evoke a passionate reaction within me is when people say, "You can't believe in the Bible these days," without having any idea what they are talking about and never having read the book! It is similar to those on the fringes of Christianity who mutter, "Well I don't go to church but I believe in God and try and keep the Ten Commandments." The greater the distance from the source, the greater the degree of nonsense that is invariably uttered on these matters. Maybe it is more a symptom of wanting to appear open while actually having a very closed mind with uninformed and prejudiced reasons. Then again, to be fair, if the people who claim to read the Bible don't appear to be enjoying the meal and come across as miserable and suffering from indigestion much of the time, it's hardly likely that I will be wanting to join them at their table!

●　●　●　●　●

**Be careful how you live;
you will be the only Bible
some people ever read.**

—William Toms

●　●　●　●　●

We do not have to strain every fragment of historical and scientific evidence through the grid of the Bible and reduce everything into black and white indisputable facts in order for it to be authoritative. For instance, we don't have to beat the topic of evolution to death to enable someone to believe in God. It is quite possible to believe that behind all of history the cause is indeed God, and still concede that how life evolved continues to be a fascinating discussion that probably integrates evolution and God's purposes. I find that attempting to provide blow-by-blow accounts of every detail relating to how the world was created, or speculating how it will end, is an exercise in futility when carried to some of the extremes we hear about. As far as I'm concerned there is plenty of material to keep me challenged by focusing on the present where I, where we, live in the here and now!

The primary focus of the Bible is to answer the question about why human life exists at all. It explains and guides us into enjoying a spiritual life rooted in relationship with God that completes "life" as we are created to experience it, instructing us that a robust spiritual life is as fundamental to a healthy life as is eating well and exercising regularly. Its purpose is to convey all that God has already done to facilitate human beings participating and interacting in a life-giving relationship with him on a daily basis.

Here are some quick facts about the Bible:

1. It consists of two sections: a) the *Old Testament* (used by Jews and Christians), originally compiled in Hebrew and Aramaic to describe the Jewish history and relationship with Yahweh/God; God's interaction with human beings from creation until the early Roman Empire; and b) the *New Testament*, which together with the Old Testament forms the Christian Bible. Originally written in Greek, the New Testament describes the coming of the Messiah/ Jesus as prophesied in the Old Testament and recounts the growth of the early Christian Church.

2. The whole Bible consists of 66 separate books written over a period of 1000–1500 years by about 40 different authors from a wide variety of backgrounds and professions: scholars, kings, peasants, fishermen, doctors, and so on.

3. It was written on three different continents (Africa, Asia, Europe) and in many different contexts and places: wilderness (Moses), prison (Jeremiah, Paul), mountains and palaces (David, Daniel), on the road traveling (Luke), Island of Patmos (John).

4. It captures different moods: praise and joy, despair and grief, confidence and hope, repentance and sorrow, love songs and adoration, prophecy and teaching, history and eyewitness reports.

5. It is the first major book ever printed (the Latin Vulgate on Gutenberg's press in 1455).

I remember as a teenager learning that the book of Isaiah had been written about 800 years before the birth of Christ and that it contains very specific prophetic words about Jesus' birth, life, and death. I thought that fact was amazingly exciting because it strengthened my very young confidence in the trustworthiness of the Book!

Some examples from Isaiah:

- *Birth of Jesus:* "The Lord himself will give you a sign: The virgin will be with child and will give birth to a son, and will call him Immanuel" (Isaiah 7:14).

- *Jesus as Son of God:* "To us a child is born, to us a son is given, and the government will be on his shoulders. And he will be called Wonderful Counselor, Mighty God, Everlasting Father, Prince of Peace" (Isaiah 9:6).

- *Jesus crucified:* "He was despised and rejected by men, a man of sorrows, and familiar with suffering. Like one from whom men hide their faces, he was despised, and we esteemed him not. Surely he took up our infirmities and carried our sorrows, yet we considered him stricken by God, smitten by him, and afflicted. But he was pierced for our transgressions, he was crushed for our iniquities [wickedness], the punishment that brought us peace was upon him, and by his wounds we are healed. We all, like sheep, have gone astray, each of us has turned to his own way; and the Lord has laid on him the iniquity of us all. He was oppressed and afflicted, yet he did not open his mouth; he was led like a lamb to the slaughter, and as a sheep before her shearers is silent, so he did not open his mouth" (Isaiah 53:3-7).

It would be easy to get carried away here, but the point I want to really emphasize is that the Bible is not some flaky piece of writing without integrity or foundation. There are in fact more historical manuscripts around the world verifying biblical source documents than exist to support the authenticity of any other piece of literature (by far). If one compares major works by famous historical figures such a Caesar, Plato, Tacitus, Pliny, Sophocles, and Aristotle (to name only a few) the biblical writings are significantly more reliable in terms of proven authenticity. One example:

| *Iliad* | New Testament |
|---------|---------------|
| Homer's *Iliad* was written in 900 BC. The earliest existing copy of his work is dated around 400 BC, giving a time span between his life and the first known copy as 500 years. | The New Testament was written between AD 40 and 100 and the earliest copy in existence is dated at AD 125 (25 years later). |
| The number of manuscript copies that exist are estimated to be 643. | There are over 24,000 pieces of manuscript in existence. |

The accounts of Jesus' life are recorded at the beginning of the New Testament in four books called the Gospels (meaning Good News). Four different people (Matthew, Mark, Luke, and John) provide complementary descriptions and insights into the life, death, and resurrection of Jesus Christ—all very aware of his audacious claim to be the Son of God.

*Matthew* was a Jew and he wrote (AD 70 to 90) specifically for a Jewish audience. He emphasized how Jesus was the long-awaited Messiah who was the fulfillment of ancient prophesies as contained in the Old Testament (remember Isaiah for instance—there are many more but we don't have time to open up that treasure chest).

*Mark* is the shortest and most crude writing (AD 50 to 70) and merely outlines events as they happened. His writing is believed to be the first recorded document of the New Testament. It is also thought that much of Mark was actually gleaned from Peter and maybe was even written down in his presence.

*Luke* was a Gentile (non-Jewish) physician who wrote (AD 60 to 80) specifically with a Gentile audience in mind. He emphasized how Jesus had broken down the distinction between Jew and Gentile. God was speaking through him to all people everywhere and no one was/is excluded. Luke is also a very careful and detailed writer, and because of his training some medical references and details are included.

*John* wrote (AD 80 to 100) as an older man reflecting back, with the benefit of many years having passed since he had been with Jesus in person. He had no doubt pondered deeply the significance of the amazing events that unfolded before his eyes when he was a younger man. When John wrote his book he was aware of the accounts written by Matthew, Mark, and Luke. In his writing he therefore sets out to interpret and explain what God was doing through this person Jesus, and why. He pays more attention to providing meaning then he does to accurately recording historical events in sequence (because he knows that the other three have already recorded that). John's Gospel possesses a wisdom and depth that continue to yield new insights and angles the longer one examines it.

I visited Patmos, the island off the coast of Turkey not far from Ephesus where John spent years in exile and also wrote the last book of the Bible—Revelation. An Orthodox monastery sits atop the hill overlooking the harbor lined with tasty Greek eating places and brightly painted boats rocking on a turquoise sea. At the bend in the road leading from the town up the hill to the monastery is a dazzling whitewashed wall draped in an explosion of colorful bougainvillea. It marks the location of a cave with a sweeping view of the bay and the distant islands.

Approaching the cave's interior the guide showed us silver inlays in the cave wall where John prayed and a fissure across the roof that we were told resulted from the intensity of the vision he received from God. I don't know why we have the need to embellish what God does. Jesus was born is a stable and as soon as he left the scene we have to sweep the place out and line it with gold and silver. Anyway, this cave is reputed to be where John lived and recorded the book of Revelation. The point being made is that he is a historically verifiable figure like all the others whose works are recorded in the Bible. I sat in a restaurant up on the hill that evening chatting with a young soccer player from England about God and Jesus as we munched on a delectable Greek salad. The moon rose like a giant golden orb and invigorated by the whole setting I ran all the way down into town under the musky glow of its beams and joked, "Poor John, must have been tough being an exile in a place like this. I also had some eye-opening revelations on the beaches—but they would not find a place in the Bible!"

Luke, a Greek doctor, wrote the book of Acts, which follows the four Gospels. He describes the growth of the early church, the persecution of Christians, and the subsequent dispersion of the new faith across Asia and into Africa. Christian (meaning little Christ) was a name given to believers by others after the movement began to spread. The rest of the New Testament consists of letters written by Paul explaining core Christian teachings, and letters by other disciples (who were eye-witnesses to Jesus' life on earth—Peter, James, John) addressed to various young churches that were emerging in the Middle East.

During a six-week sabbatical in Israel in the wake of the 1990 Gulf War, I traveled around the country studying the land, archaeology, history, and culture against the backdrop of the biblical records. What a fascinating and stimulating experience! I did not particularly care whether this particular rock was where Jesus had lunch or that tree was where Peter hung his coat; it was being in the region where the Bible was written that was deeply meaningful. Everywhere one travels in Israel you trip over history, pieces of clay jars, and mounds in the ground that mean something.

Near the Dead Sea, and not too far from Masada, you can travel to the site where a shepherd boy found some scrolls quite by accident. It was around the time of the Second World War and he was trying to maintain control of his goatherd. One of the goats disappeared into a cave so the boy threw a stone to "encourage" the animal to come out. Instead of the bleat of a goat he heard the stone smashing against something that sounded like a clay jar. He went in further to investigate. Inside the cave he found a number of jars containing ancient scrolls. He did not realize what they were and took a few pieces home with him—which apparently were promptly recognized as ideal material with which to make sandals! Fortunately, a relative concluded that these pieces of parchment might be valuable and subsequently the rest were salvaged and studied.

Exploration in the region uncovered more caves with a multitude of scrolls stored in jars that had remained untouched for nearly 2000 years. Over 12 copies of Isaiah were among these scrolls; one at least was written 1000 years later then anything that had ever been discovered before. When a comparison was made between the "old" and "new" scrolls they were found to be completely accurate except for some very minor details.

The scribes writing these scrolls were meticulous, and understood their task as a spiritual service. We regard "old" as antique and valuable, but in those days "new" was valuable and "old" was thrown out. We're talking about the Dead Sea Scrolls discovered in caves not far from where the Qumran scribes were writing on the shores of the Dead Sea. It's a hot, rusty-brown sandy region where these scribes lived and toiled. There's nothing romantic about the Dead Sea; it doesn't come close to John's high-rise cave on Patmos, and neither is the Dead Sea great for swimming after work. It is thought that when the Romans were laying siege to Masada the scribes hid their precious work in jars in the nearby caves for safekeeping.

Masada is a flat-topped rock surrounded by steep valleys and is a natural fortress to which Herod the Great fled in 40 BC. He feared Jewish revolt and fortified Masada, building huge water containers into the rock that are now great empty caverns, which one can access down steps today. After the fall of Jerusalem in AD 70 it became the last refuge for Jewish resistance fighters battling against the Romans. Two years later the Roman general Flavius Silva decided to end the resistance at Masada and marched to the area with the Tenth Legion and an estimated ten to fifteen thousand Jewish slaves.

The Romans laid siege around the mountain and if you stand at the summit (about 50 meters above sea level) their camp locations are still visible down below today. One can only imagine what it must have been like to watch the Roman army from that vantage point as they slowly built an earthen ramp up the side of the mountain and eventually destroyed the settlement. The fall of Masada is one of the greatest and most moving stories in Jewish history. When the rebels saw that they could not resist any longer, ten men were selected to kill everyone else in their camp—approximately 1000 men, women, and children. They then committed suicide themselves and the Romans entered the fortress to find themselves surrounded by silence and dead bodies. Josephus the historian wrote,

> *And so met [the Romans] with the multitude of the slain, but could take no pleasure in the fact, though it were done to their enemies. Nor could they do other than wonder at the courage of their resolution, and at the immovable contempt of death which so great a number of them had shown, when they went through with such an action as that was.*

Two women and five children survived after having hidden in a small cave and they recounted what had transpired. In the complexity of human behavior brutality and heroism, courage and cowardice, cruelty and compassion so frequently emerge and are present within the same dramatic event.

The Bible contains many images of God as being referred to as the only fortress and shelter that is truly secure for us; a refuge in relationship with him that no other human can destroy. Those were more than mere words when Roman gladiators and crowds taunted Christians in the Colosseum in Rome for their refusal to bow before Caesar as the ultimate god. It was the inner fortress with God that was their shield as they allowed their bodies to be gored by wild animals, but their spirits were never defeated. They learned the courage and power of God from Jesus hanging on a cross, his side pierced and bleeding from a Roman sword and his feet and hands broken by the nails that pinned him to the wood.

*You O Lord are a safe place for me*
*You O Lord are a safe place to be*
*You calm my heart*
*And you take all my fear*
*You draw me near with your love*
*You draw me near, with your love you draw me near*

*That you should be my Father*
*And I should be your child*
*Beloved by your side*
*In mercy reconciled*
*It's a wonder, it's a mystery*
*It's a joy to be told*
*Abiding in your love…*

*You O Lord are a safe place for me*
*You O Lord are a safe place to be*
*Like a mighty river*
*From your heart to mine*
*Let your Spirit flow*
*In your love let it flow…*

Christianity is not, and has never been, a refuge for the weak or an insipid alternative to those who cannot face life. It does not take much moral fortitude to live like a chameleon changing color to "fit in" with every passing trend, or to blend in with the crowd so as not to cause offense.

●　●　●　●　●

**The Bible is God's chart for you to steer by,**
**to keep you from the bottom of the sea, and**
**to show you where the harbor is, and how to**
**reach it without running on rocks or bars.**

—HENRY WARD BEECHER

●　●　●　●　●

To be a follower of Jesus means to stand out from the crowd with love, conviction, and courage. His call through the pages of the Bible is more radical but in the same vein as the famous and stirring words of Prime Minister Winston Churchill addressing the British nation in the House of Commons (June 1940) during the Second World War:

> *We shall go on to the end, we shall fight in France, we shall fight on the seas and oceans, we shall fight with growing confidence and growing strength in the air, we shall defend our Island, whatever the cost may be, we shall fight on the beaches, we shall fight on the landing grounds, we shall fight in the fields and in the streets, we shall fight in the hills; we shall never surrender, and even if, which I do not for a moment believe, this Island or a large part of it were subjugated and starving, then our Empire beyond the seas, armed and guarded by the British Fleet, would carry on the struggle, until, in God's good time, the New World, with all its power and might, steps forth to the rescue and the liberation of the old.*

The number of manuscripts and the volume of archaeological evidence verifying the accuracy and authenticity of the Bible is very impressive indeed and nothing to be ashamed of, nor to be apologetic about. We really do not have to deny our intellects or conjure up faith out of nothing to believe in God or conclude that the Bible is reliable.

Allow me to share with you some of the snapshots I carry around in my head and heart as I have explored these issues with a Bible in one hand and a camera in the other. It is when one walks the land that the words and teachings root themselves in the crooks and crannies of one's imagination, understanding and soul, providing substance and conviction to what sometimes can seem such wisplike and invisible strands of faith. Of course, faith inevitably has to spring from such a seed but the biblical accounts are not fairy tales either and they provide deep nourishment out of which faith is forged as tough as iron.

Sometimes the most exciting discoveries are relatively small. I was standing on a high place with a commanding view of a wide valley stretched out in front of me. It was the mound of Megiddo overlooking the Jezreel Valley where the Battle of Armageddon is described in John's book of Revelation concerning the end of time. Megiddo was an ancient and strategically important city guarding the international trade route between Egypt and Mesopotamia from about the sixth century BC until New Testament times. This was why it was constantly a scene of battles and over the centuries the city was destroyed 25 times and rebuilt 25 times. Behind me was a circular platform constructed of stone, raised from the ground, measuring about 10 meters in circumference. This was where sacrifices were offered and jars containing the bones of children/infants have been found in this place to indicate clearly that human sacrifice was also practiced.

From this historic vantage point I looked out over the plains and in the distance I saw cypress trees bending in the breeze. At first my eyes just flicked over them as I absorbed the whole picture and then it hit me and I let out of a cry of exclamation, "That's what David meant!" I suddenly understood some words in the Bible that had always puzzled me—I had thought it was David but it turned out to be Isaiah. One day Isaiah was sitting at his office rock sheltering from the midday sun in his cave, feet up writing chapter 53 of his book. Inspired by God who was working with him, Isaiah recounted the fact that God's mind is so different from the way our minds work. Nevertheless he gave us the assurance that despite all the obstacles God will actually accomplish his purposes in the world. Nearly 3000 years ago Isaiah wrote,

> "My thoughts are not your thoughts, neither are your ways my ways," declares the LORD. "As the heavens are higher than the earth, so are my ways higher than your ways and my thoughts than your thoughts. As the rain and the snow come down from heaven, and do not return to it without watering the earth and making it bud and flourish, so that it yields seed for the sower

*and bread for the eater, so is my word that goes out from my mouth: It will not return to me empty, but will accomplish what I desire and achieve the purpose for which I sent it. You will go out in joy and be led forth in peace; the mountains and hills will burst into song before you, and* all the trees of the field will clap their hands."

—ISAIAH 53:8-12

When I saw those cypress trees swaying and moving in the breeze, they looked like fingers clapping together and I shouted, "That's what he saw and was talking about...they really do look as if they are alive and clapping with joy—because the oak trees back at home certainly don't!"

I spent a day walking alongside a riverbed, the Wadi Quilt, that more or less follows the road from Jerusalem to Jericho. The Judean desert region is barren, chalk dry, and dusty. Most of the way we followed an aqueduct built by Herod's slaves to convey water down to Jericho where one of his residences was situated. Lining the wadi are cliffs with holes high up in their walls where various hermits lived out their ascetic lifestyle according to their understanding of obedience to God. When the water spilled over the aqueduct or melted into a stream with fresh clear pools vegetation sprung up in rich succulent greens.

● ● ● ● ●

**The Bible is not man's word about God,
but God's word about man.**

—JOHN BARTH

● ● ● ● ●

The Bible often mentions deserts and "streams of living water." The images tear themselves off the pages and come alive as you walk through the land from where they originated. We clambered down a steep path at midday and ate our lunch under palm trees at St. George's Monastery. The first monastery was built here in the fifth century near the cave where Elijah sought refuge and was fed by the ravens with the food God provided for him (1 Kings 17:2-6). The monastery was very active in the sixth century until it was destroyed by the Persians and then abandoned by the end of the seventh century. Most of it was rebuilt in the late 1800s and the skulls of some of those early monks (AD 600) are still visible in the chapel today. One visits these places that are so devoid of any living thing, in such stark contrast to our entertainment-addicted culture, and it is hard to ignore the sacrificial lives people undertook in their quest for God.

It was hot, about 120 degrees F., when we finally completed our trek at the ruins of Herod's winter palace. King Herod was not fictitious, and neither was he pleasant. He was so paranoid to hold onto power that he had his own relative and uncle drowned in his swimming pool. No surprise therefore that when Herod heard about the birth of a king (Jesus) from the "three magi (wise men)" who came looking for him he attempted to trick them into stopping by on their way home to update him (they chose to quietly decline the invitation and traveled by another route). However, Herod still issued a decree to murder baby boys and then later agreed to the beheading of John the Baptist. Anyone who thinks Christianity is an escape from the real world has never read the Bible or the birth of the Christian church in the first few centuries—it is quite a sobering reality check. Why would people endure such suffering for nothing but a lie?

I hopped on a bus and traveled down to the Sea of Galilee to spend a day or two wandering around the hills where Jesus had spent his time teaching, healing, and training his disciples. I've already mentioned some of that visit. The shoreline is flat and it is easy to see how Jesus could climb into a boat and push out a little way from shore to address a crowd of people.

There's a place where seven springs pour into the Sea of Galilee—it is known as Tabgha and commemorates where Jesus called his disciples to follow him. An ancient rock harbor is still visible where the fisherman would moor their boats—in fact they have recently discovered a fishing boat buried in the shoreline in the region that dates back to Peter's time. It has been restored and is now open to the public.*

*I always thought I'd be a fisherman*
*Working by the sea—in the burning sun*
*Sailing out my boat*
*Pulling in the nets*
*Blistered hands on ropes*
*Body dripping sweat*
*I always thought I'd be a fisherman*
*Working by the sea—in the burning sun*

*Then passing by he caught my eye*
*Said, Follow me, I'll set you free,*
*There are bigger fish on the land*
*Then in the sea*
*Come fishing with me*

*The people standing 'round shook their heads*
*"Don't you be a fool and be misled*
*You've a family and wife*
*And the business you've made*
*For freedom in life you've gotta be well paid."*
*The people standing 'round shook their heads*
*"Don't you be a fool and be misled."*

*Then passing by he caught my eye...*

*My heart was torn in two—what should I do?*
*Stay here with my friends or follow you?*
*You say you're the Son of God*
*Maybe just a mad man*
*I guess I'll only find out if I take your hand*
*My heart was torn in two—what should I do?*
*Stay here with my friends or follow you?*
*Then passing by he caught my eye...*

---

* See www.jesusboat.com/imgs/site/site/boat.html.

I picked up a small stone with a hole in the middle while sitting on the rocks at Tabgha drinking in the scene and fumbling among the rocks. Could it have been fastened to Peter's net! They used stones like this one to weigh down the fishing nets; you bet I was thrilled to find it.

We had supper one evening on the shores of Galilee just below the Golan Heights. As I sat munching on my very tasty "St. Peter's" fish I could see the twinkling lights of Tiberias and the hills rising above the town leading to a higher plateau in the direction of Nazareth. In the afternoon the winds can sweep down from there and whip up the waves on the Sea of Galilee in no time and some of these sudden storms are described in the Gospels. My most abiding memory of that evening meal was the color of the sky at sunset. The hills darkened to black as the clouds above the skyline glowed in red and orange so brightly it was almost like fire. Such a scene was a familiar sight to Jesus and the Galilee fishermen Peter, John, and James. They could predict the fishing weather for the next day by looking at the sky, and Jesus, being a good teacher, used it as a teaching aid.

There are literally hundreds of places to visit where we could read the biblical account and then see the land and the structures that are referred to. I picked up five stones in the riverbed of the valley where David killed Goliath; it's a broad flat valley where it was not difficult to imagine two armies facing off on either side and shouting insults at each other. The contrast in the terrain is dramatic. One minute we were hiking across the hills in white chalk dust and boulders and after another hour's walk we descended into the beautiful green En Gedi Gorge where mountain goats fed on the foliage and we swam under a cascading waterfall. David hid in this gorge and could have killed King Saul as he was relieving himself in one of the caves (1 Samuel 24). David chose not to take advantage of the situation displaying enormous integrity, as well as the realization that God had not granted him the right to take the king's life saying, "I will not lift my hand against my master, because he is my LORD's anointed" (1 Samuel 24:10).

We strapped lamps to our heads and splashed through water flowing around our knees along the ingenious tunnel King Hezekiah had constructed in the sixth century BC to bring water into the city of Jerusalem (certified as consistent with the biblical account using radiometric dating). The tunnel is about 540 meters long running 150 feet underground and emerges at the Pool of Siloam, where Jesus sent a man born blind to wash his eyes—and he was healed (John 9:7). Way out in the desert I sat in the dirt gazing at bits of straw embedded in mud bricks in the tumbledown wall of a building in the ancient village of Beersheba. The bricks had been slapped, molded, and baked in the sun during the lifetime of Abraham—more than 3000 years ago (Genesis 21:33).

These are some of the places mentioned in the Bible where God revealed himself to men and women throughout the ages. While we cannot bring the people back to life at least we are able to learn where and how they lived and can continue to construct a picture that helps us to substantiate what we read. The other link is the human element present in every line of biblical history. It is often said that we don't read the Bible but rather the Bible reads us. There is great wisdom in those words. While history moves relentlessly forward and technology changes, the human beings beneath these outer vestiges remain consistently the same. When one considers our emotional needs, relational behavior, and individual mannerisms, the same concerns and cries from the heart blend in harmony through the centuries. In the written words recorded in these ancient and remarkable biblical manuscripts God addresses the commonality and universality shared by human beings throughout the generations.

The Old Testament as we know it was the same book read by the Jewish teachers in the time of Christ. It was the book they all used to reference and teach about God's dealings with Israel. Within its pages were prophecies telling how God would provide another exciting and powerful way for people on earth to know him; the coming of the Messiah! One day Jesus held the

Old Testament scroll in his hands and addressed the townsfolk in his home synagogue in Nazareth, audaciously claiming to be that very person! He read the prophecy from the book of Isaiah, looked up, and announced to everyone, "Today this scripture is fulfilled in your hearing" (Luke 4:16-21). The religious leaders were infuriated. Somewhat understandably, as it is far easier to talk about possibilities then it is to embrace them, particularly if they are hard to comprehend anyway. To compound the matter, when you have known the person who claimed to fulfill this holy word since he was a kid it is all the more difficult to swallow. However, this inability to allow for the possibility that God's Word might indeed be in the process of being realized ultimately led to Jesus' crucifixion. It's the same reality for all of us isn't it? Although many claim to believe in God, ingrained within us is a profound reluctance to actually acknowledge that he can do anything at all.

And so we come full circle as the message of God is written in words recorded in history and also read and translated through the hearts and lives of those who inhabit this earth in every generation. We have a well-known phrase we frequently use when we try to be efficient, "We don't have to re-invent the wheel, you know." Meaning that we can utilize what others have already learned and done and springboard off their discoveries and efforts in tackling the task, thereby saving ourselves time and trouble. The same principle holds true for our spiritual growth and learning quest. The Bible records how those who have gone before us have walked, fled, argued, and been overwhelmed by the living God and we are invited to learn from them.

I can't remember where we were traveling one day across the Judean desert but it was hot. We stopped at the side of the road to visit some Palestinian boys watching over their herd as the goats grazed on whatever they could forage between the boulders in the middle of nowhere. Our guide knew the boys and they beckoned us to come over to a large rock that resembled any other boulder strewn around the hillside. Pushing it aside we were invited to see what was underneath. To our astonishment we were greeted by our reflections staring up at us from a deep pool of crystal clear water—cold and fresh to quench our thirst. Strangers like us in this foreign land would never even have realized fresh water existed in such a barren environment.

Sometimes as we wander through the Bible there will be occasions when it seems to be devoid of life and relevance. If we persist we will find wells of fresh water in the most unlikely of places because God is like that, when we are curious and teachable he reveals his resources to nourish us. My daughters used to love playing hide-and-seek in the garden, particularly for Easter eggs. God loves to surprise his kids as well—with good things! Jesus promised that to be true: "Seek and you will find…" (Matthew 7:7).

# 12

# Good God, Why Does It Hurt So Much?

*It's hard to live this life*
*For any length of time*
*Without shouting*
*At God to do something*
*About all the pain*
*And senseless suffering*
*That goes on and on*
*Polluting*
*Every corner of the earth*
*Documented through newspapers*
*Magazines*
*Documentaries*
*Movies*
*Radio broadcasts*
*And news bulletins*

*We begin with ideals*
*And visions of a new world*
*"I can make a difference"*
*Time passes*
*Not much appears to change*

*And we always seem to be*
*Debating God out of trouble*
*Manipulating faith until it fits*
*And covering the "but why's"*
*With palatable reasons*
*And intellectually thin veneers…*

*Until finally*
*Maybe if we persist*
*With our stubborn inquisitiveness*
*We are fortunate enough to catch a glimpse*
*Of heaven*
*Through the rubble of shattered ideals*
*Dismembered beneath the twisted steel of our intellect*
*And stand with Jesus*
*Weeping over Jerusalem crying "How I longed…"*

*But most surprisingly*
*After wandering in the barren wilderness*
*Where hopelessness stretches as far as the sand*
*And cynicism sprouts like cactus with angry thorns*
*Those ideals resurrect*
*And tiptoe back to inhabit our soul*
*Returning*
*In a deeper*
*Richer form*
*Cast no longer amidst frenetic rhetoric*
*And rules but*
*Now gently cocooned*
*In love laid down*
*With mercy and peace*
*And a humble whisper that*
*There but for the grace of God…*
*Go I*

Paul was a small five-year-old boy with brown hair, bright eyes, and dimples that lit up his cheeks when he dissolved into giggles. I used to tickle him until he begged me to stop as we rolled around the living room floor—I was eleven. Paul was the younger brother of my friends Bill and Michael, and I would often walk down the road to play with them after school. We rode bikes around the garden, played cricket and rugby, and we were always hungry and thirsty. Paul would usually tag along with us, sometimes disappearing in tears when he could not participate or his brothers "banned" him from the room.

One day I was visiting and the doctor came to see Paul, who was apparently sick with a cough. I thought nothing of it until a few days later I heard Paul had died. I can't remember what the cause was. I do remember the devastation I felt at the loss of my little friend. It was the first time I had experienced death snatching away someone I loved, and it made no sense to me at all. I can feel the emotions even now as I write these words after 45 years have slipped by.

Twenty years later I sat beside Jack's hospital bed. He was 14 years old. As his anesthetic wore off after surgery on his leg, "I can still wriggle my toes," he said, smiling weakly. Except he had just had the leg amputated below the knee and those phantom sensations were a normal tease after such an operation. Around the same time I spoke at the funeral of a young father who drowned trying to rescue two young people struggling in the surf at one of the beaches in Cape Town. He saved one of them and succumbed in his efforts to retrieve the other victim. He left behind a wife and three young children.

My younger brother nearly died of cancer but miraculously survived and is still alive today. My mother died at the age of 43 and my brother-in-law was killed in a futile automobile accident on the Angolan border the night before he was scheduled to return home—he was 27 years old. My sister-in-law's brother was killed with his fiancé in a freak airplane accident when their small plane smashed into a mountain. Her father was shot and killed a few years ago by a random thief. Four senseless shootings involving deranged killers and innocent young children have been reported in North American schools as I write these words. What is fair or deserved in any of these instances?

I don't know how to understand suffering or how to link the dots together to produce an acceptable picture that will explain why terrible things happen to innocent people. I do know that life is not fair and that most of us do not deserve half of what happens to us during our lifetime. We don't deserve the pain and suffering that comes with drug abuse and alcohol addictions, the curse of AIDS and the ravages of cancer. We don't deserve the chaos of floods and earthquakes, the trauma caused by abuse and rape, violence, and psychological mind-games. We don't deserve to live in countries where there is corruption and poverty, lawlessness and dictatorship. We don't deserve to live in places where it is hard to gather enough to eat and where your children die hungry or malnourished.

We don't deserve to live in tidy suburbs with two cars in the garage and a fridge and a basement filled with food. We don't deserve the privilege of running water, abundance of space, leisure time unknown to most, the ease of travel and the means to vacation anywhere we choose. We don't deserve to be able to retire and have a holiday cottage and to have more wealth than the vast majority of this earth's population could ever hope for. One person's suffering is probably another person's dream, "If that is suffering I wish I had your problem."

Whenever God (in the Judeo-Christian tradition) becomes the topic of conversation it does not take long before the reality of suffering emerges as a problem. How can God, who claims to be the essence of love, allow such misery and suffering in the world that he created for generation after generation? Look at the atrocities carried out in the name of religion and the barbaric cruelty human beings inflict on each other. The list we can construct is a tragedy of epic proportions: the Crusades, the Huns, the Nazi Holocaust, ethnic cleansing, genocide, pedophiles, rape, murder, torture…I doubt if any group of people would walk away innocent from a comprehensive list that spanned the entire human history.

What is the answer here? How do we reconcile the suffering we see all around us, and the questions we have about the unfair and random destructiveness that impacts so many individuals, families, and countries? What is the right question to ask regarding suffering? Do we pound on the throne of God for an explanation demanding to know why he allows it? Is suffering an indictment upon God?

It's a fair question to initially be angry with God for suffering because that's where the buck stops. Our immediate assumption is that God causes suffering, or at least allows it, and that must mean that he is indifferent to the reality of suffering in people's lives.

●　●　●　●　●

## If you are going through hell, keep going.

—WINSTON CHURCHILL

●　●　●　●　●

There is a huge difference between "cause" and "allow." I allow my children freedom to leave the house and meet with friends, to travel in cars, and to participate in countless other activities. If during the course of their daily lives they get hurt that does not mean that I am the cause, or that I desired that pain to be inflicted. The possibility of pain and suffering is the underbelly of freedom. The only alternative would be to restrict freedom for "your own protection and safety." We all know what response that rationale will evoke. We would all be exclaiming, "I'd rather take the risk of getting hurt than endure this safe and sterile padded environment!"

Years ago I traveled up the west coast of South Africa to the Orange River on the border with Namibia, which drains much of the southern Africa hinterland. Over the millennia vast quantities of silt have been deposited at the river mouth where pounding surf and desert converge. It's a place that few people would ever dream of living without some real incentive. And in this instance diamonds proved irresistible; particularly in the quantities that were found at this muddy river mouth. Oranjemund is the company town built to support the vast diamond mining operation in the area. No one enters or leaves the town without passing through X-ray machines, and all vehicles used in the facility are destined to stay there forever. Security is very tight to protect the valuable stones they keep finding in the sand dunes and to minimize theft.

What have diamonds got to do with suffering? Let's step back from the individual instances of suffering that cause us such excruciating pain and questioning. We'll try not to take suffering personally; instead we'll see how it might fit within the context of the biggest picture we can comprehend. In order to do that I invite you to join me on a sand dune on the edge of the Namibian desert where we can watch the diamond mining operation take place.

It is an impressive sight to observe huge earthmoving vehicles remove load after load of earth to be processed on conveyor belts equipped with the latest technology for collecting the diamonds. If you were to stand next to the wheel of one of these machines, you would not even be able to reach halfway up to the top rim; they are huge! When the heavy equipment hits the bedrock then men follow behind on foot and dig and sweep until the rock is bare and naked under the sun. Everything possible is done to ensure that not a single diamond is lost or overlooked.

What we are observing is actually the end of a process that has taken millions of years. While these diamonds are found relatively close to the earth's surface that is not where they were "born." It is estimated that diamonds were formed between 45 million and 2.5 billion years ago at depths within the earth's crust averaging 165 kilometers (95 miles). They are the only gems made of pure carbon, resulting from melting rocks subjected to extremely high temperatures and submitted to intense pressure. Over millions of years these diamonds have eventually been squeezed to the earth's surface, where rivers wash them downstream and deposit them carelessly wherever they may fall.

Nature often gives us clues into "super-nature," the supernatural, or the spiritual world. God is very consistent and creative. As we stand on our dune pondering the big picture the exposed bedrock lies beneath our feet and the vast expanse of space rises above our heads. We all live between these two realities of solid hard ground and open space stretching to infinity.

The bedrock upon which our lives are founded is the freedom of choice that we enjoy. Freedom to make decisions about what we do, where we go, how we treat one another, what we eat; the choices and possibilities are endless. The limitation is that gravity keeps our feet on the ground and therefore we are restricted to exercise our freedom on this planet. We are indeed making very limited trips into our "outer space," but in the vastness of the galaxies and the cosmos these epic voyages are scarcely more impressive than fleas hopping on the back of an elephant and marveling at how high they can jump. Everything is a matter of perspective.

The space above our "limited freedom" is infinite and beyond our comprehension. Nevertheless, where "space" touches this earth it sustains life and encapsulates us in layers that enable us to continue to live here. Astronomers aim their telescopes and sophisticated gadgets out into that great canopy and attempt to understand what they see, establish some order, and identify patterns in the movement of objects that appear in the night sky or flash across it. They take some of the principles they have learned while examining life on earth and translate those into their research into outer space. What they learn by looking "outwards" is then applied to inform the ongoing research "down here." They tell us how meteors have crashed into the earth and probably eliminated dinosaurs, and how continents drift apart, and why earthquakes occur. This is a living, active, and interacting universe in which we live, constantly changing and adapting.

These same principles can be adopted to inform our understanding of the less tangible aspects of life as we explore spirituality and the human emotions, psyche, and behavior patterns. Without getting lost in abstraction and philosophical complexity how might our perspective change if we do not view suffering as a personal attack, or God's way of punishing us. Perhaps suffering can be viewed as an invaluable by-product of the interplay of patterns and principles that are essential to sustain life intersecting with human will and freedom. Perhaps "freedom" extends to every part of the universe where there are set patterns and yet there is also room for randomness that allows for some degree of uncertainty?

We return time and again to the question of "perspective." What happens if in the big picture suffering is embraced as essential to the molding of human character as heat and pressure is in the forming of diamonds? Some of these "harsh realities" in this vibrant and dangerous world can be harnessed to enable us to avoid suffering, while others do indeed harm or even kill us. Our challenge is to learn how to embrace both realities creatively rather than merely sulk when we have to sweat the tough stuff. This is not at all about suggesting that suffering is "fun." How we accept, acknowledge, and embrace its existence makes all the difference in the world in determining whether real diamonds are the end result or cheap glass beads roll out at the "bitter" end.

It is frequently noted that when things go wrong people turn to God. The insinuation is "How convenient" or "How weak." It is not particularly surprising that when circumstances finally bring us to the end of our resources we find ourselves at God's doorstep as a last resort. Alcoholics Anonymous discovered long ago that people seldom get help until they admit they actually have a problem. They have to want to change and be willing to take responsibility for doing something themselves. More than anything else, adverse conditions and suffering tend to bring out the quality of our inner resources. At these times some of us are surprised at the strength within us, while others finally come to grips with how distorted our priorities and investments of time and money have been.

Visit the African men and women living in squatter camps outside Cape Town and witness their dignity and "life"; it was a humbling and yet exhilarating experience for me. They do not shy away from suffering even though they would rather not have to endure it. When someone dies, they take the time to mourn and grieve as a community, expressing their sorrow openly and often loudly. When there is something to celebrate exuberance abounds and the singing, dancing, and laughter is infectious and vibrant. In other words the up and downs of life are all accepted and woven into spirits and lifestyle as an integrated whole. There is no sense of entitlement as is often the case in our Western cultures. In the "First World" we tend to regard affluence and peace as our inherent right (without requiring sacrifice or personal effort), and all negativity and hardship is an unfair intrusion and interruption.

In the 1970s there was tremendous political upheaval in South Africa and one of the flashpoints was the "Group Areas Act" that stipulated who could live where according to the color of their skin. Common practice was for the government to issue work permits permitting Black men to provide the menial labor required in the cities. Wives and families had to stay behind in their designated "homeland." Many families quite rightly refused to submit to this barbaric ruling. The squatter camps mushroomed around all major cities and ongoing tension continued between the quiet but determined defiance that was displayed within these camps.

At one point the situation between "squatters" and police boiled over and one area was bulldozed and destroyed by police workers, leaving thousands stranded with no shelter. Displaying remarkable courage the Anglican priest in our White middle-class suburb, Christopher Gregorowski, invited a group of these displaced families to live and camp on the church property. You can imagine the consternation that arose, particularly as the bold move found its way into the spotlight of the international media. I visited the group on site and attended a service held in the half-demolished squatter camp where a large cross stood silhouetted against a blazing wood fire. In both places the atmosphere was charged with a defiant joy with singing and laughter and a spirited resilience that I will never forget. The people who lived in such harsh conditions embraced their suffering and refused to allow a political system or difficult conditions to break their spirits or cause them to cower in self-pity. They supported each other and were enormously gracious in the midst of all the chaos.

Years later when Nelson Mandela emerged from prison after so many years in captivity the world witnessed the same dignity and quality of character. Are the brightest diamonds in the human character only produced under the heat and pressure of some form of suffering? Maybe when the basic material has become polluted and flawed it is the only way to get rid of the impurities. Not because God wills it that way but because he is able to take what is normally destructive and transform it into something beautiful. Understanding the risks and costs of freedom he has to permit these various realities to work through the system clogged full of choices and consequences, both good and bad. In the midst of all the chaos he continues to invite us to participate in producing diamonds through refining rather than settle for glass beads.

Rolfe Harris was an Australian singer and artist who was humorous and entertaining in his live shows that I enjoyed in Cape Town. At some time during his performance an enormous blank screen was wheeled onto the stage. He picked up a pail of paint and with a large paintbrush began slapping black paint around while he chatted over his shoulder to the audience. He painted a broad flat line here and a squiggly line there, flicked paint and dabbed with his brush until most of the area was covered—all in a matter of three or four minutes. The trouble was it looked totally unrecognizable. Rolfe Harris would step back, turn to smile and bow as the audience politely applauded amidst a sense of anticlimax. Moving back to the screen he would dip his paintbrush once again and add one or two more brush strokes with boldness and flair. Suddenly confusion was lifted and out of the black and white "nothingness" emerged a sailboat on a moonlit lake, or a mountain scene. The transformation was greeted with a rapturous and loud applause!

Suffering without God is like watching Rolfe Harris paint the first part of his picture. All we're left with is confusion. Maybe that is where many of us find ourselves. The final brush strokes illuminate the whole picture; sometimes we have to wait a long time for those strokes to appear and it is hard to be patient. It has taken almost ten years in my case; at times I thought God had left the building and thrown away the paint and the brushes. However, he does not play sadistic games—even though, as I reflect on that dark decade, I shake my head at questions that remain unanswered for me. The truth is that on occasion I became so fed up and impatient that I left the building for a long time myself, deciding to do my own thing and paint my own picture. Eventually I had to eat humble pie and acknowledge that my "alternative sketches" were so pitiful in comparison that even I wearied of my efforts. God was still waiting with paintbrush in hand when I returned, no need for a lecture as the lesson was already learned. Jesus is an incredibly creative artist when it comes to working positively and beautifully in our lives. He will sculpt and paint with great delight when he is invited and welcomed, never violating the bedrock of freedom upon which we live and stand—in happiness or in suffering.

●　●　●　●　●

**Character cannot be developed in peace and quiet. Only through experience of trial and suffering can the soul be strengthened, ambition inspired, and success achieved.**

—HELEN KELLER

●　●　●　●　●

Sometimes in the more affluent West we mistakenly believe that sickness, suffering, and death are unfair inconveniences beset upon us by the Almighty. The real miracle is that God can take hold of suffering and transform it into an opportunity for remarkable and wonderful possibilities for victory within every human spirit. I have seen more joy on the faces of the Africans living among sand dunes than I have witnessed upon the faces of affluent Westerners mowing lawns in suburbia, shopping in the streets of Zurich or Manhattan, or sightseeing in Auckland or London. That is not romanticizing poverty but rather suggesting that in the real world ironically a richness of spirit (diamonds) may be most abundant in places of material scarcity. Why? Because with the absence of pressure, heat, depth, cutting, and polishing no character gemstones of great value and beauty are pro-duced—it is another principle embedded into life on earth. Unfortunately there is a lucrative market peddling superficial substitutes that look like the real thing from a distance.

Pete was a man of mixed race who clawed his way into adulthood under the shadow of Table Mountain in Cape Town. He lived in a tough community and it was not long before he socialized with the "wrong" crowd and began to drink heavily. Some days he would buy a bottle of wine, skip work, and walk up onto the mountain slopes and remain there the whole day. He drank through his marriage and the birth of his children year after year after year. Eventually under South African apartheid laws he and his family were forcibly relocated. With virtually no resources he scrounged enough secondhand material to build a small shelter in the sand dunes on the outskirts of Cape Town's southern suburbs.

Through these turbulent years his wife patiently supported him, parented the children, and prayed for her wayward husband. A church was built not far from their little home in the dunes and every Sunday his wife attended the morning service and became actively involved in the community. Pete would lie in bed and listen to the bells ringing and somehow God spoke to Pete through their peals week after week calling people to worship him. One Sunday Pete could not resist any longer; he rose from his bed, swallowed his pride, and went to the church himself. There he met God and encountered his love personally; it was liberally and freely poured out, forgiving him for all those wasted years and healing his alcoholism as well.

Pete and I used to talk of these life-changing events years later after he had been free of alcohol for a long time. His life had new meaning and purpose and he always choked up when he recounted that first meeting with God. He worked as a janitor, participated in music enthusiastically sing-ing and playing his guitar and demonstrating much wisdom and some real leadership skills. I was a young pastor in that church and many men and women in the congregation told similar stories of lives changed, particularly overcoming deep-seated drinking addictions.

There are many remarkable stories around the world of God working in the lives of people to bring healing, hope, and courage in the face of adversity. Consider Mother Teresa ministering to the poor and the dying in the streets of Calcutta and starting a movement of care for the poor in many nations. Jackie Pullinger, stepping off a boat in Hong Kong in her early 20s with a conviction that God wanted her to work among the chronic drug addicts in the Walled City. She started a recovery work rooted in prayer (seemed naïve at the time) that has been underway now for 30 years (google her name to read some fascinating stories). Joni Eareckson Tada speaking and modeling God's love and faithfulness after becoming a quadriplegic resulting from a random diving accident in her teens, the books and artwork she has produced have encouraged others to overcome their circumstances. In Canada we could talk of Terry Fox and his magnificent run across Canada while dying of cancer, Rick Hanson pushing himself around the world in a wheelchair to show that anything is possible. These are merely a few people who make the headlines.

There are countless unsung heroes around us (you may be one of them) who are seldom noticed but who demonstrate remarkable fortitude and courage every day. Paul Simon captured it eloquently in his song "Diamonds on the Soles of their Shoes." In Africa the worn-out soles of shoes with holes in them are called diamonds—they have taken a sign of poverty and trans- formed it into an emblem of elegance and wealth with unabashed humor!

Another reality in Africa, Asia, India, and many other parts of the world is a heightened awareness of evil and the power of "the dark side." If we read the Bible and God's perspective on the world and human suffering, also magnified through the life and teaching of Jesus, this cosmic intersection between freedom and "scientific" principles is further complicated by the introduction of yet another dimension that for many of us borders on the fantastic or fringe of science fiction. The realm of good and evil where we encounter angels and evil spirits, and the possible existence of satan as a real power.

●  ●  ●  ●  ●

## Reality leaves a lot to the imagination.

—JOHN LENNON

●  ●  ●  ●  ●

In the West we tend to joke and play down any insinuation that we are not totally in control. However, a reading of the Bible and a study of the life and teaching of Jesus reveals a perception that some aspects of suffering might well be caused by the influence of evil at work. We're not going to dwell on this topic but there may be room for reciprocal humility with our Bushman friend. When he holds the Coke bottle we are introducing him to a world he cannot even begin to imagine. When he tracks animals and demonstrates a sensitivity to nature and the spirit world that our sensitivities have forgotten, then maybe we should pause and consider more graciously possibilities and insights that are no longer intuitive to many of us.

Christianity is the only world religion where God is known as one who cares about our feelings or our life on earth in an empathic way. In the person of Jesus, God enters into the world and suffers with us and for us—and that is a real mystery in itself. Therefore the logical place to look and learn about how God responds to suffering in the world is to explore the life and teaching of Jesus, his Son.

It is only when God is distant and impersonal that blaming him for suffering really sticks. I have found to my shame that the further I am away from God the easier I find it to blame him for everything I don't like or understand. If God is identifiable and can be known personally might the question change to not only *Why do you allow suffering?* but also *Where are you in the midst of it?*

The astounding and unique revelation the person of Jesus Christ introduces to the world stage is that God is personal, that he suffers and grieves with us, and that he offers us help and strength. Like a mature parent he provides the resources for life and then he encourages his children to grow into their freedom. He agonizes at some of their choices but he never forces his will. He warns of consequences and provides counsel when asked, his love is always offered but he imposes himself on no one.

One of the most moving moments for me in the Bible is when Jesus looks down on Jerusalem traveling from the village of Bethany. I've walked that road, and as you come over the hill the whole city unfolds before your eyes. Jesus knows his death is fast approaching as he senses the opposition mounting against him. He did not admire the view that day—instead the sight of his beloved city broke his heart and the voice of God the Father resonated through him...he wept,

> *O Jerusalem, Jerusalem, you who kill the prophets and stone those sent to you, how often I have longed to gather your children together as a hen gathers her chicks under her wing, but you were not willing.*

> —MATTHEW 23:37-38

This is the gift of free will at work, where God himself weeps at the implications of his own creation and the choices he has permitted with all the subsequent consequences. No parent in their right mind would allow such a situation to evolve unless there was a deeper reason and purpose being accomplished through such a process. How often do I stone the very initiatives that God sends my way to rescue me because it is not how I thought things would be? And then I blame him, while I am locked up in my narrow preconceptions and arrogant disposition. To say that God is indifferent or uncaring in his response to suffering in the world is misguided.

Jerusalem, the ancient city situated at the crossroads of history and a symbol of God's love for every individual and of all of creation at the same time, broke Jesus' heart. His response to the suffering he witnessed was to lay down his life for those who suffer. Nowhere else in any religious or spiritual movement is God revealed as one who suffers with us like that.

> How I weep for my broken body
> Scattered over the land
> Wounded and bleeding
> Loveless limbs and hardened hearts
>
> O Jerusalem, Jerusalem
> How I longed that you would come to me
> O Jerusalem, though you called out my name
> You stoned the ones who came
> And my tears flow over you
>
> How I weep for my broken body
> With tears from deep within
> Blind children denying
> Believing a lie
> They crucify
>
> O Jerusalem, Jerusalem…
>
> How I weep for my broken body
> Singing Rachel's lament
> For loved ones now lost
> Father forgive them
> They know not what they do
>
> O Jerusalem, Jerusalem
> How I longed that you would come to me
> O Jerusalem, though you called out my name
> You stoned the ones who came

*And my tears flow over you*
*Now I lay my body down—for you*

Suffering is never something we desire nor should we wish it on anyone. It is not a virtue and God does not give each of us "our cross to bear." That term is a gross misrepresentation of his purposes. Let us remind ourselves again of the difference between what God allows and what he desires. Suffering is acknowledged as a reality in this world and God never promises that any of us will be immune from it. However, when suffering occurs it is not punishment from God nor is it his method of getting our attention. That would be as bizarre as my deliberately causing my child to have an accident so that she will listen more carefully to what I have to say.

What God does promise is that he will provide us with the inner resources to deal with suffering when it comes, and therein lies the determining factor as to whether suffering ultimately destroys or enriches. The fact that God can take very negative circumstances and events and create positive outcomes despite their harsh cruelty does not mean that he prefers to work with us like that.

When Jesus prepared to suffer on the cross and wept in Gethsemane he had no desire to enter into that suffering, but he ultimately accepted that there was no other way. His wrestling and agonizing in Gethsemane is important because it gives each of us permission to "be spiritual" and to wrestle with some of the challenges we face. There can be a tendency in some spiritual circles to behave in a manner tantamount to denial by not acknowledging the very human process of coming to grips with pain. "Name it and claim it" is not faith most of the time; it is avoidance of dealing with the struggle in Gethsemane that authenticity demands. God is not at the beck and call of the loudest voice or a genie that is activated by the rattling off of Scripture verses, or a "prayer in the name of Jesus."

This question of suffering and healing is extremely puzzling, complicated, and often an elusive mystery. All I would assert is that in the final analysis when I sit down with Jesus and ask, *Why?* his response will be perfectly fair, perfectly reasonable, and perfectly loving. That is why it is ultimately into his hands I commit and entrust all my unanswered questions and my frustrations in a cruel, unjust, and unfair world.

Meanwhile the big picture is exactly that, bigger than we can comprehend. So in order to get a glimpse of how we comprehend a loving God and the reality of suffering we need to walk out of the desert into a beautiful garden.

# 13

# Suffering—A Cosmic Victory

MY TWO YOUNG DAUGHTERS WERE PLAYING IN THE GARDEN AND ONE OF THEM WAS WEARING A T-SHIRT WITH THE NEW SOUTH AFRICAN FLAG EMBLAZONED ACROSS IT. It was Christmas time in Cape Town and my first visit to the country since the end of apartheid. For the first time in my life I was proud of the country and particularly of the leadership. I sat in the sun and read from Nelson Mandela's biography, *A Long Walk to Freedom:*

> *To be free is not merely to cast off one's chains, but to live in a way that respects and enhances the freedom of others...*
> *I have walked that long road to freedom. I have tried not to falter; I have made missteps along the way. But I have discovered the secret that after climbing a great hill, one only finds that there are many more hills to climb. I have taken a moment here to rest, to steal a view of the glorious vista that surrounds me, to look back on the distance I have come. But I can rest only for a moment, for with freedom comes responsibilities, and I dare not linger, for my long walk is not yet ended.*

The words I read moved me, primarily because South Africa, a country so twisted in hatred and prejudice, was hearing a voice in leadership that was moderate and generous in spirit. If anyone had a right to be angry and vengeful it was Nelson Mandela. Instead the years in confinement on

Robben Island taught him lessons only learned in the deepest part of our souls in the places of intense pressure and fire. That's where the diamonds come from, diamonds of insight, compassion, grace, courage, forgiveness, and mercy.

It is easy to hate and to accuse. In the Christian church there is so much bickering and arguing over who is right about which segment of theological truth. The Christian community is divided by every conceivable issue one can imagine and is a shameful model to the rest of the world of what it means to be gracious. I love Graham Cooke's comment on the church as the Bride of Christ. He imagines Jesus looking down at the church and saying to his Father, "Dad, please, do you really want me to marry that?"

A tragic example of the grace and mercy of God was witnessed in North America recently when one man shot and killed a number of young Amish children in the school before committing suicide. The Amish community was devastated but still recognized that the love and compassion of God reaches out to all people. They extended forgiveness and support to the family of the man who had killed their children, demonstrating powerfully and deeply what the love of God truly means. That quality of love and integrity is far more powerful and challenging to live than is the easy road of hate and revenge.

Imagine that we all stand before Jesus with our particular "issue" clutched in our hands. He asks us what we feel most strongly about and then listens to our presentations. I hold up issues of gender and sexuality, you hold up issues of baptism, another thrusts forward poverty, another wealth, another biblical inerrancy, another gifts of the spirit, and so it goes on down the line.

When we have finished Jesus approaches each of us accompanied by two people, one on either side of him. They introduce themselves. One is Peter and the other is Paul. Peter speaks first, "I understand your desire for truth and commend you. I had some strong convictions as well..." He pauses and gestures to Paul who says, "Peter my brother was a fisherman,

I was highly educated, steeped in the Jewish faith, and very eloquent about God's Word, but on the road to Damascus it all changed."

•  •  •  •  •

**As soon as questions of will or decision
or reason or choice of action arise,
human science is at a loss.**

—NOAM CHOMSKY

•  •  •  •  •

"John, I hear the cry of your heart and those issues are indeed important. But can you give them back to me now because they are getting in the way. What happens if I agree with you and you are absolutely correct about your issue? What then?" asked Jesus.

The silence hung between us, I said nothing. Jesus continued, "Being right does not really mean much if love has been sacrificed. I'll ask you the same question I always ask—Do you love me?" I could hardly nod but Peter reached out and touched my arm..."Then feed his sheep, my brother."

The ancient Hebrew people were a loose conglomerate of tribes and kinsmen who had become enslaved to the powerful Egyptians. They had entered the land of Egypt under Jacob's leadership and the promise of God that he would make them into a great nation. They settled in the land of Goshen after Joseph, his son, had negotiated with Pharaoh on their behalf. For many years they enjoyed increased prosperity and peace in their new homeland.

Years later after Joseph and Jacob had died the Israelites continued to increase in number and became a significant population group throughout Egypt. The new pharaoh grew concerned about their numbers and the potential for armed revolt and introduced a policy of oppression and slavery. A brutal decree was introduced whereby every Hebrew boy was to be killed at birth. Consequently when Moses was born his terrified mother placed him in a reed basket on the Nile with the hope that he would somehow miraculously survive. Throughout these years, with their riches and peace dashed under the yoke of slavery, the Hebrew slaves cried out to God for help and rescue.

Meanwhile Moses had grown up within the courts of aristocracy with Pharaoh's daughter as his adopted mother. He was evidently a powerful young man and one day when he witnessed a fellow Hebrew being badly treated. He killed the Egyptian who was doing the beating, and thought that no one had seen him. His action however had been witnessed and fearing for his life Moses fled and spent the 40 forty years of his life as an alien in a foreign land.

However, God was not finished with Moses, and while tending the sheep of Jethro, his father-in-law, God told him to go to Pharaoh and ask him to let the Israelites go. Moses was totally shocked at this suggestion and started making all kinds of excuses, but God reassured him and eventually he agreed to do as instructed. Various plagues were sent by God to counter Pharaoh's obstinate refusal and to persuade him to set the Israelites free. In the encounter recorded in the book of Exodus between Pharaoh and Moses it is made clear that neither the stubbornness of the king, nor the weakness of Moses, would ultimately prevail against the will of God.

Even after the promise of a plague on the firstborn, where every firstborn Egyptian son would be killed, Pharaoh would not relent. Then came the Passover. Instructions were given to the Israelites in captivity. On the tenth day of the month each man was to take a lamb, which was to be a year old and without defect, one for each household, and care for it until the fourteenth day. They were then told to slaughter the lamb at twilight and paint the sides and top of the doors of their homes with its blood. The meat was to be shared and eaten by the family together with a variety of other herbs and rituals. That same night God said that he would pass through Egypt and strike down the firstborn, animal and human. This was to be a judgment upon Egypt and their gods. "The blood will be a sign for you on the houses where you are; and when I see the blood, I will pass over you.

No destructive plague will touch you when I strike Egypt" (Exodus 12:13). That night Pharaoh relented and the people of Israel were released from slavery and began their journey—their long walk to freedom. (We will return to this event later.)

The symbolism of the sacrificial lamb, the judgment of God, the blood over the doorways protecting those who were inside, were all deeply rooted in the subsequent Jewish faith. They were then interwoven in the Christian Gospel and the crucifixion of Christ (the Lamb of God). But...

...Animal sacrifice was ultimately insufficient because it dealt with only half the problem, the consequences of our actions. It did not really resolve the issue of *why* we kept making the wrong choices in the first place. As is the case with most rituals, before long human beings were using sacrifice as some kind of magic rite. They deceived themselves into believing that by merely going through the motions God would be satisfied and even impressed (back to religion again).

We witness this dynamic throughout the biblical accounts of God and humanity—God seeking relationship and humanity glimpsing moments of that possibility and then quickly degenerating back into religious ritual. Similar, I suppose, to a married couple that within a short while has lost their "sparkle" and passion, cohabit in the same building, and communicate in monosyllabic responses. Such is hardly the interaction from which great relationships are sustained and enjoyed—they all require some give and take—including the relationship with God.

A frighteningly dark side of our culture in North America is the prevalence of missing children. It is far too common to see pictures of smiling kids pasted on the walls of supermarkets and other public places with the word *missing* above them. One can only imagine the pain of a parent whose child has disappeared like that. A few years ago the CBC ran a documentary on drug use in Vancouver. They interviewed a brave and resilient mother and father whose daughter had lived on the streets for many, many years.

The mother recounted in an interview how she would sometimes take supplies down to her daughter and leave parcels at her feet without much recognition, acknowledgement, or thanks. On other occasions she would go downtown and stand and watch her discreetly from a distance, to reassure herself that her beloved daughter was still alive.

Human mothers and fathers aching for reconciliation with their children is an inadequate analogy for God seeking the same with every human being, including you and me. That is why Jesus walked on this earth—God becoming like us in order to reunite us with himself. It had nothing to do with ego gratification and everything to do with a restored relationship forged and bound in love.

But there was more to Jesus on earth than even that immense task and reason. Remember when Adam and Eve were in the Garden of Eden the penalty for disobeying God was death? Instead of them dying for their wrongdoing they had to live outside Eden and the covenant involving sacrifices was instituted. Instead of my death, God would accept the death of an animal sacrificed as my acknowledgement that I had grieved him and that I was genuinely sorry.

Some people will struggle here and protest that all we are faced with is an angry God who loves killing things. That would be as blind a conclusion as if you were to take one day out of my life and profess to know me. The only way to know God is to meet him where he has revealed himself most fully, in the person of Jesus Christ. From that meeting place we then move back and forth through the pages of the Bible unashamed to be puzzled at times while also asking tough questions. However we do recognize that there will be occasions when specific questions are unanswered, because by definition God's ways are not intuitively obvious to us. When that happens we are left having to trust the character of uncompromising sacrificial love he revealed in the person of his son, Jesus.

In Moses' day the gift of animal sacrifice still meant that a barrier existed between God's heart and the human heart, because the animal sacrifice alone was only sufficient to forgive behavior. It did not go deep enough to impact attitude and facilitate a lasting change within the human heart. A sacrifice of that magnitude would demand that a human life be offered, Adam to die for Adam's disobedience.

It is tempting to react and state that this all sounds barbaric, yet the whole structure of our society is laced with rules and regulations. In fact it is one of the great ironies that our attempts at democracy contain so many restrictions and regulations for it "to work" at all. It is an illusion to believe that freedom exists within our democracies, although despite their imperfection they are still probably the best we can reasonably expect to accomplish. When we experience injustice or serious crime are we not the first to demand "justice" and consequences for crimes committed? If we explore the meaning and intent behind these biblical accounts we will invariably uncover integrity and depth of meaning within the parameters of unconditional love.

The problem is that we are so "dead" spiritually that we have become similar to the Bushman (in terms of Western culture), lost in a spiritual desert and out of touch with an entire "other world" or realm. Consequently when these topics are under discussion we respond like the Bushman holding the Coke bottle. We look at "it" in bewilderment and then discard "it" as useless because instant gratification is not what is being offered. Another barrier for many is a memory of a shouting, sweating, Bible-thumping evangelist who has used "the Word of God" to pummel us into submission with volume of speech and intensity of accusation. Such an image and practice is unfortunate, and is another testimony to our propensity to take what originates from God, cheapen it, and pedal it in a manner for which it was never intended. Human nature gravitates toward legalism much more naturally than it is able to embrace unconditional love.

Jesus presents a very different model to the world. The Pharisees (who were the religious leaders of Jesus' day) could not come to terms with his insistence that the purpose of the law was to draw people into the love of God. For the Pharisees love was "touchy feely" nonsense relegated to the Human Resources Department; the really important issue was obedience! Jesus was furious with them for the way they misappropriated God's word. If you ever want to see the tough side of God, eavesdrop on some of his conversations with the Pharisees! Mincing no words he berated them, "You are like white-washed tombs, which look beautiful on the outside but on the inside are full of dead men's bones and everything unclean" (Matthew 23:27).

●　●　●　●　●

**Human beings are perhaps never more frightening than when they are convinced beyond doubt that they are right.**

—SIR LAURENS VAN DER POST

●　●　●　●　●

Jesus walking on earth was Adam walking in the Garden of Eden *before* he and Eve were seduced by the lies of the snake. John was very young when he first met Jesus and wrote as a much older man, "God so loved the world that he gave his one and only Son, that whoever believes in him shall not perish but have everlasting life" (John 3:16).

Why was this so important? In order for God to restore the heart of humanity to be able to comprehend him and the meaning of their own existence, radical surgery was required to remove the source of the infection (the venom from the snake bite) that had occurred in Eden. God created the world with all life contained within it, and he takes responsibility for humanity—without transgressing his own laws and justice. The radical surgery is only possible if Adam dies—a perfect human sacrifice for a human transgression that violates the very core of human existence. The penalty for rebellion/disobedience against God was death (separation from God is the same thing). Through Jesus, God was paying the price for the penalty he himself had imposed. Providing the only "perfect One" who would satisfy his law and open a way back to Eden, where you and I could once again experience the relationship he always intended for us to enjoy with him.

Mike was almost 16 when he lost his boat to the wind and the weather. It was a two-foot long sailboat he had spent years building from scratch. Three years earlier he and his grandfather had built the keel and ribs of the boat—as his grandfather remembered them being built outside his home on the shore when he was a boy. They had shaped the wood and carved the white oak, glued and nailed every piece until the skeleton lay before them strong, naked, and proud. Mike had been so thrilled. Seven months later his grandfather sailed away in his sleep and Mike vowed to finish the boat no matter how long it took him.

He kept his word, and over the months and then years a beautiful sailboat began to emerge until in the early spring of his sixteenth year it was finished. Complete to the very last detail. That summer Mike frequently carried the boat down to the shore and watched it sail, carefully setting the line and then letting it go. Until one afternoon in the fall the wind began gusting and instead of maintaining its line the boat was pushed farther and farther offshore. Mike could do nothing but watch, hoping that it would return when the wind changed as it usually did later in the day, but not this time. Instead it was broadsided by a large wave and capsized, disappearing altogether. Mike went home devastated and for the next few weeks walked along the shoreline every day hoping to find his boat washed up on the beach. Nothing.

Five years later Mike returned home for a few weeks during the summer and was walking down the main street when something caught his eye. There in the main window of an antique store was the boat he had carved with his grandfather! Someone had painted it and cleaned it up so that it looked quite smart, but there was no mistaking the model he had carved, glued, and constructed. Excitedly he rushed into the store, "Excuse me, that's my boat in the window. I lost it off the beach here five years ago!" he exclaimed. "Can I have it back please?"

The storekeeper took a while to comprehend exactly what Mike was telling him. After listening politely to his story he replied, "You may have the boat, sir, if you pay the price I am selling it for, because it is mine now, and has been for quite some time."

"But it's my boat, I built it. I know every nail and fitting that went into its construction," Mike explained.

"That may be so, but the boat is mine and if you want it back you will have to pay for it."

Mike left elated and frustrated, having asked the owner to keep the boat for him while he collected the money to buy it back. It took him the whole summer but eventually he earned enough, the transaction was made, and he was reconciled with his precious boat again. The next time he went sailing with it he made sure that he secured a safety line to it, just in case.

What God accomplished through Jesus dying on the Cross and placing the death penalty for human rebellion upon his shoulders was similar to "buying back" his creation but not quite the same. Jesus' "perfect sacrifice" paid the price for our separation from God and opens a door inviting us to return to the garden (life in relationship with him). While satan rebels against God and messes around with his creation, God is not buying us back from him as satan does not enjoy that level of status and is not God's equal. Therefore the "buying back" is about paying the price of rebellion in order that justice may be honored as well as God's love for his creation. It is about redeeming and restoring what was lost.

I was walking down Ben Yehuda Street in the new section of Jerusalem when suddenly a commotion erupted in front of me as someone started throwing T-shirts out of a window above into the street below. "Free shirts," was the cry and everyone scrambled to grab hold of one or two. I picked up two for my daughters and was very pleased with myself. Imagine if the person in the upstairs window had thrown shirts out into the street shouting, "Free shirts," and people had ignored him and the T-shirts falling all around. The only "catch" is that in order to take advantage of the offer you have to pick up a shirt. The same is true with what God offers us through Jesus. It's all been thrown out onto the street in front of us but we still have to pick it up and wear it, make it our own. Nothing is forced. God makes reconciliation possible but still leaves us with a choice of whether we want to appropriate his gift—or not.

Adam cast out of Eden re-emerges with Jesus in Gethsemane on the hillside ten minutes walk beyond Jerusalem's old city wall. Gethsemane is another garden, full of olive trees. Olives are crushed in order to release their oil—a staple resource in the Middle East. Olive oil was used for cooking, lighting lamps, and providing illumination and comfort in the darkness of night. Gethsemane is a garden every bit as symbolic as Eden. That is where Jesus spent his last night alive as a human being on this earth, sweating blood as he agonized over the decision he had to make and the violence that lay ahead of him. He would be crushed like an olive releasing the oil of forgiveness to be poured out for you and me. Some will take hold of his sacrifice with the deepest gratitude; others will walk by totally unaware and indifferent.

* * * * *

**They were so strong in their beliefs that there came a time when it hardly mattered what exactly those beliefs were; they all fused into a single stubbornness.**

—LOUISE ERDRICH

* * * * *

Jesus on the cross is at last the sacrifice that will completely atone for the sin (transgression/wrong choice) of Adam and Eve, and ultimately of all of humanity. Justice is finally satisfied. The radical surgery on the heart is completed as Jesus is falsely accused, mocked, whipped, beaten, nailed, hung, stabbed, and left on a wooden cross to die. One man spilled his blood on a cross as a sacrifice for every other human being, one individual at a time. There is no hiding here behind "humanity" and hoping to get lost or found in the crowd. The ramifications impact all of humanity and every individual.

Jesus responded to one of the criminal's hanging next to him while they hung on crosses dying together. The criminal asked to be remembered by Jesus when he entered into his kingdom. Jesus responded to the cry from the heart of a condemned man and promised him, "Today you will be with me in paradise" (Luke 23:42-43). Even in such a weak and decimated condition, Jesus' spirit was not broken. His trust in his Father was implicit and he was confident of what lay beyond physical death. Perhaps he could even see over the garden wall.

No other religion reveals God as one who loves so personally and intimately as a father loves a child. Nowhere else is God revealed as one who agonizes over his creation and who enters into the midst of humanity as a suffering servant in order to intervene in their plight. A king who descends all the way down to our level, leaving his majestic throne to be born in a stable; specifically to open and restore the pathway for reconciliation between himself and each one of us.

> *Evil meets good*
> *Hammered nail on wood*
> *Iron through flesh*
> *Pierced bleeding hand*
> *Men crucify*
> *What they don't understand*
>
> *Crowds jostle jeer*
> *Laugh, spit, and sneer*
> *Soldiers squat lazy*
> *Throw dice around*
> *Bleeding feet, crazy*
> *Figure makes not a sound*
>
> *Mother stands still*
> *Tearfully gazing*
> *Love submits will*
> *Upon the hill*
> *Rain falls and shadows*
> *Sweep over her Son*

*Love hangs suspended*
*On heaven and hell*
*Father's departed*
*Why...?*
*Long lonely cry*
*Dying to live*
*And living to die*

*Evil meets good*
*Hammered nail on wood*
*Iron through flesh*
*Pierced bleeding hand*
*Men crucify*
*What they don't understand*

After the crucifixion, Joseph of Arimathea gave Jesus a traditional burial in a garden tomb without the slightest inkling as to what was about to happen. A large round stone was rolled in front of the entrance to the tomb and that was that. These are big stones about 12 to 18 inches thick and can be six feet in circumference, or more! The stone could have been 20 feet thick and weighed 20 tons. It wouldn't have mattered. But God...

But God, after three days, demonstrated his power and authority by raising Jesus from the dead. No one could believe the news at first because nothing like this had ever happened before. People who die do not rise from the dead! Dead people do not appear to their friends as Jesus appeared on a number of occasions—unless of course you are God.

Some have suggested the Roman soldiers removed the body. If they had hidden the body why did they not produce it when rumors of the resurrection began to surface? After all, they were left looking rather foolish when they had placed guards to watch the tomb for fear of political ramifications. Others thought the disciples stole the body. But they never admitted to anything like that and, furthermore, many of them later died violent deaths precisely because they refused to renounce the resurrection of Jesus, their Lord. Would you die a cruel death for a lie, which you would only need to renounce in order to be free? Another desperate explanation was that Jesus never actually died but rolled the stone away and went into exile somewhere else. After the damage done to him from the Roman whipping, scourging, crucifixion, and spear wound—it takes more faith to believe such a fantasy than to accept that God did indeed reveal his miraculous power by raising his Son from the dead on that first Easter morning.

Paradise (or heaven) is where God lives—the original Eden—where there are no tears and there is no longer any suffering. It may be a place or another dimension, or a state of being. In the middle of Paradise is the Tree of Life and God's desire is for each of us to eat as much as we can from that special tree; Jesus is the only one who can lead us there to pick the fruit. Within Paradise there is also an enormous mansion. Jesus told his disciples that one of the reasons for his walking on this earth was to invite us all back to his house for eternity—beyond death. "In my Father's house are many rooms; if it were not so, I would have told you. I am going there to prepare a place for you. And if I go and prepare a place for you, I will come back and take you to be with me that you also may be where I am" (John 14:2-3).

I am the proud father of two beautiful daughters and my house has a place that is prepared for them—and it will always be that way as long as I live. Why? Because they are dearly loved and precious to me and there will always be room for them and an unconditional welcome for them wherever I live. I carry my daughters in my heart, and my home is a tangible symbol of what is in my heart as it relates to them. Every parent will identify with what I am saying. Our parent hearts receive their beat from the heart of our Creator Father. He spoke to us through Jesus about the place he has prepared beyond death for us, and the place that he has in his heart for each one of us right now. Just for you—whom he calls by name even as you read these words.

Close this book for a moment and think about that possibility. Feel what it would be like to have someone love you unconditionally…someone who is quite able to sift through the jumble of your life and understand why you are who you are. Someone who genuinely desires to be in the midst of your life with you, and who is more than capable of helping you find a place of hope and peace and joy—and to be safe and secure in his love. He is not impressed with your accomplishments one way or another, and he is certainly not disillusioned with you! He really doesn't care whether you're a professor draped in degrees and academics, a socialite desperately hiding behind appearances, or a bum on the street addicted to drugs. You're his kid and he will never ever give up looking for you. Furthermore, he has a room in his mansion that was built for you, and a place in his heart waiting for you to come home to.

The fact that this accommodation is freely offered and can be freely received is because God and Jesus have already paid your and my outstanding debts. Imagine scraping and saving all your life paying visa bills and accounts and discovering right at the end that it had all been taken care of, but you were too busy to sign the agreement lying at your bedside waiting for a signature!

Many of us come from all sorts of backgrounds where our experience of fathers and parents is very battered, broken, and distorted. We are even afraid of those words because we have been abused and betrayed, sometimes abandoned and neglected, and tragically not the recipients of the love and nurture that God the Father designed for us to receive. Jesus was very secure in the love of his Father. I know from my own experience, as well as having worked with many others like me, that Jesus is the only one who can truly restore us to know the Father's love—which is the deepest cry of every human heart.

My father was a good man but emotionally distant and somewhat crippled by his own emotionally impoverished childhood. He did not know how to verbalize love or to encourage and praise his children. He was not able to be generous in spirit and share his heart openly and freely. It took me many years to begin to embrace and respond to the reality that Jesus and God the Father are not like that at all. They are embarrassingly kind and overwhelmingly generous, never really wanting to say "no" to you and me. All they have is our well-being at heart but they love us too much to merely give us whatever we want or to be swayed by our mood swings and tantrums. That is why we will usually have some "unlearning" to do when we enter into a relationship with Jesus and God the Father. We will keep mistrusting them because we will find it hard to believe that they mean what they say, that their love is absolutely constant and unconditional, and that they will watch over us and impact our lives right on earth. We don't have to wait until we die to get started on this new journey!

Jesus said as much: "If anyone loves me, he will obey my teaching. My father will love him, and we will come to him and make our home with him" (John 14:23).

That's why Christianity is such good news. No other religion, faith, or belief system ever comes close to understanding and knowing a God who pays your Visa bill and embraces you with this kind of radical and generous love. When my daughters were very young I would always reach down and pick them up saying, "Give me the biggest hug in the world." They would respond by hugging me as tightly as possible to the accompaniment of giggles and smiles as an added bonus. As a father, I soaked up their love maybe even more than they did as they were embraced and carried by mine. That is the relationship Jesus came to reveal as possible for each of us with God; nothing stagnant and boring, formal or too intellectual. It is a relationship between a Father who adores his children and who looks forward to "the biggest hugs in the world" from his kids—who in turn know that they are secure and safe in his embrace.

# 14

# Expecting Miracles

JANE WAS 22 YEARS OLD, A BEAUTIFUL YOUNG GIRL ON THE THRESHOLD OF LIFE. She had a very close family, a younger brother and parents who adored her and loved one another. When I met her she was propped up in bed dying of leukemia. I had been asked to visit her at the family home on the outskirts of Oxford, which I did with some trepidation as I was still trying to learn how to find God in the midst of these situations myself.

Jane's mother was a devout Christian; her father was an academic who quite understandably could not tolerate any sense of God as his daughter slipped from his helpless and angry grasp. I wondered what I was going to say and do as I rang the doorbell for the first time. *I'm the one who is meant to believe that God loves and heals and that he cares for those who suffer,* I thought to myself. *What does all that information mean here and now for this family writhing in agony and sobbing with unanswered questions?* I didn't know how else to answer other than to merely step into their space and share that vulnerable place with them.

I thought that this would be a great opportunity for Jesus to work a miracle, as he did in Capernaum with the Centurion's dying slave. But in my heart I didn't honestly expect too much. What would a miracle look like in this situation? Instant healing? That's what I would go for! Which is a typical response from someone so close to the situation that they don't even see the big picture at all, there's no time or energy for that.

We live in a very cynical age where it is easy to think that because we can provide explanations or scientific reasons the miraculous is diminished. Is the Coke bottle appearing to the Bushman in the Kalahari a miracle? For him it definitely is. Because we can explain it and place it in a larger context from our vantage point does that diminish the fact for him? I'm not sure. I'm wondering whether the term *miraculous* does not better describe statements related to timing, meaning, substance, and relationships rather than explanations of how?

Maybe miracles are in the eye of the beholder and appear rather mundane to the onlooker, while being quite extraordinary to the recipient. The deception of the desire for an abundance of "miracles" is that we can have heaven on earth and that God should wave a wand and make what is not right perfect—now. That longing within all of us, to have the power to eliminate all sickness and "bad things," is played out in movies and fairy tales. When Jesus was tempted by satan in the wilderness he was taunted to demonstrate his power through miracles and Jesus refused (Matthew 4:1-10). Later during his public ministry Mark tells us that he could not do many miracles in his hometown because of the lack of faith, he was Joseph the carpenter's son after all (Mark 6:4-6).

Let me recount a simple example to illustrate how faith and miracle can occur because there is no doubt that Jesus expected "signs and wonders" as a normal part of his "ministry." Quite a few years ago now I was working with a small group of about ten Christians and we were talking and studying around this question of God healing today and miracles. After an interesting and fruitful exchange of ideas and stories we came to that moment where we could either have coffee and say, "Interesting discussion. Thanks for a great evening," or we could put what we said we believed into practice. I asked if anyone had any physical ailment they would like prayer for. Glen, an older gentleman, told us that his knee had been bothering him and was quite painful. We gathered around and started to pray for God to heal

Glen's knee. A number of people prayed and then we stood back as if to say, "Whose next?" "Are we finished?" I teased them. "Has God answered? Is Glen's knee healed?" There was some spluttering and Glen admitted to not feeling much different.

"How many of us are afraid of this kind of praying, really don't believe anything will happen, and certainly are scared to ask if anything is happening?" I asked. Everyone put their hands up and we laughed together with relief. "That's great, now we know that we are all nervous and God knows that. So why don't we try again? Last time we prayed out of our fear and unbelief. Now that we have admitted our weakness why don't we start by asking God how he wants us to pray for Glen? Let's be silent for a minute and see what happens." We prayed in silence and tried to listen. Then someone suggested that they had a sense that Bobby should pray. He was a little taken aback but was sporting and agreed. She started praying all kinds of wonderful things for Glen and was clearly nervous. "Bobby, what do you want Jesus to do for Glen?" "Heal his knee," she replied. "Well let's ask him to do that very simply." "Okay. Dear Lord, please heal Glen's knee and take away the pain."

"Glen, is anything happening?"

"Well, it feels warm."

"Let's keep praying...Remember, the effectiveness of our prayers is not based on what Glen feels but upon the promises of Jesus, and our authority to pray and defeat the enemy in his name. We check in with him because he is obviously an important part of the process, but even if he felt nothing happening, God could be doing a powerful work. Our task is to be obedient and recognize why we are doing this, but knowing at the same time there is an element of mystery that will always be present."

Glen left that evening saying his knee was feeling better. The point of the story is to illustrate that we all need encouragement in learning how to listen to God, how to pray, how to build up our faith in order to see God work and to be used by him to bring about miracles in others. It is not magic; it is the outworking of growing in a relationship with the living God day by day. Look what ice dancers accomplish after much practice together honing their routines and establishing the rapport and trust required to produce stellar performances. Trust in God grows in direct proportion to the time spent investing in the relationship and becoming familiar with who he is and who we are in relation to him. I picked up one of my philosophy books and looked at the chapter on miracles. They were buried under mountains of sentences, definitions, and intellectual musings that would have squeezed the life and faith out of any potential miracle.

●　●　●　●　●

> **Miracles are a retelling in small letters of the very same story, which is written across the whole world in letters too large for some of us to see.**
>
> —C.S. LEWIS

●　●　●　●　●

Is there a secret to discovering miracles? Maybe the answer is "Yes!" Jesus encouraged people to come to God as little children. Not childishness, but, childlikeness; the disposition of most children to innately trust, to believe with imagination, and to approach life with a genuine and open innocence. Jesus kept most of the key elements of faith very simple and direct, "What do you want me to do for you?" (Matthew 20:21, 32). "Follow me" (Matthew 9:9). "Don't be afraid" (Mark 6:36). "Come to me all you who are weary and heavy laden and I will give you rest..." (Matthew 11:28).

Is the true miracle that moment when, despite all the heartbreak, disillusionment, and darkness, we learn to accept and live with hope in the midst of ongoing death? The miracle is surely finding hope in the midst of what is not yet true—but with faith one day it will be. Is the real miracle trusting God's faithfulness even to the threshold of death and then beyond and being able to understand a life with God that transcends our present mortality?

⊕

I visited Jane every day in the afternoon. Some visits were short, others were longer. I don't recall what we talked about but I do remember that it was not long before I was wrestling with God about what he had to offer in this situation. I felt such a fraud talking about God's power and love and yet seeing nothing obvious happen. I always seemed to be explaining the mystery but never celebrating the victory. Jane was incredibly stoic and brave and politely chatted through our visits having more or less accepted her fate. She had traveled to the Far East in the hope of finding some cure but by now it was evident that nothing was working and that her time was running out—at 22 years of age!

Desperate in my turmoil to know what to do, I called a good friend and asked for advice. During the conversation I also expressed my struggle with the apparent inefficacy of this Christian ministry that seemed so pathetically inadequate. It was good to have someone to vent with but in the end nothing earth-shattering transpired.

Jane's mother suggested that we meet with another couple in the church and pray together for her daughter. She was very sensitive about not imposing anything at all upon Jane and quite rightly did not want to surround her with people desperately praying for a miracle.

Tuesday night came and we all gathered in the living room of Bill and Dawn to share our struggles and to pray for Jane. I had thought a great deal about this situation and really concluded that I did not have the faith to pray for Jane to be healed of leukemia—it was too big, and I did not want to offer false hope in a vulnerable situation. However, during my frustrated and frantic musings I recalled an incident recorded in Luke's Gospel (5:17). Friends carried a paralyzed man to a house where Jesus was busy teaching. There was such a large crowd gathered around the house that they could not even get close to the entrance. The friends had nowhere else to go and refused to be deterred. With stubborn tenacity and creativity they scrambled onto the roof, removed some of the tiles, and lowered the paralyzed man on his mat right down in front of Jesus.

Luke tells us that when Jesus saw the man at his feet and his friends staring down through the hole in the roof he was amazed at their faith. He looked at the paralyzed man and said, "Friend, your sins are forgiven." Of course all the Pharisees and spiritual leaders gathered in the room began to discuss and argue about the political correctness of Jesus' words. Without going into the details Jesus proceeded to address the paralyzed man again, "I tell you, take up your mat and go home." The man got up and the people who witnessed the event were amazed and praised God saying, "We have seen a remarkable thing today."

What about Jane?

We read that story together and I certainly could identify with those friends who did not really know what to do with their paralyzed friend except...except bring him to Jesus. And that is what it seemed we were being prompted to do. It did not matter whether we had the faith to pray for Jane to be healed of leukemia, what did matter was where we carried her. We could have left her alone and done nothing other than wait for death. We could have fed our anger and been overcome with helplessness and despair. Or we could do whatever would be constructive even though we were staring into the face of death. Reading that account in Luke encouraged us to persevere and to keep trying different approaches. What would "breaking through the roof and removing the tiles" mean in this instance?

That night in our weakness and with our little faith we carried Jane in prayer to Jesus and laid her at his feet and asked him to heal her. It did not seem like much but it felt profoundly worthwhile, to lower the one whom we loved into the presence of Jesus and to entrust her to him—whatever that might mean.

Have you ever been at a loss for words and not known how to convey what was inside? Sometimes silence, or tears, or even shouting in frustration at God is the most appropriate action we can take. I have mentioned that I went through a period of my life where I was completely broken and bereft of hope. And I'm talking about five years (not days) shrouded in various shades of black and gray. My faith in God was in shreds for most of that time. Faith in God for me has always been similar to traveling on a train with its wheels rolling "clickety-clack" along two parallel rails. One of those rails is the conscious daily sense of "faith and hope in God" that builds and maintains living out the Christian faith on a daily basis. My wheels slipped off that track completely and bounced around on rocky ground for a long time, making for a very uncomfortable ride. However, the other set of wheels never left my second "faith rail." That rail is like bedrock for me and sits secure undergirding everything I am. It is a faith that trusts that the God I have come to know, who is revealed in Jesus, is compassionate and kind, strong, and indescribably committed to holding onto me and never letting me go, no matter what I do, or what other people think. There were times where I shouted extremely abusively at God in my anger and hurt—but even as my surface emotions were almost out of control I still cried out from a deeper place, "Oh God please don't let me go. Please disregard this pathetic outburst, but I don't know how to deal with my life, my thoughts, or my emotions anymore." (I am censoring my vocabulary in the recounting of the tale.)

●　●　●　●　●

**Love anything and your heart will be wrung and possibly broken. If you want to make sure of keeping it intact you must give it to no one, not even an animal. Wrap it carefully round with hobbies and little luxuries; avoid all entanglements. Lock it up safe in the casket or coffin of your selfishness. But in that casket—safe, dark, motionless, airless—it will change. It will not be broken; it will become unbreakable, impenetrable, and irredeemable. To love is to be vulnerable.**

—C.S. LEWIS

●　●　●　●　●

My writing this book is a miracle. It is a testimony to God's faithfulness and the stability of that deeper "faith rail." It is an affirmation that God's grip on us is far more secure and strong then anything we can throw at him. It is an encouraging reminder that he doesn't take much of what we say in our emotional outbursts too seriously; or at least not seriously enough to throw us out of his presence in disgust and disown us altogether. He is more loving, mature, and stable than sometimes we might give him credit for. There is a great deal that transpired in my situation that I still do not comprehend and that remains a real mystery to me. The bottom line (or rail) though is that any relationship we have with him is based upon his stability and wisdom, not ours. That might come as a surprise for some who tend to speak and behave as if God is their servant who runs and jumps at their beck and call. I am extremely grateful indeed that my relationship with him is established in the quality and integrity of his character rather than mine—that's for sure!

We knew that Jane had leukemia and that somehow prayer was important, but how did we continue praying for God to heal her without repeating the same thing over and over again? Or how did we know what it was Jesus would pray for if he could guide our praying? Don't you sometimes quietly, or angrily, say to God, "If you were here what would you do?" At those times we gently have to remind each other, "He is here, remember his promise...'For where two or three come together in my name, there am I with them'" (Matthew 18:20). We were encouraged to come before him with a confidence that his love for Jane was greater than ours affections, and that we were not on opposing sides of her bedside engaged in a tug of war and wills. Furthermore, we sensed that he was giving us permission to be reckless and to knock a few tiles off the roof. In other words, to "for God's sake," be real and open and uninhibited in our prayers and conversations with him—he could cope with who we were and accepted us completely.

We prayed together, affirming God's faithfulness; we were going to trust him with the outcome and were quite transparent in prayer about our unbelief and fears. It's not a bad idea to be honest and open with yourself and with God...not to justify staying in a "faithless" position, but rather to acknowledge weakness and request help where you are in the present. A distraught father came to Jesus asking him to heal his son of seizures and dumbness and admitted to Jesus his unbelief, "I do believe; help me overcome my unbelief!" (Mark 9:14-29). Paul wrote to the church in Corinth that our weakness is God's opportunity to work in power because we are less likely to grab the wheel and wrench back control: "God chose the foolish things of the world to shame the wise; God chose the weak things of the world to shame the strong...so that no one may boast before him" (1 Corinthians 1:27-29).

Faith is a funny thing. Sometimes you have a sense that God is at work without being able to provide any rational explanation; that's how we parted company that evening. A few hours later, I received a call from Jane's mother who said she climbed in her car and just sat there and asked God to speak through her and he did! She made a fool of herself and alone with God she trusted him like a child and received his gift. All the pent-up emotion began to pour out of her. She found an outlet for her own pain and grief as well as new way to bring Jane before Jesus in a new freedom to pray authentically. That night she experienced a wonderful sense of God's loving presence and the gift of his empathic strengthening. Is that a miracle?

We continued to visit and pray together during the course of the following week. Jane's white blood cell count went very high; she became increasingly jaundiced, she gradually lost more of her sight and taste, and her ability to move her muscles and control them began to deteriorate. "How do you pray for God to heal someone with leukemia?" was a question that still plagued me.

When we gathered the following Tuesday we shared our experiences and feelings, our confusion, fears, and lack of faith. Then we prayed for Jane, but this time instead of "big" prayers praying for the healing of leukemia we prayed for those "smaller" things we could see. We prayed for the blood cell count, for the jaundice, for the restoration of Jane's sight and taste and muscle movement. I remember Jane's mother saying as we left that night, "I have a real sense that God has done something tonight."

Over the next ten days everything we prayed for appeared to begin to heal and be restored and we could scarcely believe what we were witnessing.

One day Jane was strong enough to be assisted into the sitting room, I played the guitar and we sang some familiar songs by Bob Dylan and John Denver that we all knew. There was laughter and an intangible sense of hope and life in the air that afternoon. I helped Jane back to her bed later in the afternoon and I think that was the last time she walked. Two days later I received a call that Jane had taken a turn for the worse and the next day she died early in the morning at about six o'clock.

The evening before she died I spent some time alone with Jane. She was conscious and we had by then met every day for almost three months. We didn't have many in-depth discussions about God, she was usually too weak or tired but she allowed me to pray; most of the time we just visited together. On this particular occasion it was clear that despite the resurgence she might not have long to live. Jane understood that reality as much as anyone can comprehend these things. I told her a story about a time when I had nearly drowned a few years earlier; I didn't know what else to do…

> I was at Cape St. Francis visiting my godfather, whose white-washed, gray-thatched holiday house overlooked the bay; famous as one of the premier surfing spots on the South African coast. From the sitting room you could see the waves pounding onto the beach leaving white strands of foam streaming behind them in the deeper water as they curled and surged up the beach. We were assured that it was safe to swim there, even though there had been a recent storm and the surf was quite high.
>
> Juliette (my future wife), William (an old school friend), and I swam into the breakers and then beyond them into deeper water. Everything appeared normal until William shouted that he was having trouble swimming back to shore. Juliette, who is a strong swimmer, swam over to him and together they moved through the breakers making some headway. I attempted to swim in but discovered that I was also being swept backwards

*out to sea, and afraid of tiring myself I decided to wait. I could feel the panic rising up through my chest to my throat and I kept telling myself to relax and someone would come and rescue me, but it was hard to stay calm. I remember thinking, God, is this the way my life is going to end? Help!*

*Then I heard a shout. As they were trying to get through the breakers Juliette had let go of William and he was being washed back to where I was paddling around putting on a brave face. "Don't panic, someone will soon come out and get us," I said as I watched Juliette finally scramble ashore and run up the beach for help. Sure enough in a matter of minutes a young surfer came riding over the waves with his board and two grateful guys hitched a ride back to dry land. It was with indescribable relief that we clutched his board and surfed to safety. One minute we were nearly drowning and the next minute we were rescued and safe.*

"Jane," I continued, "I don't begin to understand why all of this is happening, but you have tried everything and are tired. I think God is saying that he is going to come and take you to safety and a place where you will be at peace. Our perspective is so limited that we think this is the only place to be, maybe it's time to give him permission to put you on his surfboard and allow him to take you home through the waves where you don't have to struggle anymore."

Jane quietly nodded and we held hands and prayed together, both of us drowning in life and death in private and very personal ways; both of us rescued and supported in life and death in very different ways. I had tears in my eyes as I kissed her forehead and said goodbye for what was to be the last time.

There are few experiences that I can imagine are more heartbreaking and traumatic than for a parent to witness their child being wheeled out of the family home in a body bag. I was there when the attendants wheeled Jane out of the house the next morning; words then and now are totally inadequate.

It was my task to preside over the funeral for a young girl of 22. What was I going to say that would be meaningful and have integrity and maybe even hope? I wept during those days for Jane, her family, the senselessness of this death, and the frustration with a God who seemed so powerless and almost predictably inadequate when there was a real crisis at hand. I argued with him about how healing Jane would have shown so many people that he was indeed loving and powerful. Instead we always seemed to be shaking hands and making excuses with comforting words but so little power.

"Why, God? Why did you answer those prayers when Jane started getting better and then just turn it all around again and allow her to die so quickly after that? Why are you so cruel?"

I don't recall precisely how or when God's voice began to penetrate through my consciousness but he answered something like this:

*John, I did respond to the prayers, you prayed about the specific conditions relating to Jane's illness. I wanted you to know that I was listening and that I am not indifferent or powerless to act. There is a life that is far greater than that which you experience within the confines of your human body, and that is the life I have given to Jane. I have answered your prayers for her healing.*

*If you, who are for a while imprisoned on earth, could see what lies over your horizon beyond death, you would accuse me of cruelty for not allowing you to embark on that journey sooner rather than later.*

*The resurrection of Jesus showed you that in the greater perspective death is indeed just a matter of surfing through the waves into a place of warmth and safety. Know that I have heard your cry and I share your grief. I do care and love deeply and my comfort will be present as you gather to remember, grieve, and give thanks. I know what it is like to watch my only child suffer excruciating pain and one day you will understand what is impossible now to comprehend or explain. My Son Jesus died and rose from the dead so that in the midst of Jane's death you will know comfort, love, faith, hope, and even life.*

The church was filled with flowers on the day we gathered to say our last farewell to Jane. The music was powerful with grief, thanksgiving and even joy, and the words and memories people shared were genuine and true. In the sadness and the profound loss we found a measure of hope and comfort. Is that a miracle? I think so.

In contrast I have presided over many funerals where faith has not been obviously present and the absence of hope has been deafening. It is a sad predicament when one tries to hook faith and love onto an infrastructure that has never been built, and the words seem to deflate and collapse into nothingness. Faces stare back with no comprehension, wrapped in their silent pain but unable to receive the comfort of a God who is a stranger in their midst. All I could do was try to introduce them to Jesus at that place of sorrow and to encourage a relationship to begin there. After witnessing the absence of faith one begins to appreciate the miracle that is manifest with the birth of faith in a human soul.

Jake was a big, tough guy who lived and worked on the West Coast of Vancouver Island all of his life. He was emotional and kind, and had lived life to the fullest, draining every drop from each day in some wild and often very amusing way. One day his wife came to speak to me about her teenage boys being baptized. I was in the middle of a conversation when the door flew open and Jake appeared in working clothes in the doorway. "Excuse me," I said, "I am busy with…" "I know," he said, hitching his pants. "That's my wife. Thought I'd come and see what's going on here."

● ● ● ● ●

**There are two ways to live: you can live as
if nothing is a miracle; you can live as if
everything is a miracle.**

—ALBERT EINSTEIN

● ● ● ● ●

"Oh, hello, I'm John." We introduced ourselves, Jake seated himself in a chair, and we continued our discussion. What followed was some tough talk on both sides and a few more meetings with the family and the boys. We discussed Christianity and I made it clear that baptism was not something they were entitled to as if they were driving through church ordering a pizza. One of the boys told me later that he was fuming inside thinking, "Who the **## do you think you are?" I admitted I went home after one of our sessions wondering whether I had been too tough but also asking God, "How do you challenge and love and not offend all at the same time?" A few days later Jake walked down the hallway holding a booklet in his hand I had given him about knowing God. "You were right; I didn't know anything about Christianity or what I was talking about. I've asked Jesus into my life and wanted to say thank you…" He dissolved in tears and I wasn't far behind. Later he was driving down to the coast with his oldest son and both of them were quiet for a while. Then Jake said, "Well I'd better tell you…I became a Christian." "Really," said the boy with a sigh of relief and a smile, "So did I, but I wasn't sure how to tell you."

That incident happened over 15 years ago and their Christian faith is still "sticking." No question in my mind of the miracle that took place in the midst of all our fumbling and stuttering…it was wonderful! I could relate to you the story of Anne who thought she would remain a single mother forever and cried out to God in despair for years, and she is now married, with another child and a devoted husband. Or I could talk about her husband and how he came to faith or how a mutual friend of both of ours met Jesus and his life was transformed. Changes of heart and attitude are very much underestimated in qualifying for "miracle" status—when in fact they are the greatest work of God that has an impact for all eternity. The physical healings are of course dramatic and wonderful and I will pray for lots more; but our bodies still end up as ashes or in a hole in the ground when we die—apologies for being so crude.

God is so not like we are at all. We need to be continually aware of that reality. His sense of time and what is important is on a different scale to ours altogether. His agenda involves far more than whatever is the focus of our attention as we are praying for our miracle. His perspective (it's that word again) is able to comprehend the greater expanse of life beyond our finite horizons. Which is why his definition of miracle might be quite different from ours.

Frankly our view of miracles has become so childish and sensational that it often borders upon immorality. I am talking about what gets beamed into our homes from frothing TV ministries where "we're expecting and believing God for a miracle tonight" is the focus of every broadcast. I'm speaking strongly because people with genuine hurts and needs are whipped into a frenzy and paraded before TV cameras, pushed and shoved around in the name of Jesus, and treated like little more than evangelist and faith-healing fodder. I'm speaking strongly because I am convinced that so much harm is done by this prostitution that is carried out in the name of Jesus—where money, power, and human ego slink just below the "spiritual" surface like a giant anaconda in a murky jungle river (the snake again). I'm speaking strongly because many reading this book will have been "turned off" by Christianity because they too have witnessed these spectacles and shuddered in disbelief. If that is your experience then I want to offer you a genuine apology because God is not cheap or plastic, and never abuses people or masquerades their pain before TV reality shows to feed the insatiable appetite of spiritual voyeurism.

You know what is a miracle? The fact that in the midst of these presentations God does actually heal some of the people. Not because of the ministry being broadcast but despite it. Not to legitimize the whole bizarre aberration but because he deeply loves the poor woman who is in constant pain and he honors her faith and responds to her trembling outstretched hand. Jesus was often asked to "do" miracles and to perform in order to impress others. Jesus never complied because he doesn't have an ego that needed to prove anything or impress anyone. His priority is responding to the person before him appropriately and with the utmost love and sensitivity.

His priority is not "doing any miracle." The miracle is an insignificant by-product of the love of God the Father meeting the need of one of his beloved children.

I digressed because I was talking about God's ability to see the big picture and maybe a miracle in his eyes looks different than it appears to us. Let's use a familiar metaphor: the caterpillar slowly crawling along the branch of a tree and beginning to spin a cocoon into which it will disappear and "die." Imagine that we are fellow caterpillars and we are watching our friend slowly become encased in the cocoon—which we have never seen before. We pray to God to please work in Harry's life and to heal him so that he can join the rest of us further down the branch nibbling on leaves in the sun like we used to. Nothing happens, and Harry continues his work until he finally disappears and all becomes quiet and still. We grieve Harry's death and crawl off into the rising sun with heavy hearts wondering why life has to be so cruel? Why birds kill some of our friends, some fall from branches; others are crushed by huge creatures that wander around where we live? Life is tough for a caterpillar at the bottom of the garden.

• • • • •

**The most wonderful thing about miracles
is that they sometimes happen.**

—G.K. CHESTERTON

• • • • •

We're busy debating the disappointment we feel because God has not heard our prayers for Harry when the cocoon starts moving and coming to life on the branch we abandoned weeks ago. After much wriggling and squirming the most brilliantly colorful butterfly emerges, slowly tests its delicate wings, and then flies off in search of a flower. The caterpillars never see the transformation that has taken place in Harry. But God smiles as he watches his creation soar beyond its wildest dreams and fly into a bigger picture and a more majestic sky than it could ever envision from life on a branch with the vision of a caterpillar!

What happens if our lives on earth are part of a greater whole and that we are actually as limited and confined as the caterpillars were on that branch? Would the miracle of a loving God be to prevent death in a cocoon just to keep us happy within our small world? Or would the miracle be to comfort us in our limited capacity to understand and to also allow death to liberate and free others? When Jesus was resurrected he demonstrated the existence of a real life beyond death in a realm and a dimension of which we have little awareness and almost no knowledge. When Jesus appeared to the disciples it was as if Harry appeared to those caterpillars in a recognizable form to help them understand that what they thought was the end is, in fact, only the beginning of something much more exciting and wonderful.

●　●　●　●　●

### Miracles are not contrary to nature, but only contrary to what we know about nature.

—SAINT AUGUSTINE

●　●　●　●　●

The miracle is that God has promised to be with each of us throughout our lives and by our sides in the midst of all that life presents. He does not promise peace, wealth, or freedom from pain and suffering any more than a parent guarantees them for their children. He does promise, "I will be with you always, until the very end of the age" (Matthew 28:20).

As we wrestled to come to terms with how to accompany Jane through her illness God was true to his word even though it was exceedingly painful. The hard question is, *Do I want to keep Jane here for my sake, or release her to God where she can be at peace?* Maybe through death she enters into a quality of life that I would be crying out to God for if I had known what lay ahead, shouting, "Take me now, please!" That is the miracle within the midst of a multitude of unanswered questions.

I remember as a small boy lying in bed thinking, *Tomorrow I will be going to the big school. I wish I could stay at the school I'm at now forever.* That little boy was seven years old and nursery school was familiar and safe. He did not want to change and be out of his depth. That was why he was very apprehensive about moving to a much larger school. In the broad eternal reality this life is like nursery school. God sent Jesus to meet us in the playground and invites us to prepare for an unimaginable future where death is merely the door between two very different worlds.

The more we invest in our relationship with Jesus now the more we are allowed to sense and smell the fragrances of Eden blown through our lives by the wind of God's Spirit. It is similar to the heightened sensitivity people who have been at sea for a long time describe when they approach land. They can't quite see it yet but they know it is beyond the lip of the horizon.

> *I've read of sailors*
> *who have plied long voyages across wide oceans*
> *without glimpse of land nor hint of ground*
> *and when at last there is coast to explore*
> *they can sense the shore long before*
> *their eyes spy vegetation rising*
> *from that spindly distant line*
> *where sea and sky do meet*
>
> *In Africa*
> *there are times when*
> *one can smell the rain approaching*
> *before the sky grows clouds*
> *and big wet drops*
> *splash craters in the mud*
> *with God*
> *I think it's also sometimes like that as well*

*you can sense Him when definition has not yet formed*
*and understanding and faith drench your soul*
*(from the poem "River," from Into Depression and Beyond)*

Faith ultimately believes in the power, love, and faithfulness of a very gracious and kind God; it is not limited or restricted to having to understand how everything operates and hangs together. It is about knowing and trusting the one in whose hands all things work together for the good of those who are loved by him…

*PS—I am revising this for the last time before the book goes to print. The truth is, I have been learning so much more in the last year or two about how God's power and kingdom breaks through into the world we know and experience naturally. I am seeing him at work in people and through people, performing miracles of healing very powerfully and gently. I want to describe it all to you, but there isn't the time or space—so that will need to be saved for the next book. However, I couldn't refrain from telling you. There's so much more—and it's mind-boggling, wonderful, and puzzling—which leaves me more spellbound by God's love and grace than ever before!*

# 15

# Faith

I HAVE A LIFELONG FRIEND WHO LOVES TO JUMP OUT OF SMALL AIRPLANES FROM 13,000 FEET. For most of his life he has been involved with highly specialized research exploring the intricacies of the cerebral cortex in the brain. Maybe it is therefore appropriate for him to leave the world of the microscope and jump into the vastness of space and view the larger context in which we all live. I visited him recently in Europe and we half-jokingly (I think) discussed whether I might also like to jump out of the plane "for fun." When I asked whether I would take the plunge with him he said "no" (even though he has done more than 1000 jumps), it would be with an instructor "who knows what he is doing."

Fortunately or unfortunately for me the weather was questionable so I have not had the opportunity to participate in that particular activity. But I learned enough to know that I would not be pushed out of a plane at 13,000 feet with only a few instructions about what to do. Instead I would be strapped to an experienced instructor and take my first jump with nothing to do other than experience what it is like to free-fall and to cooperate and follow his instructions. That is what faith is all about—trusting in the instructor and the parachute and jumping, experiencing, and learning—repeatedly, for over 1000 jumps!

Back on earth I have always been intrigued by the grace and beauty of divers as they bounce and twist from diving boards to enter the water below with hardly a splash. Diving is not possible unless one is willing to jump and eventually leave the security of the diving board. No amount of reasoning or chatter can circumvent that reality; eventually if we want to dive then we have to pluck up the courage and jump. And if we want to dive—well, then we have to be prepared to start by making a big splash! First we begin with baby steps jumping off the side of the pool into the water. We "learn by doing," growing in confidence so we can travel between the board and into the water below without mishap. Overcoming the fear factor is important if we are going to progress further. After that hurdle has been overcome regular practice and training will lead to greater proficiency and assurance. Confidence and ability grows with regular coaching and practice. The principles are the same whether jumping into a diving pool, leaping "into thin air" from an airplane, or following Jesus.

●　●　●　●　●

**Faith is like radar that sees through the fog—the reality of things at a distance that the human eye cannot see.**

—CORRIE TEN BOOM

●　●　●　●　●

Jesus invited the disciples to "take a running jump" with him when he first called them to follow him. They were strapped to him for three years as he flung himself out of the plane into all kinds of situations demonstrating God's love, power, and faithfulness. It was only after the crucifixion, resurrection, and ascension to rejoin his Father that he sent them out as "faith instructors" having earned their "wings" after one of the most grueling boot camps in history. Yet even when he sent them off into action he whispered so that everyone could hear, "You'd better strap yourself to the Holy Spirit if you want to be effective. That's what I did when I was in your situation."

We all jump and leap into, and out of, all kinds of relationships and circumstances every single day of our lives. Everyone lives by faith and believes in something. Whether an atheist, an agnostic, a vegetarian, a fish-eating Christian, an athlete, or anyone else you can imagine. Everyone lives by faith.

Faith is the framework for reasoning and thinking that informs our actions. A key to determining what is important to a person is asking them to review their calendar and their bankbook. How do we spend our time and what do we invest our money in?

The question of knowing God and personally experiencing his reality is very similar to the process of learning to dive. No matter how much reading and talking we do, eventually each of us has to jump "and discover for ourselves" whether it works!

We often make the mistake of believing that faith means gritting one's teeth and jumping into blackness, hoping there will be something out there. That is superstition and stupidity; it is not faith with integrity. It is as outrageous as jumping out of an airplane at 13,000 feet without a parachute! Faith is what I choose to place my trust in *after* I have done the research and collected as much information as I possibly can. Such a process takes time and frequently helps to support or refute the particular object or focus of faith under examination. Some people require more evidence, others respond to their "gut feeling"; others are led by friends whom they trust and respect. The way to faith in God varies and no matter where we begin the journey, we ultimately all converge at the point of personal decision and a willingness to "jump."

In 1973 I was a student at the University of Cape Town, not very diligent in studying or focused about what I was going to do with my life. I would have called myself a committed Christian and in those days had been encouraged by the more "cool image" of the hippy Jesus people. Peace, love, and contemporary songs with guitars, leather-bound Bibles, sandals, beads, headbands, long hair, and wooden crosses on leather straps around the neck.

During the summer I hitchhiked north to visit friends and see some of the country. On my travels I passed through the town where my godfather lived (in some churches when a baby is baptized the parents ask close friends to be godparents, who agree to pray, support, and encourage the child in the Christian faith). The town is nestled inland from the humid coast of Durban at an elevation on the slopes of the Drakensberg Mountains that makes the climate far more bearable. I can't remember whether I had met Tony, my godfather before, but he had dutifully sent me cards every birthday and Christmas all of my life. He had been a school friend of my father who also grew up in that part of South Africa. Over the years they had drifted apart and did not maintain much contact.

I turned up on Tony's doorstep one day and was welcomed into his home with open arms. His wife and children were very hospitable and I enjoyed getting to know them. During the course of my visit the topic of Christianity came up in a conversation with Tony's wife. Tony was a successful general practitioner and she said something along these lines, "John, Tony is very much head of the house and a wonderful man, but this family will never take Christianity seriously unless he does." I wandered off on my travels and didn't really think too much about the conversation after that.

In those days the mail was still delivered by hand to private homes by a postman, even on a Saturday morning. One Saturday a letter addressed to me arrived totally out of the blue. It was one page and read,

> *Dear John, Being a true Christian yourself you will be interested to hear that Mary and I have had a wonderful conversion and are Christians too. I did not recognize your religious status, as I was not a Christian myself when you came to stay. Jack told me subsequently. Of course I can see it all in retrospect now. David [his son] has also committed himself…*

The following Christmas Tony and his family visited Cape Town and he related to me the story. He had a good friend (Jack) who was an enthusiastic Christian and they spent many evenings arguing and debating about the existence of God and so on. Tony claimed to be an agnostic and enjoyed the discussions with his friend—however, he dismissed much of what he heard as psychological mumbo-jumbo. But then…

> We had just come back from a holiday on the coast and Jack turned up and we had one of our usual chats, then he went home. I headed for bed and in the early morning could not get to sleep. I went into the bathroom and thought I may as well get up so I started to shave—except I couldn't finish. It was as if I was wrestling with God and I found myself weeping on my knees by the bathtub saying, "Jesus, you are Lord." When I accepted that reality as pertinent to my life my whole perspective changed.

The event was not a flash in the pan, and Tony quite unashamedly told his story when asked to do so, and he continued to grow in his new Christian faith for many years. True to his wife's prophetic words, the rest of the family embraced the faith of their father and husband as well.

●  ●  ●  ●  ●

**Where there is hatred, let me sow love. Where there is injury, pardon. Where there is doubt, faith.**

—St. Francis of Assisi

●  ●  ●  ●  ●

I lived on a community in Cape Town for nine months with Bill Burnett, the Archbishop of Cape Town. Desmond Tutu followed him in that leadership position a few years later. Bill told me how he came to appreciate that Christianity is a living relationship with Jesus Christ who empowers people with his Holy Spirit. Bill had spent years on committees in the church hierarchy and worked with great passion and conviction for political change and an end to apartheid. Eventually he became Bishop of Grahamstown and that was where his life changed, or rather was turned inside out! By then

Bill was in his 50s, had done well in his "career," and was greatly respected. He told me about what happened then.

> *I was sitting reading the Sunday paper around midday when I felt God prompting me to go to my chapel. That kind of thing didn't happen to me but I could not shrug it off or ignore it. Reluctantly I put down the paper and went to my chapel and when I was up at the front it felt like I was pushed to the floor. A great power came over me and I started praying with a new vibrancy, freedom, and enthusiasm; and it was as if a deep refreshing well had opened up inside me. My whole focus was turned to Jesus and to worship him. Now I was a respectable liturgical bishop at the time and this event turned my whole life and ministry upside down and inside out. Thank God!*

Bill subsequently became a very significant leader of Christian renewal in southern Africa for the next 10 to 15 years. He never doubted the authenticity and integrity of that Sunday surprise from God. I saw the results over many months and he had a huge impact on my life. There were so few Christian men around with passion and integrity who were role models one wanted to follow. Bill told a story of when he was visiting New York attending a conference. He was seated at a restaurant dressed in a suit wearing his purple bishop's shirt when the waitress approached him and said, "And pray, Robin Redbreast, what kind of a holy man are you?" Then he would laugh because he loved to poke fun at the self-importance of church officials and reflected, "...and I wondered, *Well, what kind of a holy man am I?*"

In Bill's case he had a genuine Christian faith but during the course of his life it was reinvigorated and revitalized. There are many "tired" Christians hanging around the fringes of churches who have lost sight of what inspired them at first. It is a sad reality that many church activities are also tired and consequently everything limps along with little sense of life or joy.

The key to a rejuvenated faith is to find a plane, climb to 13,000 feet, and rediscover the thrill and terror of the first jump all over again. Peel away all the layers that have grown over and encrusted your faith and look for Jesus again. Let him know that you're as bored and disenchanted with the relationship as he probably has become. Take responsibility for undoubtedly having followed your own footpaths for quite a while, and then give him permission to set you firmly back on both of your "faith rails." Be expectant and watch what happens. Don't worry, the parachute will billow open above your head and you'll begin to feel the adrenalin of faith surging through you as you rediscover your first love—after you leap! (Then please write to me at www.googleforgod.com and tell me the story—maybe we can write another book about jumping into faith!)

If Roundup is very effective at killing weeds right down to their roots, then pride is the equivalent "killer" when it comes to building a strong and worthwhile spiritual faith. "Feeling stupid," being "out of my depth," saying, "I'm so nervous!"...are all normal side effects of "faith in action." It is all about displaying a willingness to learn by being vulnerable and open to taking a few calculated risks. The disciples did not learn by spending three years with Jesus sitting at desks reading and listening to lectures in the Galilee Fishers of Men Bible College. They learned by talking, reading the Scriptures, making lots of mistakes, and being mentored and coached by Jesus on the road. The reason so much of our Christian ministry is so dull and unattractive is that many "disciples" have very little life experience and enormous amounts of "theology" and "Bible classes." I am the first to advocate education, but learning Jesus' style involves doing and being, reflecting, unlearning, and seeing beyond the obvious and the predictable, the safe. It means venturing beyond the crumbling edges of the deep ruts formed by religious wheels incessantly turning in unquestioned traditions.

A hallmark of dead faith and dry rot are people constantly bickering about doctrine and theology. We teach that God's ways are not our ways and his thoughts are not our thoughts, that we see through a glass darkly and that we do not have perfect knowledge. Then, as if we have 20/20 vision, we tie up our beliefs so tightly that faith is squeezed out and no mystery or surprises are left. When that occurs, life and joy vanish in a heap of dust and ashes. In desperation we resort to thumping the desk, haranguing the "godless world out there" and withdrawing even further from the people who need salt the most.

Christian faith is only effective when it remains in the hands of Jesus. Faith in the Bible or the Holy Scriptures sounds great but it is misguided. It is as ridiculous as saying in a restaurant that I believe in the menu, talking about what it says all night long, then paying a bill for the items we selected to talk about! Tell me about the food that the menu describes and that you actually consumed and enjoyed! Whet my appetite with your excitement and then I'll accompany you to the restaurant and "taste and see" for myself. But if you don't have the honesty and courage to live the faith you talk to me about the hypocrisy will soon be more obvious than we would like to acknowledge. "Nonbelievers" can discern sawdust and emptiness a mile off and most of the time they are absolutely correct in steering clear of a superficial faith that will only get them into more trouble and feed their cynicism of "religion." Sound like tough talk? It is. I've been there and have been as guilty as anyone else. But I've learned that the beginning of change starts with owning my responsibility rather than blaming others.

One of the aspects of public ministry I was most nervous about was public speaking. I was terrified of standing up in front of people. Thirty years later people flatter me, "It's easy for you, John; it's so natural." Well, that was not true. It took time, practice, and many awkward moments before I learned to relax and think on my feet in front of people. The bottom line is that the majority of us are not going to wake up one morning and automatically be good at something just because we asked God to work in us. We're not going to bypass fear and feelings of awkwardness. The process of learning skills is usually the way God refines us and keeps us humble. God actually has quite a sense of humor at times—his teaching is not necessarily stern and harsh at all!

I had been living on community with Bill Burnett and other staff for about six months when during one of our conversations over lunch I said that I didn't feel I was being challenged enough; always an unwise state-ment to make! Bill and his team were about to travel to Durban to lead a week of teaching and "renewal of faith" in a local church. In the light of my utterance he decided that maybe I should come along as well and help lead the opening worship, as I played the guitar and sang. As soon as the invitation was given I knew God was onto something and that this trip was more about him working on me then anything I had to offer. Frankly I was still a bit nervous about all the talk about God empowering us with his Holy Spirit and working through us. I mean I believed it, but Bill was taking it to another level—where he actually expected something to happen! I was used to people praying but not expecting anything vis-ible or tangible to take place—it was much safer that way, but also very predictable and boring.

●    ●    ●    ●    ●

I have one life and one chance to make it count for something...I'm free to choose what that something is, and the something I've chosen is my faith. Now, my faith goes beyond theology and religion and requires considerable work and effort. My faith demands—this is not optional—my faith demands that I do whatever I can, wherever I am, whenever I can, for as long as I can with whatever I have to try to make a difference.

—JIMMY CARTER

●    ●    ●    ●    ●

On the first night of the teaching week Bill said that he would talk for a while after the opening worship. When he was finished he would invite people to come to the front if they wanted prayer for God to work more powerfully in their lives. He then proceeded to include me among those who would pray with anyone who came forward. My heart sank, I didn't want to do that—nothing ever happens when I pray. But I couldn't get out of it; after all he had paid for my ticket to come along and I had said that I wanted to be stretched! I voiced my concerns and Bill merely smiled and said God would equip, laid hands on me and prayed, and off we went. I didn't feel any different at all.

To cut an even longer story shorter, when the moment came for people to come forward I was sort of hoping that they wouldn't. Unfortunately that was not the plan and I ended up with some poor fellow who had to suffer through my stuttering and awkward counsel and prayer. It all felt very pathetic to me and I finished the evening quite dejected. The following night the same thing happened. This time I was with a lady who felt that she was spiritually "stuck" and for some reason I sensed that God wanted her to receive more of himself and his gifts; except I didn't pray for that kind of thing. I looked up and Bill "just happened" to be walking down the aisle. I waved him over and told him that this lady would like prayer for God's power to work in her life in a new way. Bill smiled and told me to sit on the other side of her. He was a tall and very gentle man and he spoke with her for a while and removed any sense at of anxiety or pressure.

He talked to her mostly about God's great love for her and his faithfulness and then suggested that we pray and trust God to answer however he wanted to. She might receive a gift right then, or some time in the future and encouraged her not to worry about that. We prayed and nothing visible happened; Bill confidently and joyfully thanked God that he would respond to the cry of her heart, gave her a hug, and went on his way quite assured that God would honor what we had requested.

Meanwhile, as Bill had been praying God seemed to speak to me quite clearly and gently, "John, you thought that if you prayed for that woman nothing would happen, and if Bill, the Archbishop of Cape Town, prayed it would make the difference, didn't you?" "Well, I guess so," I muttered. "What happens when someone is healed, who gets the glory?" "You do, Lord, no matter who prays," I replied. "John, if that is true then what's the problem? Your task is to bring people to me and allow me to determine how I will answer and what will happen. Stop worrying about the answers, just do your part—bring people to me and don't be so afraid."

I was stunned and thrilled, relieved and excited all at the same time. God had actually spoken to me! For the rest of that week I relaxed into doing just as I had been told—it was so liberating not having to play God or be responsible for outcomes. My job was to love people where they were, to assure them of his love and faithfulness, and then to provide an opportunity for all of us to chat together (pray). That encounter in 1978 expanded my understanding of faith in a profound way, and set me free to expect and ultimately see God work so much more powerfully in the years ahead. As with everything else in life, faith grows with exercise, mistakes, practice, wise mentoring, and coaching. We are usually much more teachable when we have been on the road for a while. We always think we know more than is really the case when we hide behind desks and pulpits and dissect the theory in an attempt to arrive at some purely distilled… what?

●　●　●　●　●

### Faithless is he that says farewell when the road darkens.

—J.R.R. TOLKIEN

●　●　●　●　●

It is impossible for the human mind and psyche to rationally lead to proof of God's existence or to the door of knowing God to be true. The furthest we can get is to a place of recognizing our finite limitations as we stand on the threshold where we are willing to jump. That is what we do in human relationships when we arrange to meet someone for coffee, when we enroll for new courses, or when we turn up for work. All those activities include a component of faith that commits us to an action in the belief that other consequences and desirable events will follow as a result. In fact, I would venture to suggest that the elements of life that most inspire us and make us truly "alive" would wither and die if they were reduced to mere reasoning and facts.

This book has attempted to provide a loose framework into which faith might grow and be developed. It has taken seriously the need to respect each person in their quest for meaning and their exploration of belief. It has also taken seriously the fact that Christianity is not about blind faith or boring ritual. Rather, at the heart of the Christian faith there is enough evidence, history, human testimony, and integrity to demand at least serious consideration.

But ultimately to know God as real demands a leap of faith, and a calculated risk.

The dilemma each of us cannot avoid is that whatever happens we will jump. The question is, in which direction? To ignore God and jump into another plan of my own design also demands a leap of faith, and is definitely a calculated risk. I was chatting with someone recently who said, "I follow God in my own way." It is actually a contradiction in terms because either you follow God in his way or you're following something else in your own way—probably your shadow.

Personally, I have concluded that it takes less faith and makes more sense for me to leap toward God than to entrust myself to the alternative—faith as I see it.

My journey with God has now traversed more than 40 years and has been anything but straightforward, naïve, or a simplistic crutch. I have known peaks of great joy and fulfillment when it felt like I was touching Jesus and was close to heaven. I have also experienced very deep valleys and deserts of undulating emptiness where it seemed that God had disappeared and faith was a cruel joke. I have sat and listened with people who have wrestled with problems of addiction, abuse, despair, indescribable grief, and many other of life's challenges. On countless occasions with no clue what to do or say myself we have simply prayed together, "Jesus, thank you for your love for…, please come into this situation and…"

Many times I prayed in faith without emotion and without any great revelation. I could write another book about the way God met people and made all the difference in the world to their lives. How he healed deep wounds of abuse and set people free from emotional captivity; sometimes quickly, and at other times gradually and quietly over months and even years.

Where do we go from here? I don't know how to answer that for you. I'll leave you with a challenge though. If you want to know God as real you can rest assured he wants to meet you more than halfway. You have nothing to lose and everything to gain by quite simply asking him to give you clues about his reality over the next four weeks. (Yes, set a timeline—it will be more interesting!) Try saying every day, "God, if you are real please show me something of yourself today and help me recognize those moments." It won't hurt to read the accounts of Jesus' life in modern English (Matthew, Mark, Luke, and John). It will also be helpful to have a friend you can chat with, argue and debate with, and generally engage in conversation with to honestly share your thought processes along the way. It has to make sense for you, and no one else can do that work for you.

● ● ● ● ●

**Faith is taking the first step even when you don't see the whole staircase.**

—MARTIN LUTHER KING JR.

● ● ● ● ●

Watch and see what happens. He'll start cropping up in conversations; you may notice a book you could read, you may even find something inside you is beginning to change or open up. Enjoy the process and at least give God a chance. The reality is that if God is real he is already trying to get your attention—you're reading this book and have already earned a medal by getting this far! He's not the one playing hide-and-go-seek; he's just waiting to show us how to see life in a whole new dimension and how to live life on earth in a new and more meaningful way.

Zacchaeus was a small man with something of an inferiority complex even though he was rich. To add to his problems he was a tax collector and therefore about as popular as a skunk in a crowd, as everyone knew that his wealth came from their excessive taxes. He learned that Jesus was going to be in town and he wanted to see him, except he could not even catch a glimpse of him through the crowd that had already gathered. But Zacchaeus was not easily deterred. Throwing dignity to the wind he ran ahead, climbed a tree, and perched there like an old vulture, awaiting the arrival of Jesus.

When Jesus walked by he saw Zacchaeus in the tree and called his name saying that he wanted to stay at his house that day. The crowd muttered in disdain that Jesus would stay at such a man's house. Zacchaeus scrambled down, no doubt more surprised than those in the crowd and probably quite flustered. The impact of Jesus' visit on Zacchaeus was that his life was turned upside down and he immediately reimbursed all those whom he had cheated. Giving away money must mean that God is at work!

God does not care about reputation or what other people think of you and me. He wants to respond and he longs to come into our homes and be our friend. If you and I do what we can to get a glimpse of Jesus—climb a tree or whatever, he will do the rest. But the principle is always the same. Jesus did not stand at the tree and wag his finger at Zacchaeus and tell him what a corrupt person he was. Instead he respected him and came to where he lived.

By showing him unconditional love openly and publicly he set Zacchaeus free to choose another path. God always begins with loving a person and embracing them wherever they are, not by focusing on the rules they have broken. Relationship is the essence of Christianity and life with God, not religion.

Jesus said,

> Ask and it will be given to you; seek and you will find; knock and the door will be opened to you. For everyone who asks receives; he who seeks finds, and to him who knocks the door

*will be opened. Which of you if his son asks for bread will give him a stone? Or if he asks for a fish will give him a snake? If you then, though you are evil, know how to give good gifts to your children, how much more will your Father in heaven give good gifts to those who ask him!*

—MATTHEW 7:7-11

16

# Up Close and Personal

THE COAST IS A RUGGED AND CROOKED LINE OF BEACHES, ROCKS, AND STUNTED CEDARS LEANING INTO THE OCEAN ON THE WEST SIDE OF VANCOUVER ISLAND. Two people stand on the beach and prepare to swim to Japan. Both have been preparing for this moment for the past two years, and are committed to the task at hand with every fiber of their being. Their goal is to swim to Japan and after a few speeches and tearful farewells they dive into the surf and head out to sea. One swimmer survives for about two hours in the cold water and then drowns. The other manages to hang on for six hours because she is a stronger swimmer and an Olympic athlete. However, she also eventually succumbs and drowns as well.

The beach from where they began their futile journey is lined with memorials commemorating others who have been brave enough to accept the challenge to swim to Japan—and drowned. The strange thing is that it didn't matter who the person was, how rich or poor, how educated or athletic, how sincere, how hard they tried, or what network of people they knew. Two miles off shore they all looked the same in the water; everyone was out of their depth attempting a journey they were never equipped to complete on their own in the first place.

The reason we will reject the legitimacy of my story about swimming to Japan is that we know the task is absolutely impossible. Nobody would ever be so foolish as to seriously try to persuade others to support them in such an endeavor, doomed from the start. Attempting to find God alone, be acceptable to him, and earn our way to heaven on our own terms is equally futile. If Japan were heaven, then God sent Jesus in a boat to fetch us because he never intended for anyone to drown trying to get there. Imagine his frustration when people splutter responses to his invitation for them to utilize his boat: "I'm sincerely trying." "Thanks, but I'll do it my way." "I don't believe you will take me to Japan. I'll swim and take my chances." Grace and mercy respond, "Get in the boat. It has been provided for you. God wants you to enjoy the trip, not merely survive—and it's free, paid for by Jesus!"

● ● ● ● ●

**I believe in Christianity as I believe that the sun has risen: not only because I see it, but because by it I see everything else.**

—C.S. LEWIS

● ● ● ● ●

God sent Jesus on a rescue mission, not on a publicity stunt because he needs our vote or craves our attention. His rescue is offered to everyone. I do not believe that all who are not "Christians" are condemned and "go to hell." That conclusion is far too obvious and too easily aligned with our somewhat superficial mind-sets and human ways of doing things. The grace and mercy of God is mind-blowing in its desire to reach out and embrace all of us. However, at the same time he is not indifferent to our attitudes, and there is definitely freedom to reject God's initiative. I don't understand how God's justice and mercy deals with all the world religions, but I am convinced that the one who is revealed in Jesus is perfectly loving and perfectly fair. Whatever his solution, I would rather entrust myself to that outcome than any silly little equation I can figure out on this side of eternity where I try to decide who are the winners and losers.

Returning to the story Jesus told of the Prodigal Son: The son has left home and squandered his inheritance in a foreign land. Eventually when all his resources have run out he "changes his mind" (repents) and decides to come home. But he is convinced that he is going be in a very awkward predicament with his father and therefore he rehearses a speech and drags his feet as he gets closer to home. In every other world religion the prodigal son has to do everything to get back to God (who is never even discussed in terms of love or with a personality). The son has to struggle through numerous reincarnations, or obey multiple laws, or observe specific rituals in order to become worthy. In the Christian revelation of God (only through Jesus), God the Father runs out to meet him, embraces him, and throws a party and a feast! All that God the Father was looking for in the son was that moment of "coming to his senses," turning toward home, repenting, call it whatever you will. Once he discerns that intention in the heart and action of any of his children he runs down the road to share "the biggest hug in the world!"

When you know you have "screwed up" and you are received home with that kind of welcome, do you think you might get a little emotional, or have a new understanding and experience of worship? You won't be able to help yourself. Furthermore, you and I will also have an enormously increased capacity to love others in similar predicaments. Particularly when we meet future prodigals who are still partying in the foreign land and have no idea that the greatest love of their lives is standing on the threshold of a mansion watching and waiting and longing for their homecoming as well. Maybe you can tap them on the shoulder or show them how to get home? That's exciting as well—similar to being present at the resurrection, or the birth of a baby!

One of the great hallmarks of Jesus' public ministry was his willingness to touch and heal people anywhere and at any time. His interpersonal style and interaction was such a contrast to the religious leaders' obsession with the law that placed adherence to rules as more important than the needs of people themselves. If we want an insight into God's heart and his priorities we only need to look at how Jesus spent his time and how he responded to people. And these were not necessarily people with any special claim or status; they were ordinary men and women hassling through life with all its joys and curve balls.

● ● ● ● ●

**Success is not final, failure is not fatal: it is the courage to continue that counts.**

—WINSTON CHURCHILL

● ● ● ● ●

There are two words that describe the heart of God that Jesus revealed. Words that absolutely contradict the knee-jerk reaction you and I frequently have when we think of God. Our reactions are impacted and informed to a significant degree by a tradition and a church that has tended by and large to use rules and "the Scriptures" to define God and his purposes. How many of us have been told that Christianity means not dancing, not smoking, not drinking, not going here, and not going there?

That is exactly what my 17-year-old daughter told me last week when I asked her about church. She said, "Dad, they all think they are so holy and I just feel out of place and judged because I am not doing what they think I should be doing—and it's so boring there. No one is my age." It is not an attractive picture and Jesus did not speak in that manner at all. This is an understandable tension and I know from my own experience as a leader how easy it is to unwittingly slide into the habit of telling people what they should be doing and using the rules and guilt to motivate change. Such tactics might work for a short while but they seldom have lasting value. Jesus' style was to emotionally "connect" with the person first by communicating unconditional and genuine love and acceptance of them as they are when he met them—*before* they changed!

The two words that most offended the Pharisees of Jesus day and certainly cause us problems are *mercy* and *grace*. At a superficial glance they can be misunderstood as "letting people get away with things," or being "weak and not tough enough." The exact opposite is true. It does not take much discipline or character to seek revenge or to act out "an eye for an eye" form of justice. It demands great maturity and wisdom to hang on a cross stinking of sweat and aching from multiple whip lashes and festering wounds, and say, "Father, forgive them—they have no idea what they are doing."

We are surrounded by expectations and attitudes that tell us that we have to work and earn our way through life and that nothing is free. However, when it comes to God the exact opposite is true. We cannot earn his acceptance or his love or his favor—precisely because the standards are too high. That is why he comes to us and invites us to receive reconciliation with him on the basis of what Jesus has done for us. If all of us are only accepted and reconciled to God because of what Jesus has done, where on earth do any of us receive the right or the gall to be self-righteous or even judgmental?

I have met with people in the midst of great crisis and turmoil including all kinds of abuse, murder, abortion, addictions, betrayals, and other secrets they have never divulged to anyone else. It does not matter what their "sin" or problem has been, as soon as a member of "their" family is involved in one of these behaviors then their attitude invariably begins to change. The judgmental response quite rightly and understandably begins to soften into an attitude praying and longing for grace and mercy to be shown. There is a creative tension between recognizing the need for "justice" as well as a plea for mercy and understanding. "Because he or she is not all bad…" Or, "They were going through a really rough time…" "I know that if they had another chance it would be different…" "Please, please don't condemn them forever!" "Is there any hope for me now? I am so ashamed."

If that wonderful tendency toward mercy and grace arises in our hearts and minds over our loved ones, then maybe we can understand how God feels over all of his creation. He has no favorites. George Bush, Osama bin Laden, Adolf Hitler, Mother Teresa, Nelson Mandela, Mahatma Gandhi, Idi Amin…and anyone else you can think of…are all alienated sons and daughters in his creation. They are all his "lost" children, so he cannot not love them. Is that sentimental nonsense? I don't think so. Each one is a created human being who once fed from their mother's breasts and slept in her arms. Any one of us could have rocked them to sleep and delighted in their gurgles and cries.

"But wait a minute," you protest. "The Bible is full of references stating that faith in Jesus is the gateway to receiving the right to become children of God, like John 1:12. Or as Paul says in Galatians 4:7, 'You are no longer a slave, but a son [daughter], and since you are a son [daughter], God has made you also an heir.' If that is true, how can you maintain that everyone is a child of God?"

It seems to me that our human nature gravitates toward exclusion or a negative interpretation too quickly. I think we are holding two truths in tension here. First, if God created all things, then every living creature is his creation whether they acknowledge him or not. The fact that his creation has become estranged, kidnapped, imprisoned, or lives in self-declared rebellion does not alter their status at the heart of their Creator's design and purpose. In fact, it is because he loves them so much that he does something about it. His intent and desire is to rescue his creatures and restore them to a renewed and fully conscious relationship between Father and child. The fact that some refuse his initiative or invitation breaks his heart precisely because he knows who they truly are—and this is a reality and truth they cannot comprehend for themselves.

Therefore every life is a gift from God. Which is why John tells us that God loved the world so much that he sent his Son into the world, so that whoever believes in him will have everlasting life (see John 3:16). Jesus lived, died, and was resurrected for every life—a tangible, historically verifiable expression of God's proactive initiative of love seeking to rescue and restore his beloved.

Paul was profoundly impacted by this revelation (we have already discussed his life-changing experience on the Damascus Road). Little wonder that he would write from jail in his letter to the Romans,

> *You see, at just the right time, when we were still powerless, Christ died for the ungodly. Very rarely will anyone die for a righteous man, though for a good man someone might possibly dare to die. But God demonstrates his own love for us in this: While we were still sinners, Christ died for us.*
>
> —ROMANS 5:6-8

However, no matter how proactive God was through Jesus, his initiative and sacrificial love await a response from us (individually and personally) in order for the impact to be fully appropriated and activated. The adults those babies became is testimony to freedom of choices…and the perversity that is also rampant in the world outside of Eden. That is why Jesus would weep over Jerusalem and cry, "How often I have longed to gather your children together, as a hen gathers her chicks under her wings, but you were not willing!" (Luke 13:34).

That is why we will get so exasperated and indignant when serial killers such as Ted Bundy confessed become "a Christian" on death row—and we are cynical. We want to see justice. The fact is, Bundy *did* die for the murders he committed (despite becoming a Christian and being forgiven, there were still consequences that could not be avoided). But we want to take it further and tell God to throw him into the fire of hell because people like him don't deserve mercy. The sentiments are no sooner out of our mouths than God places his arm tenderly around us and shows us the influences and reasons that contributed to Bundy's behavior. Before long we are in tears as he says, "Of course I don't condone any of the crimes for one moment, but what would you have done? Let me review your life under the same scrutiny and with the same legalism. Where have you failed and how have you screwed up on opportunities and the potential that was given to you? What stopped you from turning out like he did? It is mercy, and "…there but for the grace of God…"

Mercy and grace makes sense to fathers and mothers in the deepest way, not condoning the wrongdoing but always loving the wrongdoer. That is why God continues to invite you and me into his boat with Jesus no matter what we have done, because no one sails with Jesus having earned, paid for, or deserving his or her seat.

Christianity and the revelation of God's love through Jesus Christ are unique. Christianity is indeed good news! Christianity fulfills the human desire for union with God that is only partially visible in many other religious teachings. However, this is the only place where we are invited to climb into "God's boat"—*before* we die, because he wants us to start a relationship with him sooner rather than later. When we "start now" then death becomes merely a transition into another realm of being that is indeed filled with mystery. The resurrection of Jesus reveals his transcendence over death and gives us reason to entrust ourselves to him for that part of the journey as well.

* * * * *

**Everyone has inside of him a piece
of good news. The good news is that
you don't know how great you can be!
How much you can love! What you can
accomplish! And what your potential is!**

—ANNE FRANK

* * * * *

God's ultimate purpose is to support and empower us to live as well as we can in this imperfect world; it is not about making everything perfect. If the world were perfect and fair, then Jesus would not have been crucified and that certainly was not fair. God does understand what it means to not be respected, to be treated with cruelty and insensitivity, or to be rejected and misunderstood. He knows what human attitudes are like at their worst and he is under no illusion about the capacity we have to cause harm. Despite all that reality, and because of it, he is still creation's Father and therefore reaches out to each one of us through Jesus (because otherwise we would not know what he is saying or doing). He extends grace and mercy to all of us by name with an invitation to travel with him from now on. There are no proxy invitations given or received, each individual "lives or dies" with the choices they make.

We mentioned earlier that Mark's Gospel is believed to rely heavily upon the experiences of Simon Peter and it bears his fingerprints on every page. It is short, rough in language, and is the least sophisticated of the four books describing the life of Christ. It is similar in essence to the fisherman that Simon Peter always was at heart. He was a no-nonsense, hands-on man who sometimes acted impetuously, without taking the time to think of the implications or consequences of what he was saying or doing. Jesus loved him for his courage and willingness to try his hand at anything. Peter was the one who dared get out of the boat and walk on water with Jesus. He boasted that he would never betray Jesus and failed miserably. Peter was so passionate and so obviously imperfect he has always been a wonderful inspiration to me.

In his first chapter, Mark recounts the beginning of Jesus' public ministry as he invites a bunch of fishermen to accompany him. Simon Peter is among them and they walk to Capernaum. Jesus spent some time in the synagogue teaching and healed one particular individual with a demonstration of great authority. Simon Peter's house was across the road from the synagogue in Capernaum and his mother-in-law was ill. Maybe prompted by what he had witnessed, Simon Peter mentioned to Jesus that his mother-in-law was sick with a fever. Jesus' response to Simon Peter is gracious, caring, and very understanding.

What would you have done if it had been you and one of your parents was ill? Most of us would probably brush it aside and say that it was not that bad and besides, Jesus is too busy to be bothered. Others are suffering more and we don't want to create a scene. During my years of counseling two themes surfaced repeatedly in conversations. One is how quickly most of us tend to trivialize and dismiss what is of genuine concern to us. And the other is how we assume that God is not interested in anything about us apart from what we do wrong and other "more important" matters.

Jesus did have time, and he followed Simon Peter to where his mother-in-law lay sick. "He went to her, took her hand and helped her up. The fever left her" (Luke 4:38-39). That's what God does. He cares about us, our children, our parents, and all those things and people that are important to us. Jesus reveals the heart of the Father—and that's how loving father's respond to their children. The fact that we don't always understand what he is doing, or why he seems somewhat inactive, is another matter. What we are talking about here is God's heart. I have certainly struggled with wondering why God cannot be more responsive at times; however, I am confident that if I were to sit down and question him, the quality of love and care exhibited in Jesus would come through.

Jesus called Simon Peter to follow him and he demonstrated great leadership by being sensitive and responsive to Simon Peter's family needs. He is always interested in the whole person, not merely segments of life in isolation. God is not confined to the compartments we tend to erect around our lives; business, home, work, sport, sacred, secular, racial, national, age, gender, and so the list goes on. How many times do you hear it said, "That's business." I have heard those words uttered by people working in Christian organizations and in many other businesses as well. What does it mean? God does not give two codes of ethics—one for business and one for the rest of life. He does not distinguish between secular and sacred. The phrase is a false distinction that legitimizes nothing that is not consistent with the character and standards of God the Father. The trouble is it demands integrity and guts to live them out and to maybe sacrifice a little profit or extra income, and therein lies the rub.

In the next chapter of Mark's Gospel we find Jesus on the shores of Galilee walking and teaching with a random crowd who had gathered around him. It is easy to overlook the point that much of what Jesus accomplished happened on the road, in people's houses, and on the way to somewhere else. That tells us that God is not confined to religious buildings and that he is also quite comfortable bypassing religious leaders if they obstruct his ability to care for people. In this instance he saw Levi sitting in his tax-collector booth. If Jesus were concerned about popularity he certainly would have ignored this man. The tax collectors had a reputation for gouging people and were extremely unpopular with the local population.

Jesus looks at people from the inside out and responds to what he discerns. He really does not care what others think when he takes the initiative and approaches Levi. He not only engages him in conversation, but he also invites Levi to work with him. A short time later they are eating together at Levi's home. How do you think Levi felt when Jesus first approached him? "Here's another God guy who is going to harangue me, judge me, malign and humiliate me, I bet." Instead Jesus calls him by name, and I'm sure he smiles while he speaks to him, and tells him that he needed his help. I suspect that most of us react to any mention of God in a manner similar to how Levi may have responded. *What negative aspect of my life is going to be under scrutiny now?* Or *Where have I failed to comply again?*

The good news is that such images are distorted and are invariably false projections that Jesus turned upside down. He revealed a God who is so much nicer and more gracious than many of the people who speak in his name give him credit for. The reason is that we cannot handle Jesus being so gracious and we keep whispering in his ear, "But do you know who that is? Are you aware of what she has done? Do you know how he treats people?" The problem is that Jesus turns back and whispers quietly, "If I cannot extend mercy to him or her, where does that leave you? Look at all the people whispering in my ear telling me not to talk to you." And with a nudge and a wink he exhorts us to leave the judging to him; but it's hard and only God's Spirit can really help us deal with that judgmental tendency of ours.

I have been separated and subsequently divorced for almost ten years. Because I was a pastor I naturally had to resign my position, as my life was falling apart, and it took me many years to regroup. But the rumors and judgmental attitudes and statements one hears are quite astounding in terms of distortion or conclusions reached based on half-truths. Ten years later I still encounter attitudes of self-righteous ignorance that leave me shaking my head. Everything in me wants to lash back but there is a point where Jesus yanks on the chain and commands, "Enough!"

While they are sharing a meal, the other Pharisees question Jesus about the company he is keeping because they have labeled Levi a "sinner." Jesus' response is to merely underline his purpose for being on earth by using an analogy from medicine. Just as it is only sick people who need a doctor, so he has come to help the sinners. This statement is stunning in a culture where God was defined in terms of rituals and rules. The leaders spent much of their time obsessing about who is righteous and who is not. Jesus was in fact saying that God wanted to help all those who had failed to keep the rules and who were defined by the Pharisees as "sinners." He called disciples from fishing boats and tax-collecting booths, from brothels and market squares, men, women, and teenagers. The message is simple, obvious, encouraging, and clear: God calls everyone and anyone, anywhere and at any time. He steadfastly refuses to endorse the false criteria human institutions too frequently become enslaved by, and the straitjackets they try to confine him to. Mercy and grace are only possible when God's Spirit empowers our earthenware efforts. Left to our own resources we soon resort to rules, rationalization, power trips, and excuses without ceasing.

Luke was a doctor, an educated physician who recorded his account of Jesus' life and ministry with a great sensitivity to the Gentiles (non-Jews) and also with attention to medical details. The compassion and mercy of God are not lost in his accounts of how Jesus responded to people either.

On one occasion Jairus, a leader of the local synagogue, interrupted Jesus. He pleaded with Jesus to come and heal his 12-year-old daughter who appeared to be dying, and was understandably frantic with worry and concern. Jesus started to follow him to his house with a whole crowd of people jostling around him. If you've ever been in a crowd in the Middle East you will know that this would not have been a quiet, controlled group! In the midst of all the pandemonium, with a grief-stricken father probably talking his head off, Jesus suddenly stopped. Turning around he asked who had touched him. Nobody responded and Peter offered his dubious wisdom yet again, saying in effect, "Sir, there is a whole crowd of people here crowding around and touching you all the time..." (Matthew 9:18-22).

But Jesus was operating with a much deeper and more heightened sensitivity. Someone's heart and hand had reached out in a manner that no one else had, and he felt it. Sure enough when Jesus repeated with absolute assurance that someone had touched him because he had felt power leaving him, a woman stepped forward. Luke tells us that she had a condition that caused bleeding for 12 years and was probably too embarrassed to face Jesus. Again, she also no doubt felt that he was too busy looking after an important person's daughter who was dying; she could not possibly bother him. Despite all her inner turmoil she reached out in desperation, touched his cloak, maybe whispering, "God please heal me, help me!" As soon as she secretly reached out, Jesus responded.

In front of everyone Jesus had her tell him what had transpired and we read that she was shaking and trembling from anxiety and nervousness. Jesus responded with great tenderness by calling her "daughter," affirming her incredible act of faith, and blessing her with the words "Take heart, daughter, your faith has healed you."

● ● ● ● ●

You have brains in your head.
You have feet in your shoes.
You can steer yourself any direction you choose.
You're on your own, and you know what you know.
And you are the one who'll decide where you'll go.
Oh the places you'll go.

—DR. SEUSS

● ● ● ● ●

Why did Jesus insist on stopping and embarrassing her in front of everyone? Often we reach out to God for one thing and he wants to respond with much more. The woman wanted physical healing but Jesus took that healing even deeper. By talking to her and listening as he did, he touched her spirit that had been filled with shame and a constant desire to hide in the crowd. Jesus noticed her and acknowledged her publicly. I guarantee from that moment on she was no longer the woman in the village filled with shame and shunned by all. Instead, she was known as the woman who had reached out and touched Jesus and been wonderfully healed by him. God always has time; it's amazing but true, even for you and me with all our embarrassing conditions and habits. He will never humiliate us, but he will allow us to be awkward if it means he can accomplish more in our lives in the long run.

What about Jairus? Imagine his concern as Jesus stops to attend to this woman. If I had been him I would have thought to myself, *Never mind her, she's just a...My daughter is dying!* To make matters worse, when Jesus was speaking to the woman someone came to Jairus and told him his daughter had died, so it was too late anyway (Matthew 9:18-26).

How would you have felt as you looked over Jesus' shoulder at the woman who had touched him, smiling and growing in confidence and joy before your eyes. If it hadn't been for her maybe your daughter would be alive. Probably hard to be glad for her at that time don't you think? Of course all those silent little sentences would have been Jairus' self-talk, drawing conclusions before talking to Jesus. We do that every single day and it obstructs so many possibilities for good.

The older brother responded the same way when the prodigal son returned home and his father ordered a great feast and celebration to be prepared for him. He muttered that his father had never done anything like that for him and he resented the grace and mercy extended to his brother. In that instance his father turned to him and very empathically said, "All that I have is yours and it has always been like that. How could we not celebrate when you're my son, you are always with me, and everything I have is yours? But we had to celebrate and be glad, because this brother of yours was dead and is alive again, he was lost and is found" (Luke 15:31-32). The brother became caught in measuring relationships with money and things, whereas the father, God, is absolutely focused on the restored relationship as the highest priority.

Jairus tells one of the people near him not to bother Jesus anymore and we can almost hear his anger and dejection. Jesus hears it as well and responds with great compassion and authority and reassures him, "Don't be afraid. Just believe and she will be healed." Luke then recounts how Jesus leads a few family members into the room where the daughter is lying and those already there laugh at him. Once again Jesus ignores the laughter and the attitudes of cynicism and taking the girl by the hand restores life into her lifeless body. He is very pragmatic and tells the parents to give her something to eat and then leaves requesting them not to tell anyone.

How could you keep quiet about such an event? It is probable that while Jesus loved to heal and respond to the needs around him he also dreaded how they would be misinterpreted and become misused. The last thing he wanted was to become a spectacle and a "miracle worker."

The hallmark of greatness is authentic humility when it would be quite possible to flaunt status or misuse power and authority. God portrayed that quality of humility perfectly. Jesus' birth was in a stable shared with livestock, his parents were members of the poor working class, his country was under occupation, and so we could go on. It was always about God's power being made perfect in weakness with Jesus leaning away from titles and status and toward the disenfranchised, the blind, and the hungry.

If nothing else, I hope these writings have provoked some thought about God that makes it more difficult to brush him aside. I trust that in our time together we have managed to glimpse Someone who is far more likeable and interactive than you previously had expected him to be. And if you have heard that God really does delight in you and longs to break through all the "distorted messages" to prove his authenticity to you, then my purpose and prayer will be fulfilled.

* * * * *

Everything we shut
our eyes to, everything we run
away from, everything we deny,
denigrate or despise, serves
to defeat us in the end.
What seems nasty, painful, evil,
can become a source of beauty,
joy, and strength, if faced
with an open mind.

—HENRY MILLER

* * * * *

Thank you so much for accompanying me through these pages. I marvel at your tenacity. May God the Father embrace you with "the biggest hug in the world" so that you too may know beyond a doubt that you are unconditionally accepted, joyfully welcomed, and deeply loved by him. And please don't give up on the journey or the quest now—it has only just begun.

* * * * *

I have always found
that mercy bears richer fruits
than strict justice.

—ABRAHAM LINCOLN

* * * * *

# Epilogue

"JOHN, WAKE UP…JUST MADE SOME FRESH COFFEE."

"What time is it…?"

"Early, thought you'd like to check out the sunrise, seeing you kept me up looking at shooting stars for half the night. It's weird, can't remember whether I was dreaming—or did we really have quite a long discussion about God? I don't often think of that stuff too much."

"Mmm…I dunno…Thanks, this coffee is good, I always love the smell… Ever thought about what it would be like to be created as a coffee bean?"

"No, as a matter of fact I haven't…Being me is quite enough to contemplate. Oh no—don't start now."

"Imagine the coffee bean, growing up in the mountains in beautiful surroundings, only to discover that its whole purpose was to grow to maturity and then die, be crushed, and ground into coffee to bring pleasure to others…people whom you never knew or had ever seen. People like you and me."

"Hey, that's morbid, man—I want to enjoy this nectar—don't spoil it."

"No, think about it…It's actually quite beautiful…kind of like what God did with Jesus dying on the cross, being crushed so that his love could rise over all the world with the sun every morning and shine on you and me. And why the central symbols of the church—bread and wine—also speak to us, wheat ground down to make bread (Jesus' body), and grapes crushed to make wine (Jesus' blood)…Living to die and dying to live theme."

"Okay, enough for now…let's leave that one for later…More coffee?"

"Thanks…just a little cream…And thank you, little coffee beans, I sure appreciate you today."

"Look at the colors in that sunrise…makes you think, doesn't it? What an artist!"

"Mugs up to the sun!"

"And to the Risen Son on this new day! Cheers!"

• • • • •

**Please visit John's Web site:**
# *www.googleforgod.com*

• • • • •

**Why not consider using *Googling God* as a basis for discussion?**

You'll find ideas for discussion questions on the Web site and also resources for reading and exploring basic Christianity. If you want to pose a question to John, he would love to hear from you—just fill in the contact form located under the "Contact Me" tab (left side of Web-site home page).

Here are a few sample questions for discussion to help get you going:

### Chapter 1—Imagine...

1. Imagine you're sitting by the campfire with a friend...How would you describe your spiritual journey thus far? Have you even begun? What has helped you or hindered you?

2. Describe the God you believe in right now...or...describe the God you *don't* believe in right now.

### Chapter 2—Why Bother?

1. Sometimes something happens in our lives that so angers or disappoints us that we give up on faith in God. Do you have any "reaction" that you're still living with that is preventing you from really being open to knowing God?

   *Note that there is no right answer here...and authenticity is important. If you can share around this topic it is extremely important to listen and to try to empathize and understand. To correct someone or provide a quick rebuke (because you feel more comfortable) or "answer" at this stage will just shut most people down. We all need validation and understanding. Oftentimes permission to express doubt, disillusionment, anger, and so on without correction or rejection will be the key to unlocking a closed door.*

2. Can you describe any person(s) who has (have) impacted your life and been an inspiration to you? Or it could be a book you've read, a movie, a song, a particular place. The Irish talk about "thin places" on the earth, where it seems the supernatural and the natural almost touch…those moments when possibly despite yourself you have sensed there must be "something more to life."

   *Once again, be sure to listen to one another carefully… Trust and respect go a long way to building a conversation forum that tracks into an unknown future. At this stage the building of a safe environment is more important than debating points or correcting wrongs (no matter how tempting that might be—a very good discipline if you're someone like me…). Have fun!*

# Challenges and Questions About Spirituality...

## I'm Fine with God...It's Christians I Can't Stand
*Getting Past the Religious Garbage in the Search for Spiritual Truth*
Bruce Bickel and Stan Jantz

Are people getting in the way of your search for God? Many non-Christians find the behavior of some Christians off-putting rather than inviting. Many Christians do too! Are you annoyed by such things as

- judgmental attitudes, hypocrisy, and condemnation?
- confusing mixtures of politics and the gospel?
- extreme teachings about prosperity?
- uninformed opinions about others' beliefs?

Bruce Bickel and Stan Jantz take an unflinchingly honest and often humorous look at some believers' outlandish words and actions. This call to authentic Christianity will help you get past the peripheral issues and communicate openly and honestly about God.

## Five Sacred Crossings
*A Novel Approach to a Reasonable Faith*
Craig Hazen

In today's multireligious culture, how can you be sure your belief system is trustworthy? *Five Sacred Crossings* explores different worldviews in the form of a fast-paced novel—

*Professor Michael Jernigan, a Christian, is teaching a religions course at community college. A local, barely halted act of religious terrorism throws a teeth-on-edge relevancy into the class discussions, which Jernigan bases on a rare text he obtained while in Cambodia—the Five Crossings. Each "Crossing" unveils a universal spiritual question...*

As you probe and ask questions of your beliefs along with Jernigan and the students, you'll be challenged to wrestle with overarching truth about the God who transcends time and culture.

## Why Mike's Not a Christian
*Honest Questions About Evolution, Relativism, Hypocrisy, and More*
Ben Young

**So why is Mike not a Christian?** Simple. He has his reasons for not believing:

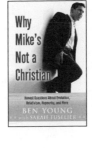

"I'm not a Christian…

- …because it's true for you, but not for me."
- …because all Christians are hypocrites."
- …because evolution is true."
- …because the Bible is full of myths."
- …because of evil and suffering."

How would you continue the discussion? Here you'll find reasoned responses to the most common challenges to the Christian faith. Whether you're a skeptic or a Christian, this book will take your conversations and your spiritual journey to the next level.

## Searching for the Original Bible
*Who Wrote It and Why? • Is It Reliable? • Has the Text Changed over Time?*
Randall Price

*Lost…destroyed…hidden…forgotten.* For many centuries, no one has seen any of the original biblical documents. How can you know whether today's Bible is true to them?

Researcher and archaeologist Randall Price brings his expert knowledge of the Bible to tackle crucial questions:

- What happened to the original Bible text? If we don't have it, what *do* we have?
- How was the text handed down to our time? Can you trust that process?
- What about the Bible's claim to be inspired and inerrant?

Current evidence upholds the Bible's claim to be the authoritative record of God's revelation—a Book you can build your life and faith on.

---

*To read a sample chapters of these and other Harvest House books,*

go to **www.harvesthousepublishers.com**

# Exploring Christian Spirituality

### Knowing God 101
*A Guide to Theology in Plain Language*
Bruce Bickel and Stan Jantz

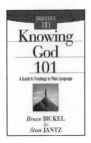

*Can I know for sure that God exists?*

*Is He personally involved in the details of my life?*

*What kind of relationship can I have with Him? Can I really know Him?*

This sensible and straightforward guide—which includes open-ended questions for discussion or reflection and resources for further exploration—will help you...

- learn about the three Persons of the Trinity—the Father, Son, and Holy Spirit—and their relationship with you
- find answers to your questions about heaven and hell, angels and demons, and sin and salvation
- see how the Bible's revelation about God can change your everyday life

### Becoming Who God Intended
*A New Picture for Your Past • A Healthy Way of Managing Your Emotions • A Fresh Perspective on Relationships*
David Eckman

Whether you realize it or not, your imagination is filled with *pictures* of reality. The Bible indicates these pictures reveal your true "heart beliefs"—the beliefs that actually shape your everyday feelings and reactions.

David Eckman compassionately shows you how to allow God's Spirit to build new, *biblical* pictures in your heart and imagination. As you do this, you will be able to experience the life God the Father has always intended for you.

> "David Eckman is a man you can trust...His teaching resonates with God's wisdom and compassion."

**—Stu Weber,** author of *Tender Warrior* and *Four Pillars of a Man's Heart*

---

*To read a sample chapters of these and other Harvest House books,*
*go to **www.harvesthousepublishers.com***

# People Who've Googled God

## Wrestling with Angels
*Adventures in Faith and Doubt*
Carolyn Arends

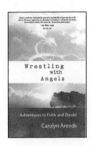

Life is messy. But life is also beautiful. These are the twin themes by which Christian singer/songwriter Carolyn Arends reveals how God meets people in ordinary moments. Her humorous, honest, and passionate personal stories delve into "the cruel short, beautiful, long adventure that is this life."

Fans of Donald Miller and Anne Lamott will discover a kindred spirit in Carolyn and her transparent and gutsy meditations on life's unanswered questions and the One who can be found there.

> *"Carolyn is a terrific writer...ruggedly tender and understanding...If you're looking for a friend to take a journey with...this book makes pleasant company."*

**DONALD MILLER**
Author, *Blue Like Jazz*

## Death of a Guru
*...One Man's Search for Truth*
Rabi R. Maharaj

*"I had been seeking union with Brahmin. Wasn't he evil as well as good, death as well as life, since he was All? Was this my true self...this evil being of great power that had momentarily shed its veneer of religion?"*

Rabi R. Maharaj grew up among the Hindus of Trinidad, descended from a long line of Brahmin priests and gurus and trained as a Yogi. He meditated for many hours each day, but gradually disillusionment and questions set in. He describes vividly and honestly Hindu life and customs, tracing his difficult search for meaning and his struggle to choose between Hinduism and Jesus Christ.

---

*To read a sample chapters of these and other Harvest House books,*
*go to **www.harvesthousepublishers.com***